Bank Costs, Structure, and Performance

James Kolari
Texas A&M University

Asghar Zardkoohi
Texas A&M University

Lexington Books
D.C. Heath and Company/Lexington, Massachusetts/Toronto

Library of Congress Cataloging-in-Publication Data

Kolari, James W.
  Bank costs, structure, and performance.

  Bibliography: p.
  Includes index.
  1. Banks and banking—Costs. 2. Banks and
banking—United States—Costs. I. Zardkoohi,
Asghar. II. Title.
HG1616.C6K65   1987   332.1'068'1   85–45295
ISBN 0–669–11282–8 (alk. paper)

Published simultaneously in Canada
Printed in the United States of America
International Standard Book Number: 0–669–11282–8
Library of Congress Catalog Card Number 85–45295

The paper used in this publication meets the minimum requirements of
American National Standard for Information Sciences—Permanence of
Paper for Printed Library Materials, ANSI Z39.48–1984. ∞™

86 87 88 89 90 8 7 6 5 4 3 2 1

To Karie, Minoo, Omeed, and Armin

Contents

Figures and Tables   ix

Acronyms   xiii

Acknowledgments   xv

1.   Market Innovation, Deregulation, and the U.S. Banking
     System   1

  Origins and Dimensions of the New Competition   5
  The New Competition and Public Policy Issues   23
  Summary and Conclusions   25

2.   Cost Economics in Banking   29

  Cost Characteristics of Commercial Banks   30
  Scale Economies in Banking   32
  Methodological Problems in Measuring the Scale Effect in
     Banking   35
  Production Functions and Alternative Methodologies of Measuring
     Scale   40
  Economies of Scale and Marginal Cost in a Multiproduct Firm   46
  Endogeneity of Bank Output and Consequent Estimation
     Problems   50
  Technology and Economies of Scale and Scope   51
  Summary and Conclusions   52

  Appendix 2A: Other Cost Functions   57

  Appendix 2B: An Alternative Solution to the Simultaneity
               Problem   59

3.   Literature on the Cost Economics of Banking   63

  Early Studies of Bank Costs   64
  Later Studies of Bank Costs   70

Recent Bank Cost Studies   79
Miscellaneous Bank Cost Studies   86
Summary and Conclusions   90

4.   **Recent Empirical Evidence in a Competitive Environment   97**

Overall Economies of Scale and Scope in the Multiproduct
   Banking Firm   98
Scale and Scope Results for Unit and Branch States   111
Summary and Conclusions   122

5.   **The Cost Economics of Banks with Different Product
Mixes   127**

Clustering Banks into Groups by Product Mix   127
Cost Analyses of Bank Groups   129
Summary and Conclusions   145

**Appendix 5A: Estimates of Multiproduct Cost Functions and
Statistical Differences across Groups, by Model
and Year   149**

6.   **The Cost Structure of Electronic and Computer
Technology   181**

Past Studies of Technology and Bank Costs   182
Cost Efficiency and Bank Technology   190
Summary and Conclusions   198

7.   **Cost Efficiency and Bank Failure   205**

Methodology   205
Summary and Conclusions   214

8.   **Bank Costs and Implications   217**

Overview of Past and Present Bank Cost Evidence   219
Implications   222

Bibliography   227

Index   233

About the Authors   241

Figures and Tables

Figures

1–1. Economic and Financial Systems 7

1–2. Ratio of Net Income to Total Assets 11

1–3. Ratio of Operating Income to Operating Expense 21

1–4. The Effects of Industry Structure on Conduct and Performance 24

2–1. Relationship between Short-Run and Long-Run Cost Curves 34

2–2. Relationship between the Number and Average Size of Bank Accounts 39

2–3. Effect of Greater Technological Divisibility on Long-Run Average Costs 53

7–1. The LOGIT Cumulative Distribution Function 209

Tables

1–1. Competition from Nontraditional Suppliers of Banking Services, 1960 versus 1984 3

1–2. An Overview of the Depository Institutions Deregulation and Monetary Control Act of 1980 4

1–3. An Overview of the Garn-St. Germain Depository Institutions Act of 1982 5

1–4. Number of Insured Banking Offices and Banks   9

1–5. The Beginnings of the New Competition   12

1–6. Estimated Earnings on Financial Operations of Major U.S. Corporations, 1981   14

1–7. Estimated Business Lending of Nonbank Firms and Bank Holding Companies, 1981 and 1982   15

1–8. Depository Institution–Broker Relationships in the Distribution of Insured Retail Deposits, 1982   17

1–9. New Competition in the Financial Industry   18

1–10. Enacted Interstate Banking Legislation   20

2–1. Comparative Composition of Total Operating Costs in Manufacturing versus Banking, 1969   32

3–1. Selected Unit Cost Results for Banks of Different Sizes, 1938–50   66

3–2. Total Operating Expenses as a Percentage of Loans and Investments, 1959   67

3–3. Total Operating Expenses as a Percentage of Total Assets, 1959   69

3–4. A Size Comparison of the Variation of Bank Costs, 1959   71

3–5. Elasticities and Marginal Costs of Basic Banking Services, 1959–61   72

3–6. Effect of Branching on Direct Costs of Selected Bank Services, 1959–61   73

3–7. Capsule Summaries of Bank Cost Studies in the 1970s   77

3–8. Scale Economy Estimates, Using a Translog Cost Function, 1978   81

3–9. Cost Complementarities between Bank Outputs, Using the Translog Cost Function, 1978   81

3–10. Scale Economies Estimates for Output, Measured in Liability and Asset Terms, 1973, 1975, and 1978   82

3–11. Scale Economy Estimates, Using Divisia Index, 1975 and 1978   84

3–12. Scale Economy Estimates for Average Account Size, 1975 and 1978   84

4–1. Estimates of Multiproduct Cost Functions, 1979 and 1980   103

4–2. Estimates of Multiproduct Cost Functions, 1981 and 1982   104

4–3. Estimates of Multiproduct Cost Functions, 1983   105

4–4. Estimates of Overall Scale and Scope Economies, 1979–83   106

4–5. Estimates of Multiproduct Cost Functions, 1979: Unit Bank versus Branch Bank States   112

4–6. Estimates of Multiproduct Cost Functions, 1980: Unit Bank States versus Branch Bank States   114

4–7. Estimates of Multiproduct Cost Functions, 1982: Unit Bank States versus Branch Bank States   116

4–8. Estimates of Scale Economies over Time: Unit Bank States versus Branch Bank States   119

4–9. Estimates of Scope Economies over Time: Unit Bank States versus Branch Bank States   121

5–1. Cluster Means for Variables as a Proportion of Total Assets, 1979–83   130

5–2. Estimates of Scale Economies for Different Bank Groups, 1979–83: Model I   134

5–3. Estimates of Scale Economies for Different Bank Groups, 1979–83: Model II   135

5–4. Estimates of Scale Economies for Different Bank Groups, 1979–83: Model III   136

5–5. Jointness Tests for the Three Models, 1979–83   139

5–6. Estimates of Scope Economies for Different Bank Groups, 1979–83: Model I   141

5–7. Estimates of Scope Economies for Different Bank Groups, 1979–83: Model II   142

5–8. Estimates of Scope Economies for Different Bank Groups, 1979–83: Model III   143

6–1   Percentage Distribution of Annual Machine Time, by Bank Function   184

6–2.   Mean Values for Measures of Bank Technology Utilization, 1980   192

6–3.   Mean Values for Measures of Bank Technology Utilization, 1982   193

6–4.   Parameter Estimates for the Relationship between Allocated Costs for Demand Deposits and Technology, 1979   195

6–5.   Parameter Estimates for the Relationship between Allocated Costs for Demand Deposits and Technology, 1980   196

6–6.   Parameter Estimates for the Relationship between Allocated Costs for Demand Deposits and Technology, 1982   197

6–7.   Estimates of Multiproduct Cost Functions for Demand Deposits and Credit Cards over Time: Unit versus Branch States   199

6–8.   Estimates of Scale and Scope Economies for the Joint Production of Demand Deposits and Credit Cards over Time: Unit versus Branch States   201

7–1.   Predictor Variables in LOGIT Models   206

7–2.   Coefficient Estimates for Stepwise LOGIT Models   210

7–3.   Classification Results for LOGIT Models: Number of Banks in Group X Classified into Group Y   213

Acronyms

ACH	Automated Clearing House
ATM	Automated Teller Machine
ATS	Automatic Transfer Service
BHC	Bank Holding Company
CD	Certificate of Deposit
CES	Constant Elasticity of Substitution
DIDC	Depository Institutions Deregulation Committee
DIDCMA	Depository Institutions Deregulation and Monetary Control Act
EFT	Electronic Funds Transfer
FCA	Functional Cost Analysis
FDIC	Federal Deposit Insurance Corporation
FSLIC	Federal Savings and Loan Insurance Corporation
MMC	Money Market Certificate
MMDA	Money Market Deposit Account
MMMF	Money Market Mutual Fund
NCUA	National Credit Union Administration
NOW	Negotiable Order of Withdrawal
RAC	Ray Average Costs
ROA	Return on Assets

Acknowledgments

Much of the research reported in this book was made possible by the generous support of the U.S. Small Business Administration under grant number SBA–8564–04–84. Any opinions, findings, and conclusions or recommendations expressed in this publication are those of the authors and do not necessarily reflect the views of the U.S. government in general or of the Small Business Administration. Dr. Charles Ou, technical research advisor at the SBA, was instrumental in the origination of the research project and was helpful in many respects throughout the progress of the research.

A number of individuals at Texas A&M University also contributed significantly to the research. Dr. Charles Cichra aided in programming some of the statistical routines and in handling associated data-manipulation problems. Dr. Fred Dahm, associate professor of statistics, originated the scope measure employed in chapters 4 and 5. Ms. Armelle Balenceu, a graduate student in statistics, ran the cluster analyses reported in chapter 5. Valuable graduate assistance was obtained from Mr. Rick Webb, Mr. Steve Holleman, Mr. Rod Van Wyngarden, and Mr. Jeff Horton.

1
Market Innovation, Deregulation, and the U.S. Banking System

C hanges in banking internal and external conditions are altering the way in which banks do business and are putting the spotlight on cost control. The most obvious internal change today is in advancing technology. Drive-in teller facilities, automated clearinghouses (ACHs), automated teller machines (ATMs), banking by phone, credit cards, and corporate cash management systems are just a few examples of the sweeping changes in bank services that technology has already brought and that continue to be refined and integrated into other computer and electronic services. Without doubt "plant vintage" in banking has evolved substantially, in the sense that the manner in which banks produce and deliver their services and products to consumers, business firms, and government customers has been transformed by technology. Although this transformation has had the salutary effect of better satisfying the transactions and portfolio service needs of bank customers, a new set of cost constraints have been introduced, and banks must learn to cope with them. For example, new technology is expensive, requires skilled operation and maintenance, can be risky from the standpoint of customer acceptance and potential obsolescence, and may be inappropriately managed to yield too much or too little service or the wrong type of service. Hence, innovative technology can provide a means to greater profitability only if its costs can be controlled.

Perhaps even more important than control of the new costs of technology are the cost implications of numerous changes in the external environment within which banks operate. Rising levels of inflation in the 1970s spawned the creation of money market mutual funds (MMMFs), which are exempt from Regulation Q ceilings on interest rates paid by banks and other depository institutions on deposits. Technology, especially in the area of telecommunications (for instance, the 800 toll-free number), enhanced the ability of MMMFs to compete for depositors' funds. At the same time, new competition from other nonbanking organizations increased.[1] Insurance companies, retailers, and security dealers have undergone a gradual structural change and now offer a wider variety of services and products, which span virtually the entire set of bank outputs. For example, these changes have allowed individuals and business firms to acquire saving, investment, and lending services from the following diversified companies:

Sears, Roebuck and Company offers insurance, brokerage, and real estate through its ownership of Allstate Insurance Company, Dean Witter Reynolds, and Coldwell Banker, respectively;

Merrill Lynch offers customers brokerage accounts, money market funds, credit cards, and check-writing privileges through its asset management accounts;

Travelers Insurance offers asset management accounts through its ownership of a trust company and a brokerage firm;

Paine Webber offers an asset management account that can be accessed through a network of automated teller machines.

Table 1–1 further demonstrates the pervasiveness of nonbank competition of recent years compared to conditions in 1960.

Partly to protect the safety and soundness of the payments system, Congress passed new legislation in the early 1980s that tended to improve the competitive position of banks in the market for deposits and to allow banks to more easily exit the industry. For example, in 1980 the Depository Institutions Deregulation and Monetary Control Act (DIDMCA) was passed. Among other changes this legislation brought was the legalization of NOW (negotiable order of withdrawal) accounts, which are essentially interest-bearing checking accounts. It also permitted savings and loan associations and mutual savings banks (as well as credit unions) to issue NOWs and engage in banking activities such as credit cards, trust services, and business loans. Table 1–2 gives a summary of key titles included in DIDMCA.[2] Because of a crisis in the thrift industry, Congress passed the Garn–St. Germain Depository Institutions Deregulation Act of 1982. The so-called Garn Bill further eliminated Regulation Q interest rate ceilings by authorizing money market deposit accounts (MMDAs) for banks and other depository institutions, effective December 14, 1982. MMDAs were directly competitive with MMMF accounts because no limits on interest applied to them and only limited check writing was allowed. The Super-NOW appeared shortly thereafter, on January 5, 1983, because of action by the Depository Institutions Deregulation Committee (see table 1–2). Super-NOWs permitted unlimited check-writing privileges and no ceilings on interest rates, but in contrast to the MMDA, they were subject to reserve requirements. Table 1–3 provides more detail on the important aspects of this legislation.[3]

The net effects of these regulatory changes have been to increase bank

Table 1–1
Competition from Nontraditional Suppliers of Banking Services, 1960 versus 1984

	Banks		Savings and Loans		Insurance Companies		Retailers		Security Dealers	
	1960	1984	1960	1984	1960	1984	1960	1984	1960	1984
Checking	X	X		X		X		X		X
Savings	X	X	X	X		X		X		X
Time deposits	X	X	X	X		X		X		X
Installment loans	X	X		X		X		X		X
Business loans	X	X				X		X		X
Mortgage loans	X	X	X	X		X		X		X
Credit cards		X		X		X	X	X		X
Insurance					X	X		X		X
Stocks and bonds brokerage		X		X		X		X	X	X
Underwriting									X	X
Mutual funds						X		X	X	X
Real estate		X		X		X		X		X
Interstate facilities				X		X		X		X

Source: Donald L. Koch, "The Emerging Financial Services Industry: Challenge and Innovation," *Economic Review* Federal Reserve Bank of Atlanta (April 1984), 26.

Table 1–2
An Overview of the Depository Institutions Deregulation and Monetary Control Act of 1980

Title I. Monetary Control Act

Uniform reserve requirements were set for all banks that are also applicable to all depository institutions. All such institutions were allowed to purchase Federal Reserve services at a price. Previously, only member banks were required to carry reserves on deposits; smaller banks carried larger proportions of reserves than larger banks; and only member banks could obtain Federal Reserve services, which were offered at no charge.

Title II. Depository Institutions Deregulation

A gradual phase-out of Regulation Q interest rate ceilings on deposits of depository institutions by March 31, 1986, was ordered. The Depository Institutions Deregulation Committee (DIDC) was established to implement this phase-out.

Title III. Consumer Checking Account Equity Act

All depository institutions were authorized to sell NOW (negotiable order of withdrawal) accounts, which were previously available only in the New England area. Automatic transfer service (ATS) accounts were also authorized. Finally, federal deposit insurance coverage was extended from $40,000 per account to $100,000 per account at all insured depository institutions.

Title IV. Powers of Thrift Institutions and Miscellaneous Provisions

Savings and loan associations were permitted to issue credit cards and were allowed to expand their consumer loans. Mutual savings banks were empowered to accept demand deposits from and make consumer loans to business customers.

Title V. State Usury Laws

State usury restrictions on maximum permissible loan rates were removed for mortgage, business, and agricultural loans at all depository institutions. States were given the right to override the preemption within three years.

competitiveness with nontraditional suppliers of deposit and loan services and, consequently, to put pressure on banks to control costs. Inefficient producers will find it difficult to attract new deposits and sell loans in this more competitive market for financial services. Moreover, nonbank organizations are not likely to respond passively to deregulation. Instead, it is expected that they will compete to retain current market shares and continue to explore and develop competitive strategies to foster their expansion. In this regard, banks can forestall nonbank entry and improve their chances of survival by operating as efficiently as possible.

The next section of this chapter elaborates on the origins and dimensions of the new competition. It is followed by a discussion of anticipated developments, especially the ongoing push toward interstate banking. The last section addresses the issue of bank size and its implications for economies of scale and scope, concentration of resources, and related public policy issues.

Table 1–3
An Overview of the Garn-St. Germain Depository Institutions Act of 1982

Title I. Deposit Insurance Flexibility

Regulatory agencies, including the Federal Deposit Insurance Corporation (FDIC), the Federal Savings and Loan Insurance Corporation (FSLIC), and the National Credit Union Administration (NCUA), were given broadened powers in aiding troubled depository institutions. They can make loans, acquire deposits and contributions, purchase assets or securities, and assume liabilities of any insured bank in an effort to forestall, prevent, or rectify the problems of troubled institutions. The organization of charter conversions and extraordinary mergers and acquisitions was also permitted.

Title II. Net Worth Certificates

The FDIC and the FSLIC were authorized to purchase capital instruments known as "net worth certificates" from qualified institutions (that is, banks and thrifts with substantial residential real estate investment) to increase or maintain their capital. Restrictions on due-on-sale provisions of mortgage contracts were preempted.

Title III. Thrift Institutions Restructuring

Thrifts (excluding credit unions) were allowed to make overdraft loans, invest in the accounts of other insured institutions, and make commercial loans. Investment capacities were improved in the areas of state and local government securities, real estate, and consumer and educational loans. Thrifts were allowed to convert from state to federal charters, from mutual to stock charters, and from savings and loan association to savings bank charters (and vice versa where state laws permit). On the liability side of the balance sheet, all depository institutions were authorized to issue money market deposit accounts (MMDAs) with no interest rate restrictions and limited check-writing privileges. Minimum balances must exceed $2,500 per account, and deposits are insured up to $100,000. No reserves need be maintained, except for a 3 percent reserve requirement on nonpersonal accounts. Also, federally chartered savings and loan associations were allowed to accept demand deposits from business customers, and the rate differential between thrifts and banks (.25 percent higher at thrifts) was to be eliminated by 1984.

Title VII. Miscellaneous

Federal, state, and local governments were allowed to hold NOW accounts.

Title VIII. Alternative Mortgage Transactions

State banks and thrifts were permitted to offer variable-rate mortgage instruments, previously available only to federal institutions.

Origins and Dimensions of the New Competition

It would not be an exaggeration to conclude that the banking industry is experiencing drastic change. However, the primary impetus does not come from forces within banking; it is from competitive pressure outside of the industry. What are the origins of this change in competition? More relevant to bank managers today—what are the dimensions of the new competition? Numerous studies have been undertaken over the years in an attempt to answer these questions. In the discussion that follows, we present some of the findings of these studies, in addition to related summarization and extrapolation, in the hope of coming to grips with what banks are up against.

Beginnings of New Competition

The new competition for financial services from nonbank firms is symptomatic of an evolving financial system. The roots of this evolution are intertwined in the growth of the U.S. economic system. Between 1850 and 1900, it is estimated that financial intermediaries (defined as those institutions that channel savings to investment by issuing their own securities) grew from about $650 million in total assets to about $20 billion.[4] This rapid asset expansion was primarily caused by two factors: (1) the growth of the U.S. economy and (2) the growing separation of saving and investment in the United States. The second factor refers to the decline in the number of self-employed individuals as a proportion of the total population. Also, people were moving from rural to urban settings to take advantage of the greater job opportunities available with the development of large businesses. Commercial banks, savings banks, building and loan associations, life insurance companies, and trust companies (including investment banking companies) experienced tremendous growth because of these changes, although the growth was along separate paths.

Figure 1–1 is a diagram relating the financial system to the economic system to illustrate their linkages. It should be clear from the interrelationships shown that economic prosperity leads to a larger and more complex financial system. The Federal Reserve System is shown on the dashed line separating these two systems, since it was created to serve as fiscal agent for the U.S. Treasury,[5] to act as lender of last resort for banks, and, in general, to control the money panics that have plagued the financial system at times. Although its original purpose was tactical, in the sense of protecting the economic system from financial catastrophes, it now actively seeks to accomplish broad economic objectives, such as full employment, price stability, output growth, and a better balance of trade.

The lower part of figure 1–1 shows the real economic exchanges between individuals, government, and businesses in terms of goods, services, and payments. The top portion of the figure indicates the savings flows, securities sales, and loans and investments that subsequently occur in the financial system. Notice that savings that are allocated to investments by financial intermediaries are known as *indirect* savings flows, obtained by the issuance of *secondary* securities (for example, certificates of deposit, insurance and pension policies, unit shares of ownership, and so forth). *Direct* savings— savings that bypass financial intermediaries—are routed to businesses in exchange for *primary* securities by brokers, who earn revenues from sales commissions and related charges. Also, notice that institutions in the financial intermediaries box have been separated into different areas because of their divergent product lines.

In the 1920s, the paths of different institutions began to cross. For example, seeking to regain deposits lost to a fast-growing securities industry,

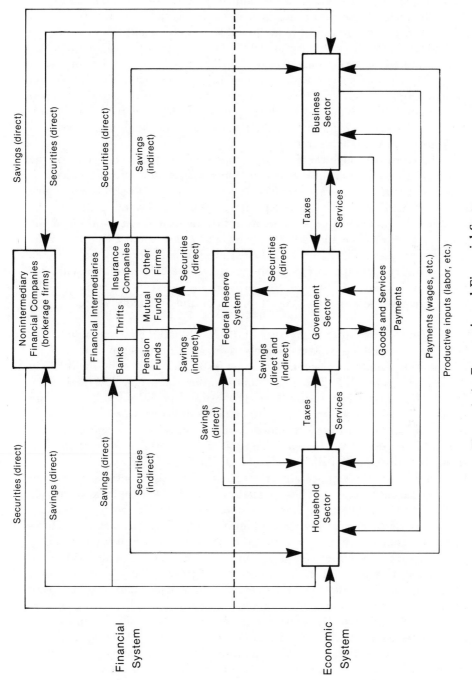

Figure 1–1. Economic and Financial Systems

banks began to issue time deposits and to acquire small deposit accounts. They channeled these new funds into securities, loans, and investments, in addition to real estate loans, made possible by new asset powers under the McFadden Branch Banking Act of 1927. Burgeoning securities markets further prompted the formation of security affiliates by banks for the purpose of supplying a complete line of investment banking services. As competition became more intense in the financial services industry, institutions diversified their product lines in an effort to recoup losses in the more traditional product lines. In terms of figure 1–1, the lines separating the different financial intermediaries became blurred.

Therefore, although there has been much publicity in recent years on the diversification of financial services, its emergence is not without precedent and can be traced to the early 1900s. It is interesting to note that the heightened competition for savings deposits in the 1920s—and probably the existence of economies of scale in prorating deposit services—thinned the ranks in banking from about 30,000 banks in 1919 to about 24,000 in 1929. By inference, a similar rise in banks exiting the industry may be expected throughout the 1980s if competition continues to escalate. In all likelihood, those banks that will survive and prosper in the years to come will be exemplified by sound management practices and (relatedly) effective cost control.

Of course, the Great Depression of the 1930s and the accompanying collapse of the banking system severely damaged the development of U.S. economic and financial systems. Congress responded by passing the Banking Acts of 1933 and 1935. These acts, among other things, created the Federal Deposit Insurance Corporation (FDIC) to insure deposits of small savers and liquidate failed banks, separate commercial from investment banking,[6] prevent banks from operating any nonbank-related subsidiary, prohibit the payment of interest on bank demand deposits, and require that interest on bank savings deposits be limited (Regulation Q). In 1934 Congress also gave the Federal Reserve Bank power to impose selective credit controls on margin credit purchases of stocks. These regulations had the effect of making the role of different financial intermediaries distinct once again. In reference to figure 1–1, much of the previous blurring of lines between intermediaries was eliminated. Of course, a major implication of these regulatory barriers to entry was an easing of the previous stress on cost efficiency (per unit risk) in the production of bank products and services. In general, banks entered a new era of regulated stability that was marked by few bank failures, which were primarily caused by management ineptitude or fraud.

After World War II, interest rates began to edge slowly upward in response to rising inflation. Since mutual savings banks and savings and loan associations were not subject to Regulation Q interest ceilings on deposits (presumably because of the desire to allocate savings to residential mortgages), banks occasionally suffered outflows of funds. To restore equity, legislators later removed thrifts from Regulation Q exemption under the Interest Rate Adjustment Act of 1966. However, thrifts were still at some advantage, since they were allowed slightly higher interest rates and lower taxes than were banks. Throughout the 1950s and 1960s, banks adapted to the competition from thrifts by expanding their products and services. For example, they expanded their use of time deposits and began offering negotiable certificates of deposit. On the asset side of the balance sheet, consumer loans, mortgages, and other nontraditional forms of lending were expanded. To service the needs of growing communities, and especially the suburbs, banks began branching in states where laws permitted it. Table 1–4 shows that the number of banking offices almost doubled from 1950 to 1970, but the number of banks stayed even. In states prohibiting branch banking, the bank holding company[7] became an alternative way of providing multi-office convenience to the public, in addition to enabling banks to diversify their interests into nonbank areas, including, for example, mortgage banking, finance companies, trust companies, insurance agencies, credit life insurance, credit card companies, data processing companies, and more. Today, bank holding companies are the dominant organizational form in banking, having grown from less than 5 percent of total U.S. bank assets in 1950 to over 85 percent at present.

As might be expected, studies of bank profitability in the 1960s pointed consistently to *cost control* as the primary determinant of success. Operating expenses, such as interest on time and savings deposits, net occupancy expenses, and other expenses, were shown to be significantly lower among banks with the highest profits.[8] This is not to say that operating costs alone were responsible for profits. Earning high gross interest on loans, investing in higher proportionate amounts (relative to total assets) of tax-exempt securities, and incurring lower losses on loans were found to increase profitability also. However, the conclusion of most early studies of bank profitability was that the most effective strategy for achieving strong net earnings is to control costs.

The aforementioned trends toward greater interbank and interdepository

Table 1–4
Number of Insured Banking Offices and Banks

	1950	*1960*	*1970*
Banking offices	18,278	23,685	35,321
Banks	13,446	13,126	13,511

Source: Adapted from Federal Deposit Insurance Corporation annual reports for the relevant years.

institution competition are notable, but they are overshadowed by a potentially much more serious threat. The 1960s ushered in a new era of participation by nondepository and nonfinancial institutions in the production and sale of financial services and products—the so-called new competition. A number of these companies entered the financial services market because of restraints on bank and other depository institution competition attributable to previously cited banking acts and other legislation. For example, nondepository companies often have no geographic restraints on permissible locations and entry into or exit from a location. Many of these companies can sell both financial and nonfinancial products and services (for instance, as cited earlier, Sears can simultaneously market insurance, real estate, and securities across the nation through retail outlets), which some customers may perceive as a convenient alternative to visiting separate suppliers in different locations. Also, these nondepository firms are not encumbered by the regulatory compliance costs applicable to banks and other depository institutions.

Another factor stimulating new competition is the profitability of the banking business. For example, figure 1–2 depicts the ratio of net income to total assets (that is, return on assets, or ROA) for different size banks throughout the period 1964–84. Since the early 1960s, the trend of bank profitability has been gradually upward. Profitability has declined substantially since 1981 in terms of ROA for all bank sizes; however, large banks experienced a reversal in this downward trend in 1984. Much of the decline in ROAs in the early 1980s can be explained by greater competitive forces because of deregulation, back-to-back recessions in 1979 and 1981, and a sluggish economy in 1981 and 1982. The continued decline of profitability in 1984 for banks with less than $100 million in assets is due to regional problems with loans in oil, farming, real estate, and export trade, which are probably temporary in nature and may be expected to be alleviated as they adjust to these problems. In light of the profit record of banks throughout the 1960s and 1970s, it is not surprising that nonbank firms have been eager to engage in the business of selling financial services.

Dimensions of New Competition

One of the earliest studies gauging the dimensions of the new competition indicates that by the end of 1970, nonfinancial corporations had invaded most of the asset-oriented activities in which bank holding companies could legally operate.[9] For example, as table 1–5 shows, manufacturers such as General Motors, Ford, General Electric, and Westinghouse and retailers such as Sears and J.C. Penney have been and continue to be in the business of commercial lending, consumer finance, real estate and mortgage banking, leasing, investment services, cash management, and a variety of other financial services. By 1981, these firms had made significant investments in financial

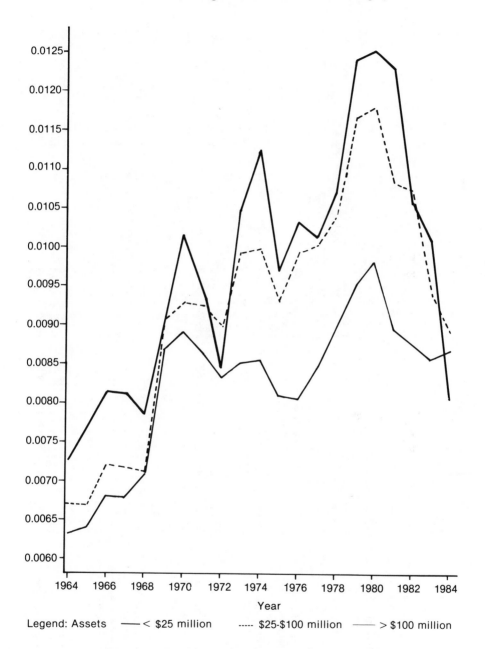

Figure 1-2. Ratio of Net Income to Total Assets

Table 1–5
The Beginnings of the New Competition

	General Motors	Ford	ITT	General Electric	Control Data	Gulf & Western	Borg-Warner	Westing-house	Sears	Marcor	J.C. Penney
Commercial Finance											
Commercial lending (short-term)		1960	1954–55		1968	1968	—[a]			1966	
Commercial lending (long-term)		1960	1954–55	1965	1968	1968		1961		1966	
Factoring					1968						
A/R and inventory finance	1919	1959		1932	1968	1968	1950	1954			
Venture capital				1970	1971				—[a]		
Consumer Finance											
Sales finance	1919	1959		1964	1968	1968	1933	1959	1911	1917	1958
Personal finance		1966	1964	19?5	1968	1968	1969		1962	1966	
Credit cards									—[a]	1957	1958
Real Estate											
Mortgage banking				1960				1969	1972		1970
Residential mortgage finance								1969	1961	1966	
Real estate development		1969	1970		1972		1969		1960	1970	1970
Real estate sales and management				1963					1960	1970	1970
Commercial real estate finance		1960						1969	1961	1966	1970
Insurance											
Credit life insurance		1962	1964	1973	1968	1968	1970		1960	1966	1970
Regular life insurance			1964	1973	1968	1968			1957	1966	1968
Property and casulty insurance	1925	1959	1964	1970	1968	1968	1970		1931	1968	1970
Accident and health insurance			1964	1973	1968	1968			1958		1967

Service									
Leasing									
Equipment and personal property	1966	1968	1968	1963	1968	1968	1960	1970	1970
Real property leasing									
Lease brokerage									
Investment services									
Investment management				1966			1969		
Mutual fund sales				1966			1969		1970
Corporate trust and agency									
Custodial services									
Business and Personal Services									
Travel services							1961	1971	
Cash management services									
Tax preparation services					1968			1966–70	1969
Financial data processing services		1965			1968				
Credit card management services			1965			1970			1969

Source: Cleveland A. Christophe, *Competition in Financial Services*, First National Corporation (New York: March 1974).
[a]Entry data unavailable.

Table 1–6
Estimated Earnings on Financial Operations of Major U.S.
Corporations, 1981

	Millions of Dollars	*Percentage of Total Earnings*
Borg-Warner	31	18.0
Control Data	50	29.2
Ford[a]	186	NA
General Electric	142	8.6
General Motors	365	109.6
Gulf & Western	71	24.5
ITT	387	57.2
Marcor[b]	110	NA
Sears[c]	385	51.1
Westinghouse	34	7.8

Source: Adapted from Harvey Rosenblum and Christine Pavel, "Financial Services in Transition: The Effects of Nonbank Competitors," Federal Reserve Bank of Chicago, Staff Study 84–1 (1984), B–2.

[a]Ford Motor Company had a net loss of $658 million in 1982.

[b]Marcor's operating loss in 1982 was $75 million.

[c]Sears financial service earnings are stated before allocation of corporate expenses to its business groups. In 1982, these expenses were $133 million.

operations, as shown in table 1–6. A total of over $1.7 billion was earned in 1981 by the ten companies listed in table 1–6.

Many of these earnings were posted in the areas of consumer and business lending. According to Rosenblum and Siegel,[10] General Motors topped the list of consumer lenders (including retail mortgage and installment and revolving loans) in 1981, with about $31.1 billion outstanding. Bank of America followed with $19.9 billion. Also, ten of the top fifteen consumer lenders were not banks. In the area of auto loans, the market share of banks moved downward from 60 percent in 1978 to 47 percent in 1981.[11] Captive finance companies of General Motors, Ford, and Chrysler accounted for much of this decline, since their share increased from 21 percent to 32 percent in these years. Table 1–7 gives some perspective on the progress of nonbank firms in the traditional business of commercial loans. Despite the predominance of the fifteen largest bank holding companies compared to thirty-two large nonbank firms, the fact that the nonbank firms made commercial loans almost equivalent to those of one-fourth of all insured U.S. banks is impressive.

New competition affected the sources of funds for banks also. As was already mentioned, the main rival has been the money market mutual fund (MMMF), which started in 1972 at Merrill Lynch as a means of managing cash for investors (that is, the Cash Management Account). MMMF accounts

Table 1–7
Estimated Business Lending of Nonbank Firms and Bank Holding Companies, 1981 and 1982
(*millions of dollars*)

	Commercial and Industrial Loans		Commercial Mortgage Loans		Lease Financing[a]		Total Business Lending	
	1981	1982	1981	1982	1981	1982	1981	1982
15 industrial/communications/transportation[b]	39,365	36,365	1,768	2,036	14,417	15,924	55,550	54,325
10 diversified financial[b]	3,602	4,705	3,054	3,451	1,581	1,419	8,237	9,575
4 insurance-based	399	827	35,506	36,419	892	737	36,797	37,983
3 retail-based	606	605	–	–	–	–	606	605
Total	43,972	42,502	40,328	41,906	16,890	18,080	101,190	102,488
15 largest BHCs								
Domestic	141,582	155,527	19,481	20,069	14,279	15,066	175,342	190,662
International	118,021	126,307	5,046	6,462	–	–	123,067	132,769
Total	259,603	281,834	24,527	26,531	14,279	15,066	298,409	323,431
Domestic offices, all insured commercial banks	327,101	379,566	120,333[c]	132,685[c]	13,168	13,738	460,602	525,989

Source: Harvey Rosenblum and Christine Pavel, "Financial Services in Transition: The Effects of Nonbank Competitors," Federal Reserve Bank of Chicago, Staff Study 84–1 (1984), B–12.

[a]For nonbank companies and for BHCs, includes domestic and foreign lending and may include leasing to households and government entities.
[b]Financing by banking and savings and loan subsidiaries has been subtracted.
[c]Includes all real estate loans except those secured by residential property.

are easy to open because of the toll-free 800 numbers advertised in the financial press, have limited draft-writing capabilities for withdrawing cash, and can be used to invest in a variety of taxable and tax-exempt money market securities' pools. By the end of 1977, a modest $3.9 billion was invested in MMMFs; however, because interest rates moved substantially higher than Regulation Q limits on deposit accounts, MMMFs expanded sharply to about $232.1 billion by the end of 1982.[12] The MMDA and Super-NOW account enabled banks and other depository institutions to reverse this outflow of deposit funds to some extent, but MMMFs still play an important role in the U.S. financial system. It is interesting that some nonbank firms are cooperating with banks to sell money market instruments issued by banks. For example, Merrill Lynch now brokers retail certificates of deposits (CDs) for numerous banks and thrifts and maintains a secondary market for such securities. Table 1–8 shows that many other firms are involved in symbiotic depository institution-broker relationships of this nature. Therefore, cooperative efforts between banks and nonbanks are blurring the lines between different financial institutions once again.

It would seem more appropriate, in view of this changing financial marketplace, to take a broader view of the phrase *new competition.* Until now, the term has referred generally to competition from nonfinancial firms in the financial service market. A more appropriate interpretation in light of recent events is *the innovation of products, services, and delivery systems taking place among depository and nondepository institutions and nonfinancial firms separately as well as jointly.* Table 1–9 provides some examples of new competition that encompasses the financial services industry as a whole. Referring back to figure 1–1, it is clear that the new competition corresponds to the breakdown of boundaries separating brokers, different financial intermediaries, and nonfinancial business firms. It is important that, in response to this new competition, banks and other financial service companies are adapting their operations to accommodate cost-efficient activities (see table 1–9 for examples). This type of cost control reaction is reminiscent of the behavior of banks in the 1920s and, later, in the 1950s and 1960s as competition from other sellers encroached on their market shares.

Another way to hold the line against the competition is to explore new opportunities for profit taking. In this regard, many banks have sought to circumvent existing regulatory barriers to entry. Kane has called this type of bank behavior "regulatory dialectic," because regulation initiates innovative circumvention, which, in turn, leads to further regulation and so on.[13] Since federal regulation of product lines and geographic barriers to entry applicable to depository institutions have not changed much over the years and since nondepository institutions are exempt from these regulations, banks have been exploring ways to bypass such restraints. One example (cited in table 1–9) of product-line circumvention is the leasing of office space in Columbus,

Table 1–8
Depository Institution–Broker Relationships in the Distribution of Insured Retail Deposits, 1982

Merrill Lynch (475 offices)
  All-savers certificates for 15 thrifts nationwide
  Retail CDs[a] for 20 banks and thrifts nationwide, including Bank of America
  Secondary market in retail CDs of 2 banks and 2 thrifts
  91-day negotiable CDs for Great Western Federal Savings and Loan, Beverly Hills

Dean Witter (8 Sears stores with financial center pilot programs and 3,200 Dean Witter offices nationwide)
  Retail CDs[a] for 2 thrifts, including Allstate Federal Savings and Loan
  Secondary market in retail CDs for City Federal Savings and Loan, New Jersey

Bache (200 offices in 32 state)
  All-savers certificates for City Federal Savings and Loan
  Retail CDs[a] for City Federal Savings and Loan and one savings and loan in Los Angeles

Shearson/American Express (330 domestic offices)
  All-savers certificates for Boston Safe Deposit and Trust Company
  Retail CDs[a] for selected banks and thrifts

Fidelity Management Group (29 offices in 50 states)
  All-savers certificates for 6 banks including Security Pacific National Bank and First National Bank of Chicago

E.F. Hutton (300 offices in 50 states)
  All-savers certificates for 15 regional banking companies

Edward D. Jones & Company (435 offices in 33 states)
  All-savers certificates for Merchants Trust Company, St. Louis

Manley, Bennett, McDonald & Company (10 offices in 2 states)
  All-savers certificates for First Federal Savings & Loan, Detroit

Paine Webber (240 offices)
  All-savers certificates for 2 banks in California, including Bank of America

Charles Schwab & Co. (offices in 38 states)
  All-savers certificates for First Nationwide Savings and Loan, San Francisco

The Vanguard Group (offices in 50 states)
  All-savers certificates for Bradford Trust Company, Boston

Source: Harvey Rosenblum and Diane Siegel, "Competition in Financial Services: The Impact of Nonbank Entry," Federal Reserve Bank of Chicago, Staff Study 83–1 (1983), 17.
[a]$3\frac{1}{2}$-, 4-, 5-year, and zero coupon certificates of deposit.

Ohio, by BancOne to Nationwide Insurance for the purpose of selling insurance, mutual fund, and annuity products. This type of symbiotic financial relationship can benefit banks because it enables customers to obtain a larger number of financial services in one place, which therefore enhances the public's convenience in depositing funds. At the same time, banks may charge a rental fee in excess of the fair market rate because the in-house financial service company picks up added business from referrals and the prime location.

Table 1–9
New Competition in the Financial Services Industry

Innovation

Products and Services

•In June 1981, Prudential Insurance Company introduced a stock fund that is available to the public and is designed to provide tax advantages for upper income investors. It is distributed by Bache.

•In March 1980, Merrill Lynch & Co. tested its Equity Access Account, which gives homeowners access to the equity in their homes through checks and debit cards. Now many banks, brokers, and consumer finance companies are offering such home equity loans.

•First Interstate Bancorp, BankAmerica Corp. and Citicorp plan to buy state-chartered banks in South Dakota in order to enter the insurance business.

•Century 21, a nationwide real estate brokerage firm, plans to establish subsidiaries for mortgage brokerage, property insurance, and the sale of real estate limited partnerships.

•Security Pacific National Bank of Los Angeles plans a new fund, the Security Pacific Futures Fund.

Delivery Systems

•In July 1982, Sears opened financial service centers in 8 stores and as of November 1983 operated 108 such financial centers. These centers offer insurance, real estate, and brokerage services, and in California they offer Allstate Savings and Loan's products as well.

•The Kroger Company is experimenting with financial centers in Ohio, Alabama, and Texas. These centers offer consumer banking and insurance products to customers at Kroger grocery stores.

•First Nationwide Savings contracted with J.C. Penney to open and operate financial service centers that offer a full range of products at five Penney stores in Northern California.

•BancOne leases space to agents of Nationwide Insurance in three Columbus, Ohio, branches. The agents sell insurance products, mutual funds, and annuities.

Reduction in Costs

•Sun Banks of Florida in Orlando acquired Flagship Banks of Miami and saved on data processing and back office operations through consolidation.

•Westinghouse Credit Corporation restructured its financial service group so that representatives are closer to their customers. This helped Westinghouse Credit decrease its ratio of direct expenses to net receivables.

•Citing insufficient business volume, Bank of Boston is phasing out the data processing service it provides to more than 100 correspondent banks.

•Bankers Trust is phasing out its less profitable retail operations to concentrate on the wholesale market.

Cross-Selling

•In June 1981, Mutual Benefit Life Insurance Co. expanded into securities brokerage through Mutual Benefit Financial Co., an in-house broker-dealer. Mutual Benefit Life sells its new service through its 1,600 insurance agents nationwide.

•American Express's insurance company, Fireman's Fund, offers an insurance and annuity plan through Shearson/American Express, and Shearson/American Express offers insured money market deposit accounts through its branch system. Shearson directs the deposit to its affiliate, Boston Safe Deposit and Trust Company.

•Prudential-Bache Securities plans to begin offering home mortgage loans as well as MMDAs and retail CDs by mail to its brokerage customers through the securities firm's Georgia bank.

•Travelers Corp. plans to offer a cash management service initially to its 10,000 independent insurance agents and later to business clients as well.

Source: Adapted from Harvey Rosenblum and Christine Pavel, "Financial Services in Transition: The Effects of Nonbank Competitors," Federal Reserve Bank of Chicago, Staff Study 84-1 (1984), B-20.

Banks have also been somewhat successful in effectively circumventing federal interstate banking prohibitions. The McFadden Act of 1927 (amended in 1933) prohibits banks headquartered in one state from operating branch offices in another state. The Douglas Amendment to the Bank Holding Company Act of 1956 prohibits bank holding companies from owning more than 5 percent of the voting stock of a bank located outside the state in which its principal office is located, unless explicitly allowed by state laws. To get around the Douglas Amendment, banks have set up production loan offices across state lines that make loans but do not take deposits. These offices have been permitted because they fall outside the legal definition of a bank as defined by the Bank Holding Company Act of 1956 (amended in 1966 and 1970)—that is, an institution that engages in the dual activities of accepting demand deposits and making commercial loans. Limited-service banks of this kind are known as "nonbank banks" because they have a bank charter and can obtain FDIC deposit insurance but are not banks by strict definition of law. At the time of this writing, Congress was considering legislation that may close the nonbank bank loophole, so the extent to which this innovation will be practicable in the future is uncertain.[14]

Another way of conducting interstate banking is through the regional compact. The U.S. Supreme Court ruled, on June 10, 1985, that such compacts are not unconstitutional. Table 1–10 shows the extent of interstate banking legislation in the United States through the mid-1980s. Most of the states restrict entry to out-of-state holding companies (the loophole in the Douglas Amendment of the Bank Holding Company Act of 1956) located in states in a specific geographic region. In all states, reciprocity provisions permit counteracquisitions by states in response to acquisition approvals in their state. Also, some states with regional restrictions have a national "trigger" provision set at two to five years, after which no regional restrictions apply. Although it is dangerous to predict the future, it appears that regional compacts will continue to grow and that federal legislation will eventually be forthcoming to phase in nationwide interstate banking.[15]

It is important to recognize that as banks explore new ways to open up forbidden markets and products and services, the need to control costs becomes more acute. The broadened scope of competition between banks, thrifts, nondepository financial companies, and nonfinancial firms, in addition to deregulatory trends and technological changes, has greatly altered the business of banking over the past twenty years. Figure 1–3 gives evidence of the subsequent cost effects (for different size banks) over the period 1964–84. Total operating income as a proportion of total operating expenses declined from the 1.35 to 1.38 range in 1964 to the range of 1.15 to 1.18 by 1984.

One of the major factors contributing to rising operating expenses has been increasing interest costs. A number of studies have noted that interest costs increased gradually over the past twenty years, as interest rate ceilings were de facto removed by banks in the 1960s and 1970s and de jure deregu-

Table 1–10
Enacted Interstate Banking Legislation (as of June 12, 1985)

State	Type of Legislation[a]	Area	Notes
Alaska	National	All states	Effective October 1, 1986
Arizona	National	All states	
Connecticut	R-R	5 New England states	
Florida	R-R	11 southeastern states and D.C.	Effective July 1, 1985
Georgia	R-R	9 southeastern states	Effective July 1, 1985
Idaho	R-R	Contiguous states	Effective July 1, 1985
Indiana	R-R	Contiguous states	Effective January 1, 1986
Kentucky	R-R	Contiguous states	Two-year national trigger (1987)
Maine	National	All states	
Maryland	R-R	Contiguous states	14 southeastern and midcentral states after 1986
Massachusetts	R-R	5 New England states	
Nevada	R-R	12 western states	Awaiting governor's signature; effective July 1, 1985; national trigger January 1, 1989
New York	N-R	All states	
North Carolina	R-R	12 southeastern states and D.C.	Effective July 1, 1985
Oregon	R-R	8 western states	Effective July 1, 1986
Rhode Island	R-R	5 New England states	National trigger June 30, 1986
South Carolina	R-R	12 southeastern states and D.C.	Effective July 1, 1986
South Dakota	National	All states	Only one bank can be acquired, and it cannot open branches
Tennessee	R-R	13 southeastern states	Effective July 1, 1985
Utah	R-R	11 western states	
Virginia	R-R	12 southeastern states and D.C.	Effective July 1, 1985
Washington	N-R	All states	Effective July 1, 1987

Source: *Financial Letter*, Federal Reserve Bank of Kansas City (June 1985), adapted from the testimony of Paul Volcker, Chairman of the Board of Governors of the Federal Reserve System, before the Senate Committee on Banking, Housing and Urban Affairs, May 8, 1985.

[a]R-R and N-R stand for regional-reciprocal and national-reciprocal, respectively.

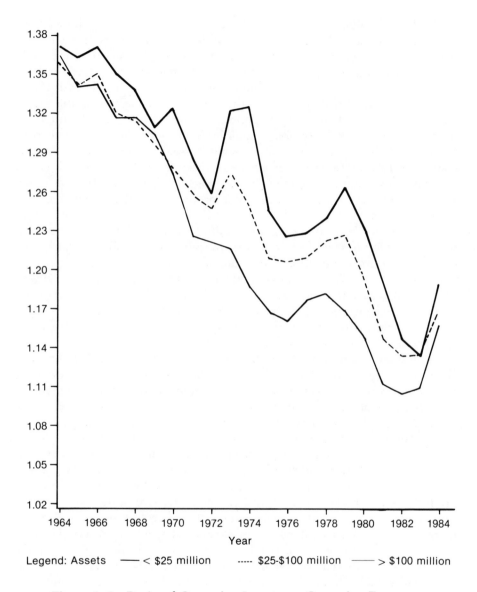

Figure 1–3. Ratio of Operating Income to Operating Expense

lated in the latter part of the 1970s and the early 1980s;[16] however, most banks did not experience an associated decline in profitability. Although the majority of banks have been able to cope successfully with higher interest rates, increasing numbers of banks are showing some amount of financial strain. In the 1960–68 period, an average of about five banks with average deposits of about $28 million failed each year. In the subsequent ten-year period 1969–78, the bank failure rate rose to an average of about eight per year, and average deposit size jumped to $514 million. The recent rash of failures—42, 48, 78, and 115 failures in 1982, 1983, 1984, and 1985, respectively—is linked, no doubt, to the economic decline and volatile interest rates that marked the 1980–82 period, not to mention isolated difficulties in the oil and real estate sectors, in addition to the widespread financial crisis in the agricultural sector. Yet there is some sense in presuming that the new competition exacerbated the problems of these failing institutions because they probably had a comparative disadvantage in adapting as easily as other banks to the new market environment prompted by the recent wave of market innovation.

It is reasonable to suspect that the failure rate in banking will not return to the pre-1980s level in the near future. Marginal banks will succumb to expected management difficulties—for example, lending, liquidity, interest rate margins, capital, and regulatory compliance—and, therefore, exit the industry. In their place, de novo banks that may be more prone to early demise in today's more competitive banking environment will enter. Be that as it may, banks that most effectively manage their costs (per unit risk) are likely to have the greatest chances of survival in the future.

Sound cost management should begin with strategic planning. This involves setting goals, developing a plan for achieving those goals, and evaluating ongoing progress toward successful goal attainment. Goal setting requires that the needs of desired customer bases be assessed. Of course, operations must be adapted to best serve the target market. Waite, reporting on a study by McKinsey & Company, has noted that deregulation in industries typically leads to a new (free market) equilibrium in which three basic types of producers emerge: (1) national distributors of a broad range of products and services over a wide geographic area; (2) low-cost producers of certain bank products and services to be delivered on a massive scale over a large geographic area; and (3) specialty banks that meet the needs of specific market niches.[17] Since banking can be subdivided as a business into five different lines—retail, domestic wholesale, international wholesale, trading, and trust—it is possible to have many alternative combinations of producer types and product lines. Banks need to choose their strategy carefully to emphasize their management strengths and to reflect the needs of their customers. In choosing a strategy, the cost efficiency of operations is perhaps the most important area, because it can be more directly managed than other areas such as marketing and finance, which are affected greatly by exogenous market forces.

The New Competition and Public Policy Issues

There is a regulatory crisis in banking today that can be traced to the considerable breadth and depth of new competition in the financial services industry. Interstate banking, as it relates to the evolving banking system, has already been discussed. A key issue involved in dismantling geographic barriers is the effect this has on the structure of banking—where structure is defined in terms of the size, number, and the organizational form of banking institutions. Banking systems in other countries are considered to be highly concentrated because a relatively small number of banks dominate the lion's share of the market (for example, in Canada, there are only twelve banks compared to over 15,000 banks in the United States). A likely reason for the large number of banks in this country is that U.S. antitrust laws cover horizontal mergers fairly well. By contrast, antitrust laws are ill-equipped to handle market extension mergers among different types of institutions or among similar institutions in different geographic markets, which are common characteristics of the new competition.[18] For these reasons, it is believed that as interstate banking grows, because of either regional compacts or federal legislation, the pace of mergers and acquisitions will accelerate.

The main fear of a consolidation movement is an excessive concentration of resources. Figure 1–4 is a standard textbook diagram of how industry structure, conduct, and performance may be related. Note that two factors directly determine structure, as characterized by whether or not there are many firms, one firm (natural monopoly), or a few large firms (natural oligopoly). The first factor comprises both the production and technological traits of the industry, which, together, shape most of the cost function of producers. The second factor is the marketplace in which the firm must compete. Structure can be affected (as shown with dashed lines in figure 1–4) by the conduct and performance of firms in the market also. Relevant questions of performance include: Are companies producing outputs at minimum cost given regulatory constraints? Are resources being allocated efficiently to maximize production (and incomes)? Is the industry expanding employment in line with market demand for products and services? Are price-cost margins competitive? Do firms achieve success based on economic rather than political criteria? And does the industry structure foster continued progress in terms of technological advancement and public satisfaction?

Although consolidation and subsequent concentration of resources in an industry can occur because of the size of the market (for example, a small community may have room only for one seller), economic events (for instance, a downturn may eliminate all but one firm), and other reasons, it is the prospect of substantial scale economies that has stimulated much interest

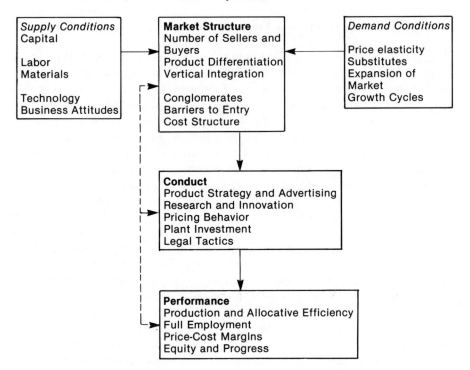

Source: Adapted from F.M. Scherer, *Industrial Market Structure and Economic Performance,* 2nd ed. (Chicago: Rand McNally, 1980), 5.

Figure 1–4. The Effects of Industry Structure on Conduct and Performance

on the part of researchers, regulators, and legislators. *Scale economies* refer to the production by larger firms of outputs at lower average cost than that by smaller firms. History tells us that specialization is one way to accomplish scale economies. For example, the use of assembly lines, melding labor and machines (performing repetitive tasks), enabled manufacturing firms in the United States at the turn of the century to cut costs and drive out smaller competitors. Of course, there must be sufficient demand to warrant mechanization of specialized operations. It should not be difficult to extrapolate the idea of scale economies to the area of banking. The majority of bank production is focused on specific types of deposit and loan accounts by the purchase of labor, capital, and raw materials. Of late, banks have been supplanting labor with machines, some of which are too costly to adopt for smaller institutions because they have not been (or cannot be) scaled down enough to compensate for idle time. Also, larger banks may have some cost advantage because of their ability to more easily handle peak load problems (for example, cyclical borrowing by the agricultural sector and transactions increases during holidays by the general public).

Another type of cost-cutting approach is to take advantage of economies of scope. *Scope economies* refer to the possibility that joint production of two (or more) products by a single firm is less costly than the sum of their separate production by two (or more) firms. Since banking is, by definition, a business that entails the joint production of deposits and loans, it is important to find out if there is any cost magic in this combination. If there is not, limited financial-service companies, whether making loans or taking deposits, would be able to hold their own against or even outperform banks. From another perspective, if there are scope economies in the production of loans and securities services, the relaxation of Glass-Steagall prohibitions on common stock purchases would endow banks with a competitive advantage over financial service companies that have not diversified into lending.

The questions of economies of scale and scope in banking, therefore, have serious implications for the structure of the financial services industry. These implications must be grappled with in order to formulate legislation affecting banks. Furthermore, the study of scale and scope economies lends itself to a better understanding of observed market forces in the financial system. In the chapters that follow, we seek to cover the following important areas relating to economies of scale and scope in banking:

The various costs of banking;

The economics of cost theory and empirical analysis;

Previous evidence of economies of scale and scope;

New findings, relevant to the last few years, on economies of scale and scope for banks of different size and organizational type;

The costs of producing electronic and computer bank services;

Related topics of special interest, especially recent bank failures and their relationship (if any) to cost control problems.

The final chapter will summarize the findings and conclusions of this and other works. Discussion of public policy issues raised in this chapter will also be provided.

Summary and Conclusions

Market innovation, new competition, deregulation, and technological advances are the primary forces shaping the way banks do business today.

The underlying motivation for the vast number of changes that have occurred in recent years is the promise of profitability. However, the ensuing struggle for financial turf will not allow that promise to be fulfilled for many of the participants. It is clear that the development of the financial services industry is at a crossroad that either will lead to congressional mandates to restrict and control the blurring of sellers' products or will liberalize further the spectrum of financial services that banks can offer to the public. Although it cannot be concluded with certainty, it would appear that the second option is the most probable outcome — that is, product line restrictions in banking will be relaxed. The extent to which this will occur is unknown at present, but it would tend to provoke reciprocal elimination of barriers to entry into banking in order to promote equity among competitors in the financial marketplace. Moreover, there is a strong interstate banking movement underway on the state and regional level in the United States that undoubtedly will intensify competition.

The central theme of this book is that the trend toward greater competition in banking will require that more emphasis be placed on cost control. Historically, successful banks have been best characterized by effective cost control. The question that naturally arises is whether small banks can operate as cost efficiently as large banks do or whether large banks are endowed with scale and possibly other benefits that cause them to be relatively more able to reduce the costs of operations.

We should caution that cost control alone is not a sufficient condition to ensure the safety and soundness of a banking institution. Goal setting, planning, and market strategy are important management dimensions. Nonetheless, banks must adapt their roles to fit both the demands of the public and the internal capabilities of management to maintain appropriate profit margins. In the process, it is likely that the banking population will become more heterogeneous in terms of the variety of output mixes. Therefore, studies on the cost economics of banking should attempt to recognize this growing divergence of bank outputs by examining banks with like outputs, rather than lumping all banks together into one group. In the chapters that follow, we discuss the notion of bank heterogeneity in greater detail and report related empirical evidence, in addition to providing a comprehensive discussion of cost theory, empiricism, literature, recent evidence, and more.

Notes

1. For more complete discussions on the new competition in banking, see Harvey Rosenblum and Diane Siegel, "Competition in Financial Services: The Impact of Nonbank Entry," Federal Reserve Bank of Chicago, Staff Study 83-1 (1983); William L. Silber, "The Process of Financial Innovation," *American Economic Review* 73

(May 1983): 89–95; and Harvey Rosenblum and Christine Pavel, "Financial Services in Transition: The Effects of Nonbank Competitors," Federal Reserve Bank of Chicago, Staff Study 84–1 (1984).

2. For additional information on DIDMCA of 1980, see Donald R. Fraser and Gene S. Uselton, "The Omnibus Banking Act," *MSU Business Topics* 28 (Autumn 1980): 5–14; Charles R. McNeill, "The Depository Institutions Deregulation and Monetary Control Act of 1980," *Federal Reserve Bulletin* 66(June 1980): 444–53; and Thomas McCord, "The Depository Institutions Deregulation and Monetary Control Act of 1980," *Issues in Bank Regulation* 3(Spring 1980): 3–7.

3. For a more in-depth overview of the Garn Bill, see Gillian Garcia et al., "Financial Deregulation: Historical Perspective and Impact of the Garn-St. Germain Depository Institutions Act of 1982," Federal Reserve Bank of Chicago, Staff Study 83–2 (1983). A synopsis of this study may be found in Gillian Garcia, et al., "The Garn-St. Germain Depository Institutions Act of 1982," *Economic Perspectives,* Federal Reserve Bank of Chicago (March-April 1983).

4. Murray E. Polakoff, Thomas A. Durkin, and others, *Financial Institutions and Markets,* 2nd ed. (Boston: Houghton Mifflin, 1981), 42. Some of the discussion that follows is based on chapter 3 of this volume.

5. The arrows between the Federal Reserve and the government represent this fiscal management role. If the government budget were balanced, and if government spent no more than its tax revenue, no arrows would be needed. As shown, the arrows illustrate a budget deficit, causing savings to flow toward the government.

6. The Glass-Steagall Act, a part of the Banking Act of 1933, is normally cited for this prohibition.

7. A bank holding company is a corporation that owns one or more banks. Under the Bank Holding Company Act of 1956, a holding company must register with the Federal Reserve Board if it controls 25 percent or more of the voting stock of two or more banks or controls the election of a majority of the directors of two or more banks. Corporations unrelated to banking must be divested by such holding companies. In 1970, Congress passed amendments to this act to encompass one-bank holding companies.

8. See, for example, John A. Haslem and William A. Longbrake, "A Discriminant Analysis of Commercial Bank Profitability," *Quarterly Review of Economics of Economics and Business* 11(Autumn 1971): 39–46; and Richard L. Gady, "Anatomy of Profitable Medium-Size Banks in the Fourth District, 1966–1970," *Economic Review,* Federal Reserve Bank of Cleveland (October-November 1972): 20–32.

9. Cleveland A. Christophe, *Competition in Financial Services,* First National Corporation (New York: March 1974).

10. Rosenblum and Siegel, "Competition in Financial Services," 6.

11. Ibid.

12. Herbert Baer, Gillian Garcia, and Simon Pak, "The Effect of Promotional Pricing on Dynamic Adjustment in the Market for MMMFs and MMDAs," *Proceedings of a Conference on Bank Structure and Competition,* Federal Reserve Bank of Chicago (April 1984), 155.

13. Edward J. Kane, "Accelerating Inflation, Technological Innovation, and the Decreasing Effectiveness of Bank Regulation," *Journal of Finance* 36(May 1981): 355–67.

14. As of April 1985, the Comptroller of the Currency had granted preliminary approval of 271 applications for limited-service banks. A recent decision by a federal court in Florida against the comptroller has prevented final approval of the applications.

Those interested in interstate banking should see David Whitehead, "Interstate Banking: Taking Inventory," *Economic Review,* Federal Reserve Bank of Atlanta (May 1983). Whitehead notes that there were 7,724 interstate offices as of late 1982, including grandfathered subsidiaries of domestic and foreign bank holding companies, agencies and branches of foreign banks, nonbank subsidiaries of bank holding companies, loan production offices, offices of Edge Act corporations, interstate savings and loan associations, and limited-service offices opened under special state laws. For further details on interstate banking, see David Whitehead, "A Guide to Interstate Banking, 1983," Staff study by the Federal Reserve Bank of Atlanta (1983), and David Whitehead, "Can Interstate Banking Increase Competitive Market Performance," *Economic Review,* Federal Reserve Bank of Atlanta (January 1984).

15. We should mention, also, that federal thrift institutions are allowed to branch, but banks are not permitted to do so unless state laws permit it. As thrifts become more like banks in terms of asset and liability characteristics, it is logical to presume that bank branching restrictions will be relaxed to promote equity.

16. See, for example, Mark J. Flannery, "The Impact of Interest Rates on Small Commercial Banks," Rodney L. White Center of Financial Research, Working Paper No. 10–81 (August 1981); Mark J. Flannery, "Market Interest Rates and Commercial Bank Profitability: An Empirical Investigation," *Journal of Finance* 36(December 1981): 1085–1101; Mark Flannery, "Removing Deposit Rate Ceilings: How Will Bank Profits Fare?" *Business Review,* Federal Reserve Bank of Philadelphia (March-April 1983), 13–21; and Michael Smirlock, "An Analysis of Bank Risk and Deposit Rate Ceilings: Evidence from the Capital Markets," *Journal of Monetary Economics* 13(1984): 195–210.

17. Donald C. Waite, III, "Deregulation in the Banking Industry," *Bankers Magazine* 165(January-February 1982): 26–35.

18. This observation is based on the following works: Stephen A. Rhoades, "Limitations of Antitrust Laws for the Analysis of Market Extension Mergers," Unpublished paper (1981); and George Kaufman, Larry Mote, and Harvey Rosenblum, "Implications of Deregulation for Product Lines and Geographic Markets of Financial Institutions," *Journal of Bank Research* 14(Summer 1983): 8–21.

2
Cost Economics in Banking

Normally, owners and customers have interests in the economic efficiency of a firm. The owners' interests stem from profit motives. The greater the economic efficiency of the firm's operations, the lower the costs and the higher the profits. The customers' interests derive from the desire to pay lower prices and obtain higher quality goods and services. Therefore, greater efficiency can lead to reductions in costs that are partly used by the profit-maximizing firm to lower prices or improve the quality of goods and services produced.

The public sector should also be concerned about the economic efficiency of the firm—to the extent that the firm's economic efficiency and behavior have external effects. For example, the public sector's concerns about the economic efficiency of banks is usually rationalized on the grounds that the efficiency of individual banks may affect the stability of the banking industry and, in turn, the effectiveness of the monetary system. A well-managed bank offers the productive sector of the economy a public service without which economic growth might be seriously hampered.

An examination of the economic efficiency, or cost economics, of banking is thus important for three reasons. First, owners of banks are interested in knowing how to improve cost efficiency to achieve higher profits and improve the chances of survival, especially in the face of the recent deregulation and its potential effects on market competition. Second, customers are interested in knowing the effects of deregulation on costs and, consequently, the prices and quality of bank services and the likely effect on the number of new services that may be offered. Finally, policymakers would like to have information on bank costs and competition under the present deregulatory regime to help them formulate policies affecting the banking industry as a whole.

This chapter examines cost economics in banking. Cost economics in banking, as in other industries, involves three aspects—cost considerations of size, scope, and technology. Our purpose is to critically evaluate the empirical models used in the literature for examining cost economics in banking. It is hoped that such an evaluation will shed some light on the practical implications of past empirical results. Additionally, an assessment of past bank cost models will set the stage for discussion of empirical models we will use in chapters 4, 5, and 6. The next section discusses the cost characteristics of commercial banks. It is followed by an examination of theoretical and empirical aspects of scale economies in banking. Other sections consider the empirical aspects of scope economies, in addition to the effects of technology on bank costs. The last section provides a summary. Also included are two appendixes with discussions of other cost functions that may be needed to properly examine cost efficiency.

Cost Characteristics of Commercial Banks

Firms in any industry are characterized by their own peculiar internal operations and external transactions, which imply unique cost structures and patterns. One way to examine the cost characteristics of banks is to compare the cost properties of banks with those of manufacturing firms. In this respect, it is important to consider the following: (1) fixed versus variable costs, (2) costs of joint products, and (3) allocable versus inallocable costs.

Fixed versus Variable Costs

Like manufacturing firms, banks generally require large fixed expenses in facilities, equipment, and full-time personnel. A large proportion of these expenses are fixed because of the nature of demand for bank services. For example, the volume of checks processed can fluctuate widely from one day of the week to the next, from month to month, and from one season to another. Similarly, the number of loans can vary from one season to another. For instance, agricultural banks face seasonal changes in their loan and deposit activities. These fluctuations require that banks maintain a sufficiently large fixed capacity in terms of personnel and equipment to accommodate service demands during peak periods, resulting in relatively large fixed costs.

Joint Products and Costs

Like most manufacturing firms, banks produce more than one product. In the shoe industry, for example, firms produce women's, men's, and children's shoes; and refineries produce different types of gasoline, such as jet fuel, diesel fuel, and a variety of other types of fuel. Banks also produce a wide variety of services, including demand deposits, time deposits, certificates of deposit, commercial loans, agricultural loans, installment loans, real estate loans, investment, and so on.

Product jointness can be important when inputs are used to produce more than one product, because the cost efficiency of the firm can depend on the output combination produced by it. In banking, demand deposits and time deposits (two distinct services) may be produced by the same employees using the same facilities. Furthermore, various types of loans and securities may be produced by the same factors of production. An examination of joint production properties may help in evaluating the cost structure of commercial banks.

Allocable versus Nonallocable Costs

Since banks produce a variety of products, as a first step in analyzing bank costs it is necessary to relate costs to the products produced. For our purposes, most banks' costs are easily traceable and can be associated directly with either a fund-acquiring activity (deposits), a fund-administration activity (loans), or a nonfund activity. This task may not be so easy, however, for manufacturing firms.

In attempting to piece together the cost characteristics of banks, we may further compare (in terms of percentages) the cost of production in manufacturing to the cost of production in banking. The primary function of a banking firm is the acquisition of deposits and the conversion of the resulting funds into loans and securities investment, or the so-called intermediation task. An important contrast between a bank and an industrial concern is that banks are peculiar in the way they pay for the acquisition of their raw material—that is, deposits. Whereas industrial firms make cash payments only for raw materials, banks pay in terms of cash (or interest payments) and in-kind services, including protection of depositors' funds, funds transfer services, collection of checks deposited, record keeping, monthly statements, and so forth. Another important difference between banks and industrial firms is that although industrial firms usually purchase their raw materials and retain the property rights of the materials until the finished goods are sold, banks acquire the right to use their raw material (or deposits) only for as long as owners of deposits allow. This factor increases risk costs of raw materials in banking as compared to nonfinancial companies.

Providing in-kind services as a way of compensating owners of deposits is an important component of the banking operation. In fact, the largest operations in most commercial banks in terms of the number of personnel are those involved in the provision of services to depositors.[1] Table 2–1 provides a comparison of costs for a manufacturing plant and a commercial bank in 1969. About 30 percent of bank costs were attributable to in-kind services rendered depositors. The interest expenses incurred for the use of funds constituted about 50 percent of total costs. The items *cost of funds* and *cost of sales* represent the total costs of producing a good in the banking versus manufacturing industries, respectively. Such costs are somewhat lower in banking

Table 2–1
Comparative Composition of Total Operating Costs in Manufacturing versus Banking, 1969
(percentage)

Representative Manufacturing Plant		Representative Bank	
Material	63	Interest	50
Labor	14	Noninterest cost of funds	30
Manufacturing overhead	13	Total cost of funds	80
Toal cost of sales	90		
		Other costs	20
Other costs	10	Total operating costs	100
Total operating costs	100		

Source: Adapted from Haskins and Sell, *Bank Costs for Planning and Control* (Park Ridge, Ill.: Bank Administration Institute, 1972), 64.

than in manufacturing. The item *other costs* in banking corresponds to the cost of making and servicing loans and to other tasks. In manufacturing, *other costs* correspond most closely with the costs of selling the finished goods, which are considerably less than such costs in banking.

Scale Economies in Banking

As a firm expands its scale of operations, economies of scale occur if it is able to reduce costs per unit of output, holding all other factors constant. However, the observation that per unit costs fall as output increases does not necessarily imply the existence of scale economies. The reduction in costs per unit of output may be caused by technological advancements or improvements in managerial techniques. To obtain the effect of scale only on cost, one must separate out the effects of technological advances and other factors. *Returns to scale* thus refer to the relationship between changes in output and changes in inputs when all other factors are held constant.

Economies of scale, or increasing returns to scale, arise when the doubling of output requires less than the doubling of every input. The causes of increasing returns to scale are fourfold.[2] First, the firm may possess unavoidable excess capacity of some inputs. Specifically, some inputs may be wholly or partly indivisible by output. For example, the cost of inventing a new technique is indivisible with respect to the level of output produced by using the technique. The cost of producing the first copy of a book is indivisible with respect to the number of copies produced. A railroad may have a tunnel that is necessary for a given level of traffic, but it can handle relatively more traffic. Similarly, a bank may have excess capacity of some inputs for most of the year, so that an increase in output may not require a proportionate increase in all inputs for the entire year. The presence of indivisibility should help reduce costs per unit of output as the output level is increased.

Second, many inputs cost less when they are purchased on a larger scale. For example, machinery, equipment, and buildings usually cost less per unit of capacity when larger sizes are purchased. The effect of large size should not be confused with the effect of large numbers, however. Economies of large size stem from a generally true physical relationship between capacity and surface area—in effect, increases in capacity (volume) are generally proportionately greater than concomitant increases in the surface area. For example, doubling the capacity (floor space) of a room ten yards in length and width requires only a 50 percent increase in the wall length and width, thus reducing costs per unit of floor space.[3]

Third, relatively large operations allow for greater input and process specialization in production than do small operations. In a small banking operation, for example, tellers may also be assigned to sorting checks and auditing accounts part-time. Greater specialization (and reductions in per unit cost) is possible with increases in size.

Fourth and last, the law of large numbers accounts for certain economies of scale. By way of example, as a firm expands sales, the appropriate quantity of inventory to be maintained need not be increased proportionately, because the demand for goods is spread across a greater number of customers. This smoothing effect may also be applicable to banking, in that large banks may not need to hold as much in inventory (cash balances) as do small banks (at least in proportion to their anticipated transactions). Since holding cash balances is costly, larger banks should incur lower costs of holding cash balances than do small banks to the extent that the law of large numbers smooths transactions demands.[4]

If these four factors are relevant, the long-run marginal cost curve of the firm will have a negative slope and, by definition, there will be economies of scale.[5] Figure 2–1 shows a declining long-run marginal cost (LMC) curve and a long-run average cost (LAC) curve with a series of short-run marginal cost (SMC) and short-run average cost (SAC) curves. The long-run curves allow for simultaneous changes in all factors of production, and the short-run cost curves represent cost changes as output increases because of changes in some (but not all) factors of production. Each set of short-run cost curves represents a different amount of fixed factors of production. For example, the fixed factors associated with SMC_2 and SAC_2 are greater than those for SMC_1 and SAC_1.

Scale economies do not continue indefinitely with the expansion of size. As the scale of operation increases, there comes a point at which limitations to efficient management set in and long-run marginal cost tends to rise. An

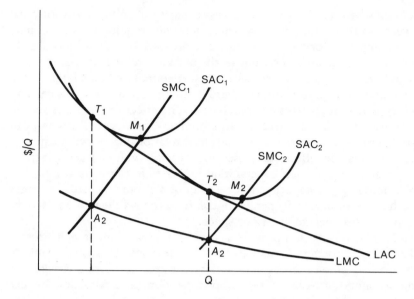

Figure 2–1. Relationship between Short-Run and Long-Run Cost Curves

important reason for this adverse effect is that as size expands, top management tends to delegate responsibility and authority to lower-echelon staff. Intimate control and contact with the daily routine of operations tends to be mitigated, resulting in organizational rigidity, red tape, increased paper work, and other consequences of size that eventually cause operational efficiency to decline.

Many firms find it necessary, at some point, to decentralize operations in order to avoid the costs of organizational rigidity that largeness entails. The dilemma, however, is that decentralization might sacrifice some of the gains from large-scale operations. In the extreme, the firm may decide to decentralize functions by dividing its operation into separate plants (or branches) to the point at which no cost gains are available from large-scale operations or joint advertising. Such a firm would consist of a set of quasi-independent branches and would probably be subject to rising long-run marginal costs.

Therefore, the most critical question facing management is how large the bank should be. Alternatively, at exactly what point should the bank branch out? For regulators and policymakers, these questions give rise to related concerns. For example, can competition with larger banks drive smaller banks out of the market? What is the most efficient bank size? Can the efficient bank size emerge naturally in the absence of regulation? Should regulation protect smaller banks from their larger counterparts? If regulation is desired, what regulatory frameworks would entail the most efficient outcome without sacrificing market competition? These questions (and others) make a careful analysis of bank cost structures imperative.

Methodological Problems in Measuring the Scale Effect in Banking

The production decision is concerned with choice among alternative production processes—that is, the selection of production techniques and the allocation of resources. How much and what to produce and the efficient combination of resources are key issues in any production problem. From the standpoint of the researcher, however, it is of paramount importance (1) to precisely define the product that the industry under investigation produces and (2) to identify as accurately as possible the production process, which we hereafter refer to as the production function chosen by the firm.

Alternative Output Measurement

Economies of scale are defined in terms of the volume of output the bank produces. An accurate measurement of output is therefore necessary for any estimation of the scale effect. Commercial banks, however, produce services rather than readily identifiable physical products, and it is not clear how to measure service output. Without question, commercial banks produce intermediation services through the acquisition of deposits and other liabilities and the transfer of these funds to interest-earning assets such as loans, securities, and other investments. But how can intermediation services be expressed as a unit for the purpose of measurement? The difficulty is that intermediation is a multifaceted task. Funds acquisition is a process that requires unique techniques, skills, and marketing expertise that are principally different from those required to extend loans and make investments. Furthermore, in the area of lending, it may not be appropriate to use the same measurement scale to quantify the relative output of commercial loans, real estate loans, consumer installment loans, agricultural loans, and international loans. Because of their peculiar nature, these loans are effectively different products that are extended in different markets, with their own specific risk, marketing, and servicing characteristics. Similar problems may arise when various types of deposits and liabilities are compared. For example, it may be more costly to maintain demand deposits than time deposits because the frequency of check clearing, balance inquiries, and deposit and withdrawal activity is far greater.

A major problem, then, is how to differentiate among various loans, deposits, and other "products" on the asset and liability sides of the balance sheet. Should all products be measured in terms of the number of accounts, or should dollar values be used? What are the criteria for choosing one type of measurement over another? Early cost studies in banking (see chapter 3) defined output as the dollar amount of loans and investments made. Later studies used the number of deposit accounts and loans processed, because it was believed that if cost efficiency were measured in dollars, economies of scale in processing larger accounts would be confused with scale economies of bank operations.

We will measure outputs in dollar amounts for the purpose of empirical analysis. Dollar amounts are preferred, because we believe banks compete to increase market share of dollar amounts, as opposed to the number of accounts. As previously suggested, the use of *number of accounts* presents a problem in that it implies that there are equal costs per account across various types of accounts. Contrary to this implication, demand deposit accounts, for instance, may be more active and thus more costly to maintain than time deposit accounts; installment loan accounts may be more costly to maintain than industrial loans; and so forth. Using dollar values as the measure of output alleviates this problem. The reason for this is that competition among banks to attract more dollars in the form of low-cost accounts raises their relative cost. In equilibrium, a competitive market should drive the marginal cost per dollar of accounts across all deposit accounts (for example) to be the same.

A third justification for dollar measurement of output is that banks are multiservice firms. As we will discuss in chapter 3, some studies have proxied bank services by a single index that combines all services into a unidimensional measure. Others have measured each bank service (that is, deposit or loan account) separately. Additionally, some researchers have chosen to measure output in terms of bank assets and liabilities by focusing either on only one side of the balance sheet or on both sides at the same time. Whatever the best way to measure intermediation services may be, *dollars* is the only common denominator (for example, securities investments can not be measured in numbers of accounts).

Some studies have used bank revenue to measure bank output. For example, Greenbaum[6] used the dollar market value of services rendered to measure output in an attempt to estimate the real social value (or contribution to community well-being) of banking services.[7] Output was defined as

$$Q = b_1 Z_1 + b_2 Z_2 + \cdots + b_n Z_n + \text{NI}, \qquad (2.1)$$

where the Z's and b's represent financial services and their corresponding market prices, respectively, and NI is the nonlending gross operating income of the bank. The b's were estimated from a regression that related gross income per dollar of assets to the types of earning assets the bank holds, ceteris paribus:

$$Y_j/A_j = b_o + \sum_{i=1}^{n} b_i \frac{Z_{ji}}{A_j} + \sum_{k=1}^{m} b_k X_{jk} \qquad (2.2)$$

where Y_j = gross income due to lending of the jth bank;

   A_j = total assets;

   Z_{ji} = i types of assets ($i = 1, \ldots, n$); and

   X_{jk} = banking structure variables ($k = 1, \ldots, m$), such as the population in the banks' market area, the state in which it resides, and the number of competing banks.

This approach considers demand and time deposits to be inputs, so that output is only in terms of assets.

A major problem with Greenbaum's approach is that observed variations in operating income can be due to changes in physical units, prices, or both. Furthermore, operating income does not necessarily provide an accurate measure of community well-being because, to the extent that banks do not perfectly price-discriminate, operating income would underestimate community well-being by the amount of consumers' surplus. Furthermore, as observed by Benston, operating income is a function of the price elasticity of demands for bank services, the riskiness of earning assets, and the production cost of earning assets.[8] These factors were not taken into account by Greenbaum in computing the output of the banks.

A recent study by Gilligan and Smirlock measured output in dollars, but only because the data source (Call Reports of Income and Condition) did not have the numbers of account available.[9] Since total operating expenses are not allocated in balance sheet and income statement data, output was measured as either demand and time deposits or securities and loans. Other potential drawbacks of using such data are (1) that input prices are assumed constant and (2) that other bank services are excluded even though they affect total operating expenses.

To our knowledge, no studies have used dollars to measure the output of banks on a conventional model of bank services and Functional Cost Analysis (FCA) data sources. In chapters 4 and 5 we present cost efficiency findings for key bank services on both sides of the balance sheet. To overcome the methodological drawbacks of the Gilligan and Smirlock study, FCA data are employed. We believe that dollar measurement of output is superior to measurement by numbers of accounts for the practical and theoretical reasons cited. Perhaps the most crucial part of our argument is that market competition will drive the cost of the last dollar acquired or invested by any given bank to be the same as all other banks (or financial service companies). This argument was less applicable to the banking environment of the 1960s and early 1970s than it is today. Regulatory control and other barriers to entry protected banks from the pressures of free-market competition. As was documented in chapter 1, however, new technology, new financial service sellers, and industry deregulation have substantially increased the exposure of banks to competition. Hence, a case can be made against the use of dollars to measure output in past studies on the grounds that costs per dollar output could differ depending on the competitiveness of the bank's market. This objection is less appropriate in the 1980s because of the growing nationwide competition for deposit funds and (to a lesser degree) credit.

Types of Banks

A problem that has not received much attention in the literature is the fact that commercial banks tend to specialize in separate market niches. For example, some banks specialize in making agricultural loans. Other banks specialize in commercial loans, still other bank groups specialize in installment loans, and so on. How meaningful are the results of the cost studies that represent all commercial banks lumped together as one group? For example, what would be the reaction of an agricultural banker to a set of estimated cost results that represented all kinds of banks? How useful would the results be to policymakers? Agricultural banks are generally more seasonal in lending and deposit-taking than other banks. In agricultural banks, the nature of risk, timing of payments, amount of loans, and customer relationships are generally different from other banks, as, for example, international banks are different from city banks or rural banks. Finally, for all practical purposes, competition normally occurs only between those banks with similar market orientations. For these reasons, the results of a cost study that aggregates all banks into one group may well be meaningless to any specific bank group. In recognition of this problem, chapter 5 presents a method for clustering banks into various groups according to their product (market) characteristics. Separate cost analyses and comparisons of cost characteristics are performed for each group of banks.

Stocks versus Flows

Another important problem overshadowing a great deal of the literature is that bank outputs are generally defined in terms of stock variables, such as loans, demand and time deposits, securities, and so forth. Stock variables do not correspond with the fundamental nature of the bank production process. Bank production is a continuous, or flow, process in which inputs are continuously transformed into a flow of services using existing technology. One way to capture flows is to define bank output as gross revenue, sales, earnings, or some market value proxy of bank output, but these measures are prone to problems of their own (for example, the previously discussed measures of Greenbaum).

Another possible solution is to define bank output as a simple average of the number of accounts outstanding at the end of each month or the number outstanding per year. As already mentioned, this measure has its shortcomings. Even if the previously cited problems with this measure are accepted, there is a major bias introduced: the output of banks with large accounts would be underestimated, whereas the output of banks with relatively small accounts would be overestimated.

Figure 2–2 illustrates this potential bias. Banks A and B are assumed to have 1,000 demand deposits accounts each. The average sizes of accounts at banks A and B are $200 and $600, respectively. The line $0R$ shows a hypothetical regression line between *size of accounts* and *number of accounts*. If operating costs depended on the number of accounts, bank B would be larger than bank A, but they would have the same operating costs. With all else the same, the rate of return on assets for bank B would exceed that of bank A. Since operating expenses per unit asset are relatively lower for bank B than for bank A, bank A should increase its account sizes to be competitive with bank B (that is, lower earnings for bank A will lower its capital and growth rate, not to mention its ability to sell services at competitive prices). Resultant

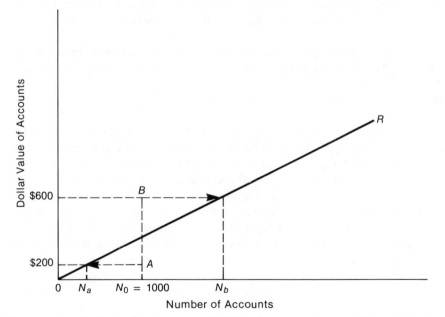

Figure 2–2. Relationship between the Number and Average Size of Bank Accounts

competition for larger accounts will proceed until, at the margin, the cost per dollar of serving small accounts is equal to the cost per dollar of serving large accounts (which includes advertising and promotional costs). Since the number of accounts treats large and small accounts as equals, bank activities to attract and service large accounts will be underestimated by the cost function, leading to biased estimated parameters. In figure 2–2, $N_0 N_b$ approximates the number of accounts by which bank B's activities in serving and attracting a large account are underestimated. Conversely, $N_0 N_a$ approximates the number of accounts by which bank A's activities in serving and attracting a small account are overestimated.

Production Functions and Alternative Methodologies of Measuring Scale

The problems of measuring output aside, there is the problem of specifying a model that corresponds with the way banks transform inputs into outputs. More specifically, what exactly are the characteristics of the bank's production function that best identify the relationship between inputs and outputs? How do banks maximize outputs per unit of input? How many units of outputs will result from the employment of given quantities of various inputs? These questions can be examined by developing a simple production function as a prelude to the more complicated situations observed in the banking industry.

A production function identifies the relationship between the quantities of output resulting from the use of various quantities of inputs. For example:

$$Y = aX \tag{2.3}$$

is a linear one-output/one-input production function, where Y measures the quantity of the output produced by the employment of X units of the input, and the parameter a gives the quantity of output that results from a one-unit change in X. Average product, or AP, is defined as the quantity of Y per unit of X; that is, $AP = Y/X = a$. Marginal product, or MP, is defined as the change in Y, or ΔY, that results from a one-unit change in X, or ΔX; that is, $MP = \Delta Y/\Delta X = a$. Obviously, in this simple linear case, $AP = MP$.

A more complicated linear production function involving more than one input is as follows:

$$Y = aX + bW + cZ \tag{2.4}$$

where X, W, and Z are the inputs. In this case, average products and marginal products are defined for each input when all other inputs are held constant. For example, the expression $AP_{x|w,z} = \Delta Y/\Delta X = a$ denotes the marginal product of X when inputs W and Z are held constant. Notice that the production function in equation (2.4) assumes that output Y always changes in the same proportion for changes in each output, no matter how many units of given inputs are employed. Thus, if all inputs are increased by a factor of $t = 10$, Y will also increase by the factor $t = 10$ times, no matter what the initial quantities of X, W, and Z are. Thus, equation (2.4) may be expressed alternatively as

$$Y' = a(tX) + b(tW) + c(tZ)$$

$$Y' = t(aX + bW + cZ)$$

$$Y' = tY \quad \text{or} \quad Y' = 10Y \tag{2.5}$$

This property is referred to as *constant returns to scale*, where the change in output is proportionate to changes in the inputs.

A major drawback plaguing production functions of this form is that they preclude estimation of economies and diseconomies of scale or, correspondingly, increasing and decreasing returns to scale. The reason, of course, is that production functions, as specified, imply the employment of no fixed factor of production. For our purposes, this assumption is not realistic, because banks do use fixed factors of production, such as land, buildings, and equipment. To rectify this problem, a constant term, A, may be added to capture the effect of fixed inputs:

$$Y = A + aX + bW + cZ \tag{2.6}$$

If A is zero, there are no economies (or diseconomies) of large size.

An improvement over the simple linear production function is the following generalized Cobb-Douglas functional form:

$$Y = AX^a W^b Z^c \tag{2.7}$$

which can be rewritten in the form of a log-linear equation:

$$\ln Y = \ln A + a \ln X + b \ln W + c \ln Z \tag{2.8}$$

where A represents fixed inputs, including the effect of technology. The parameters a, b, and c indicate output elasticities for the respective inputs. For example, the elasticity of Y with respect to X is

$$\frac{\partial \ln Y}{\partial \ln X} = \frac{\%\Delta Y}{\%\Delta X} = \frac{\Delta Y}{\Delta X} \cdot \frac{X}{Y} = a \tag{2.9}$$

where a is the percentage change in the output Y resulting from a given percentage change in the input X, holding all other inputs and technology constant. Notice that the output elasticities are not affected by the level of inputs; that is, the size of bank does not affect how changes in inputs affect output in percentage terms. To be more specific, assume that all inputs increase by the factor t so that output increases to

$$
\begin{aligned}
Y' &= A(tX)^a(tW)^b(tZ)^c \\
&= t^{a+b+c}AX^aW^bZ^c \\
&= t^{a+b+c}Y
\end{aligned}
\tag{2.10}
$$

Regardless of the initial size of the bank (represented by output level Y), output increases by a factor of t^{a+b+c} as inputs increase. If $(a + b + c) > 1$, output increases at a rate greater than the rate of increase in the inputs, and the production process is uniformly increasing returns to scale. On the other hand, if $(a + b + c) < 1$, output increases at a lesser rate than the rate of increase in the inputs, and the production process is uniformly decreasing returns to scale. Constant returns to scale are obtained when $(a + b + c) = 1$. The main disadvantage of the Cobb-Douglas production function is that it only allows for uniform scale characteristics. Thus, the cost function is restricted to reflecting increasing returns to scale, decreasing returns to scale, or constant returns to scale, but not any combination of these scale outcomes, as would be required to consider a U-shaped cost curve.

A further restriction of the Cobb-Douglas production function is that it limits the way factor inputs can be substituted for one another. Specifically, the elasticity of factor substitution, or σ (defined as the proportionate rate of change of the input ratio divided by the proportionate rate of change in the ratio of factor marginal products in the Cobb-Douglas production function), is unity:

$$
\sigma = \frac{\Delta(X/W)}{X/W} \div \frac{\Delta(MP_w/MP_x)}{MP_w/MP_x} = 1
\tag{2.11}
$$

where X and W are the units of the two inputs and MP_x and MP_w are the marginal products of the inputs, respectively. In general, however, the elasticity of substitution between two inputs can take on any number between zero and infinity for convex isoquants. The larger the elasticity of substitution, the greater the degree of substitutability between the two inputs. If, for example, σ is infinite, then X and W are perfect substitutes. If $\sigma = 0$, X and W are complementary and therefore must be used in fixed proportion. A major disadvantage of setting the value of $\sigma = 1$, a priori, is that if the bank's production process actually reflects $\sigma \neq 1$, the cost estimates may be biased.

Another major problem in using the Cobb-Douglas model has been the disregard for the existence of a dual relationship between production functions and cost functions. Specifically, corresponding to every output maximization process, there always exists a counterpart cost-minimization process, and vice versa. Firms maximize profits either by maximizing the amount of output they produce, given their resource endowments (budget), or, equivalently, by minimizing the cost of producing a given amount of output. These are not two alternative approaches to profit maximization but rather the same approach seen from two perspectives. To properly estimate cost, it is necessary that the cost function reflect the properties of its dual production function. Otherwise, the estimated costs may not reflect the true profit-maximizing behavior of the firm. Unfortunately, most bank cost studies that have utilized the Cobb-Douglas ignore this dual relationship.[10]

One way to correct for the duality problem is to derive the cost function from its corresponding production function. Following Nerlove,[11] assume a generalized Cobb-Douglas production function for a bank as

$$Y = a_o K^{a_1} L^{a_2} u \tag{2.12}$$

where Y = output per period;

   K = capital input;

   L = labor input;

   a_i = elasticity of Y with respect to the inputs; and

   u = a residual expressing neutral variations in efficiency among firms.

Given total costs equal to

$$TC = P_k K + P_l L \tag{2.13}$$

where P_k and P_l are the unit prices of capital and labor, respectively, cost minimization implies the familiar marginal productivity conditions, or

$$P_k K / a_1 = P_l L / a_2. \tag{2.14}$$

As observed by Nerlove, there are problems associated with estimating relationships between inputs and outputs whenever the prices paid for factors vary systematically from firm to firm because independence among production efficiency, output level, and factor prices no longer holds. Because of the likelihood of this factor price problem, it is preferable to derive estimates of the structural parameters from estimates of reduced-form parameters. An important reduced form of equations (2.12), (2.13), and (2.14) is as follows:

$$C = \gamma Y^{1/r} P_k{}^{a_1/r} P_l{}^{a_2/r} V \tag{2.15}$$

where $\gamma = r(a_0 a_1{}^{a_1} a_2{}^{a_2})^{-1/r}$;

$V = u^{-1/r}$; and

$r = a_1 + a_2.$

The parameter r, which is equal to the sum of output elasticities with respect to K and L, measures the degree of returns to scale. Because cost function (2.15) is directly derived from minimizing the cost relationship (2.13) subject to the production function (2.12), the duality between cost and production functions assures that the relation between the cost function, obtained empirically, and the underlying production function is unique.

Equation (2.15) can be rewritten in the log-linear form as

$$\ln C = \ln \gamma + (1/r)\ln Y + (a_1/r)\ln P_k + (a_2/r)\ln P_l + \ln V \tag{2.16}$$

Since duality requires that input prices be homogeneous of degree one, the price coefficients in equation (2.16) must add up to one; that is, $a_1/r + a_2/r = 1$. With this restriction, equation (2.16) becomes

$$\ln C - \ln P_k = \ln \gamma + (1/r)\ln Y + (a_2/r)(\ln P_l - \ln P_k) + \ln V \tag{2.17}$$

Equation (2.17) can be estimated to derive a measure for economies of scale. Once again, a problem plaguing the applicability of equation (2.17) is that it only allows for a uniform scale economy, which disallows U-shaped cost curves. Also, the elasticity of substitution between the two inputs is restricted to unity.

Constant elasticity of substitution (CES) production functions (which are homogeneous functions) allow for any degree of substitutability between two input factors and are therefore more general than Cobb-Douglas production functions. A typical CES function is

$$Y = A[bK^{-g} + (1 - b)L^{-g}]^{-z/g} \tag{2.18}$$

where K and L are two factors of production and z is the degree of homogeneity (or the measure of scale properties). The measure of elasticity of substitution between K and L is $\sigma = 1/(1 + g)$, which is constant regardless of the amount of inputs employed. The corresponding cost minimizing function is

$$C = Y^{1/z}A^{-1/z}[b^{1/(1+g)}P_k^{g/(1+g)} + (1 - b)^{1/(1+g)}r_2^{g/(1+g)}]^{(1+g)/g}$$

$$((2.19)$$

which is amenable to cost estimation. The CES production function has proved to be useful for the analysis of production with one output and two factors of production.[12] However, for situations in which the firm produces more than one product or employs more than one factor input, the CES is highly restrictive.[13]

A significant advancement over the CES production function is the translog production function. Developed by Christensen, Jorgenson, and Lau, the translog production and cost functions overcome all the problems associated with the Cobb-Douglas and CES models.[14] They allow estimation of production (or cost) functions with more than one output and more than two inputs. Further, they are flexible in form in that they allow for any degree of substitutability at all levels of input employment. Most important, translog models allow estimation of U-shaped cost curves.

Unlike the Cobb-Douglas and CES models that allowed the derivation of a cost function from specified production functions, translog cost functions are intractable from corresponding translog production functions. Alternatively, however, applying the duality properties, translog cost functions are obtained by a Taylor series expansion around a specified point of a generalized log-linear cost function of the form

$$\ln C = f(\ln Q_1, \ln Q_2, \ln P_1, \ln P_2) \tag{2.20}$$

where $Q_i(i = 1, 2)$ are the quantities of products produced by the firm and P_i ($i = 1, 2$) are the prices of two input factors. The following translog cost function is a log-linear quadratic local approximation to the arbitrary multiproduct cost function specified in equation (2.20) around a point of expansion:

$$\ln C = \alpha_0 + \alpha_1 \ln Q_1 + \alpha_2 \ln Q_2 + \frac{1}{2}\delta_{11}(\ln Q_1)^2 + \frac{1}{2}\delta_{22}(\ln Q_2)^2$$

$$+ \delta_{12}(\ln Q_1)(\ln Q_2) + \beta_1 \ln P_1 + \beta_2 \ln P_2 + \frac{1}{2}\gamma_{11}(\ln P_1)^2$$

$$+ \frac{1}{2}\gamma_{22}(\ln P_2)^2 + \gamma_{12}(\ln P_1)(\ln P_2) + \rho_{11}(\ln P_1)(\ln Q_1)$$

$$+ \rho_{12}(\ln P_1)(\ln Q_2) + \rho_{21}(\ln P_2)(\ln Q_1) + \rho_{22}(\ln P_2)(\ln Q_2)$$

$$\tag{2.21}$$

where by symmetry $\gamma_{12} = \gamma_{21}$ and $\delta_{12} = \delta_{21}$.

Duality conditions require that the cost function be linearly homogeneous in prices, or

$$\frac{\partial \ln C}{\partial \ln P_1} + \frac{\partial \ln C}{\partial \ln P_2} = 1 \tag{2.22}$$

which, in turn, requires the following restrictions on the parameters of function (2.21):

$$\beta_1 + \beta_2 = 1 \tag{2.23a}$$

$$\gamma_{11} + \gamma_{12} = 0 \quad \text{and} \quad \gamma_{22} + \gamma_{12} = 0 \tag{2.23b}$$

$$\rho_{11} + \rho_{21} = 0 \quad \text{and} \quad \rho_{22} + \rho_{12} = 0, \tag{2.23c}$$

By imposing these parameter restrictions, the following cost function can be derived:

$$\ln C - \ln P_2 = \alpha_0 + \alpha_1 \ln Q_1 + \alpha_2 \ln Q_2 + \frac{1}{2}\delta_{11}(\ln Q_1)^2$$

$$+ \frac{1}{2}\delta_{22}(\ln Q_2)^2 + \delta_{12}(\ln Q_1)(\ln Q_2) + \beta_1(\ln P_1 - \ln P_2)$$

$$+ \gamma_{11}\left[\frac{1}{2}(\ln P_1)^2 - (\ln P_1)(\ln P_2)\right] + \gamma_{22}\left[\frac{1}{2}(\ln P_2)^2\right.$$

$$\left. - (\ln P_1)(\ln P_2)\right] + \rho_{11}\left[(\ln P_1)(\ln Q_1) - (\ln P_2)(\ln Q_2)\right]$$

$$+ \rho_{12}\left[(\ln P_1)(\ln Q_2) - (\ln P_2)(\ln Q_2)\right]$$

$$+ \rho_{21}\left[(\ln P_2)(\ln Q_1) - (\ln P_2)(\ln Q_2)\right] \tag{2.24}$$

Economies of Scale and Marginal Cost in a Multiproduct Firm

The multiproduct nature of banks makes analysis and interpretation of returns to scale somewhat complex, because average cost is only defined for single product processes. Unless all products are aggregated into a single index, conventional textbook average cost curves cannot be derived for multiproduct firms. The problem with aggregating all outputs into a single index is like adding apples and oranges. An alternative approach to aggregation would be to consider the behavior of costs as the size of the firm's outputs increase proportionately. If each product in the bundle increases by a given percentage, the quantity of the composite commodity increases by the same percentage.

Baumol has shown that the concept of ray average costs (RAC) describes average costs for the multiproduct firm without recourse to arbitrary aggregation.[15] Defining RAC as

$$RAC = C(kQ_i)/k \qquad (2.25)$$

where Q_i is a vector of outputs, or the unit bundle, for a particular mixture of outputs $(Q_1, \ldots, Q_n)$ and k is the number of units in the bundle such that $Q = kQ_i$, economies of scale are present when RAC is strictly declining, or

$$C(kQ_i)/k < C(tQ_i)/t, \quad \text{for } k > t. \qquad (2.26)$$

Alternatively, economies of scale are obtained in a multiproduct, multi-input firm if for $(X_1, \ldots, X_m)$ quantity of inputs and $(Q_1, \ldots, Q_n)$ quantity of outputs, the proportionate increase in the output vector $(wQ_1, \ldots, wQ_m)$ exceeds the proportionate increase in the input vector $(vX_1, \ldots, vX_m)$, where $w > v$. The RAC definition of scale economies, however, is preferable to the latter definition because it does not require firms to increase inputs proportionately. It does require, however, that firms expand all outputs at the same rate while mixing inputs optimally.

The importance of the concept of economies of scale in a one-output case is that its existence is said to be required to have natural monopoly. In a multiproduct situation, however, the existence of economies of scale is not a sufficient condition for a natural monopoly. For example, it is possible to have economies of scale within the given range of demand for all products, yet one firm produces the products at a higher ray average cost than it costs a group of firms to produce the same amounts of the products separately. Scale economies describe only the technical gains from increases in scale of operation, rather than gains originating from the production of several goods jointly. In other words, economies of scale do not detect whether it is cheaper to produce two different output bundles separately by different firms or jointly by one firm.

A sufficient condition for the existence of natural monopoly in a multiproduct case is the subadditivity of costs. A cost function is subadditive when single-firm production of the output mix $Q_i = (Q_1, \ldots, Q_m)$ is less costly than production of Q_i using any combination or division of Q_i among a group of firms, holding technology and input prices constant. For example, in a three-product case, $Q_i = (Q_1, Q_2, Q_3)$, a necessary condition for subadditivity is that no group of firms—say, firms A and B—producing (Q_1^A, Q_2^A, Q_3^A) and (Q_1^B, Q_2^B, Q_3^B), respectively, could produce Q_i as cheaply as one firm producing Q_i combined, where

$$Q_1 = Q_1^A + Q_1^B \qquad (2.27a)$$

$$Q_2 = Q_2^A + Q_2^B \qquad (2.27b)$$

$$Q_3 = Q_3^A + Q_3^B \qquad (2.27c)$$

Hence, subadditivity holds only if

$$C(Q_1, Q_2, Q_3) < C(Q_1^A, Q_2^A, Q_3^A) + C(Q_1^B, Q_2^B, Q_3^B)$$

$$(2.28)$$

for all nonnegative values of Q_i^A and Q_i^B.

Subadditivity of cost functions stems from two sources: (1) ray economies of scale (that is, a declining ray average cost) and (2) interproduct cost complementarities, where the marginal cost of producing one product declines with increases in production of a different product—that is, for a two-product case, or Q_1 and Q_2, $\partial^2 C / \partial Q_1 \, \partial Q_2 < 0$ at point $Q_i \equiv (Q_1, Q_2)$. In short, subadditivity of the multiproduct cost function is required for the existence of natural monopoly in all the product markets taken together.

Although subadditivity is a useful concept in the discussion of natural monopoly, it is difficult to devise a direct test of its existence. A direct test of subadditivity would require knowledge of the cost function in the neighborhood of zero outputs. Many researchers have alternatively opted for a weaker test that detects the presence of both declining ray average cost and economies of scope (for example, Fuss and Waverman observe that the simultaneous existence of declining ray average cost and economies of scope is sufficient to ensure local subadditivity).[16]

A number of researchers[17] have suggested that the appropriate measure of economies of scale in a multiproduct case is the sum of the individual output cost elasticities:

$$\text{SE} = \sum_{i=1}^{n} \frac{\partial \ln C}{\partial \ln Q_i} \quad \text{for } n = 1, 2 \qquad (2.29a)$$

The basis of this formula is

$$dC = \sum_{i=1}^{n} \frac{\partial C}{\partial Q_i} dQ_i \quad \text{for } n = 1, 2 \qquad (2.30a)$$

which in percentage terms is

$$d \ln C = \sum_{i=1}^{n} \frac{\partial \ln C}{\partial \ln Q_i} \cdot \frac{dQ_i}{Q_i} \qquad (2.30b)$$

In other words, the total change in cost equals the sum of the differential changes in the levels of the n outputs. Fuss and Waverman maintain that in order to interpret changes in cost resulting from changes in outputs in terms of economies of scale, it is convenient to assume that all outputs increase proportionately.[18] More formally, $dQ_i/Q_i = d \ln Q_i = k$. Substituting k for dQ_i/Q_i in equation (2.30b) and rearranging, we have

$$SE = \frac{d \ln C}{k} = \sum_{i=1}^{n} \frac{\partial \ln C}{\partial \ln Q_i} \qquad (2.29b)$$

If SE < 1, marginal overall costs are decreasing and, therefore, production is subject to increasing returns to scale. If SE > 1, the production function exhibits decreasing returns to scale. Finally, if SE $= 1$, constant returns to scale prevail.

One obvious flaw in this procedure is that profit maximization might require differential changes in the outputs of the bank. In other words, banks may maximize profits by varying outputs at different rates. This flaw is probably a small price to pay to incorporate separate outputs as separate variables and to avoid the aggregation problems of lumping all inputs together as one single variable.

Economies of scope are said to exist if for $Q_i = Q, \ldots, Q_n$ outputs,

$$C(Q_1, \ldots, Q_n) < C(Q_1, 0, \ldots, 0)$$
$$+ C(0, Q_2, \ldots, 0) + C(0, \ldots, 0, Q_n)$$
$$(2.31)$$

This expression implies that single-firm production of all Q_i is less costly than production of each Q_i separately by individual firms. Notice that economies of scope is a special case of subadditivity in which the division of outputs among firms takes the form of zero amount for all outputs except one.

Panzar and Willig have shown that economies of scope exist between any two products when a twice-differentiable multiproduct cost function exhibits cost complementarities between the products.[19] That is, as defined earlier, cost complementarities exist when $\partial^2 C/\partial Q_1 \partial Q_2 < 0$. By implication, the marginal cost of producing Q_1 is inversely dependent on the amounts of Q_2 produced, and vice versa. A small increase in the amount of Q_2 reduces the marginal cost of producing Q_1, ceteris paribus. Thus, joint production of Q_1 and Q_2 by one firm is less costly than the sum of costs when Q_1 and Q_2 are produced separately by two firms.

Willig has observed that economies of scope due to input sharing can occur (1) when excess capacity remains after the production of a subset of the outputs and (2) if some capital inputs can be freely shared among different production processes.[20] He has suggested that the degree of economies of scope can be measured as

$$SC = [C(Q_1, 0) + C(0, Q_2) - C(Q_1, Q_2)]/C(Q_1, Q_2) \quad (2.32)$$

where SC, if positive, measures the percentage reduction in total costs attributable to producing Q_1 and Q_2 jointly. The problem with this methodology is that when it is applied to the translog cost function, it is not possible to take the log of zero. (Appendix 2A discusses the hybrid cost function as a solution to this problem.)

Endogeneity of Bank Output and Consequent Estimation Problems

A well-defined cost function requires, among other things, that all the variables appearing on the right-hand side of the cost regression be exogenous, which means that they are autonomous, or predetermined. In the banking literature, however, many studies are plagued by the fact that one or more of the explanatory variables are endogenous. To have a full understanding of this problem and an appreciation for the possible remedies, consider the estimation problems caused by endogenous variables. Regression analysis requires that the relationship between the dependent variable and the independent (or predictor) variables be one-way, or unidirectional. For example, if Y were to be predicted on the basis of some fixed values of the X_i variables, relationships would run from the X_i's to the Y. There are many situations, however, in which such a unidirectional relationship does not apply. For example, if Y were the height and X were the weight of individuals, the relationship between X and Y would be simultaneous to a certain degree, so that Y (height) would be explained in part by X (weight), but weight could be explained also by height. In this situation, there would be a two-way relationship between X and Y that would break down the distinction between dependent and independent variables.

The problem of endogeneity is recognized in many bank cost studies. For example, Benston, Hanweck, and Humphrey (hereafter BHH) have observed that larger banks produce more deposit services, including payroll, cash management, and various funds transfer services per deposit account than do smaller banks.[21] This may imply that at least some bank outputs are endogenous, because they simultaneously affect bank operating costs. In econometrics it is well known that simultaneity of this kind can bias parameter estimates and render them meaningless. The solution that BHH propose is to add a predictor variable measuring average account size to adjust the number of accounts for bank size. In our opinion, however, this approach does not necessarily resolve the problem of endogeneity and may well cause another problem, in that the inclusion of average account size is likely to create a multicollinearity situation since the number and average size of accounts are highly correlated. (In the BHH study, the logarithm of total cost was regressed on the following predictors: (1) a Divisia index, which proxied the total number of bank accounts, (2) average size of account, (3) a vector of input prices, (4) branch bank status, and (5) holding company status. Obviously, the Divisia index and average account size are directly related to each other.)

Kim has recommended estimating a system of equations as a solution to the simultaneity problem in the BHH study.[22] The system of equations consists of a translog cost function, a cost-share equation, and a revenue-share equation (with the proper parameter restrictions to ensure linear homogeneity in factor prices and symmetry). Appendix 2B discusses Kim's model in more detail.

Although Kim's procedure certainly seems appropriate, it may not be totally necessary. First, the endogeneity problem in the banking industry is probably no more or less serious than it is in cost estimations in other industries. For example, output is at least partly determined by advertising and promotional activities of a firm. Since advertising and promotional activities also affect cost, cost and output are determined simultaneously to some degree. However, although advertising and promotional expenses are incurred in the current period, their effect generally takes place only in the future. In other words, the current period's demand generally depends on the last period's advertising campaign, ceteris paribus. For this reason, we believe that the simultaneity problems that are caused by advertising and campaign activities are generally small.

Second, and most important, the point to which Kim has referred is mitigated by demand for banking services. More specifically, Kim's argument stems from the BHH observation that larger banks produce more deposit services per account to attract larger deposit balances. But this argument considers only the supply side of the market, without recognizing the demand side. In many cases, large banks may provide more services to large depositors—not only to attract deposits but also to satisfy the demand for a greater variety of services from these customers. The market for deposits (and all bank services) is most appropriately described by both its supply and demand conditions. To the extent that bank customers are sovereign, there is no problem with endogeneity, because demand is exogenous for the most part (that is, excluding the effect of the bank's marketing program on market demand). Therefore, whether or not Kim's supply-side argument is indeed a significant factor biasing the estimation of cost functions in bank studies becomes an empirical question.

Technology and Economies of Scale and Scope

There are many costs (factors of production) that are at least partly independent of size over certain ranges of output—that is, costs that are partly indivisible for output. In general, the greater the extent of indivisibility, the greater the gains from increasing scale, if all else is the same. Indivisibility in banking operations can be attributed to a number of factors, including, for example, the cost of senior management personnel, buildings, equipment, developing new procedures, and technology. Among these factors, technology is the one that has undergone substantial changes over the last decade. In particular, technology has become and is becoming more and more divisible in many industries.

Computers and reader-sorters in banking, which cost thousands of dollars per year in the 1970s, are now generally obsolete. The old equipment required large rooms with special electrical wiring and humidity and temperature control, which only large banks could install cost-effectively. Today, computer capacities of comparable size and power are available in desk-top typewriter size, without the special environmental support needed previously. If the technological trend of the 1970s and early 1980s continues, large banks may lose their comparative size advantage in using technology as a means of reducing cost per unit of services.

The rapid advancement in the divisibility of computer technology not only would aid in resolving the scale disadvantages of small financial institutions but could provide them with greater scope economies. For example, until the development of microcomputers—a highly divisible technology— only large banks could provide various kinds of electronic funds transfer (EFT) services in a cost-effective manner. Today, small banks are implementing EFT technology, either by sharing equipment with other institutions or by acquiring the needed technology on their own.

The effects of greater technological divisibility on bank average cost should be obvious. For example, the U-shaped average cost curve should be becoming flatter because of the scale effect. Also, improved scope should cause the cost curve itself to fall. Figure 2–3 depicts these effects; the AC_1 curve represents the long-run average cost with indivisible technology, and the AC_2 curve represents the average cost curve with greater technological divisibility. Notice that the advantages of divisibility are expected to be more pronounced in small-scale operations than in large-scale operations. The reason for this is that large banks are presumably already producing these products with the scope effects being reflected in the AC_1 curve. The new divisible technology should improve the ability of small banks to provide the same products as large banks.

Summary and Conclusions

This chapter has discussed the sources and measurement of scale effects for firms in general and their implications for the banking firm in particular.

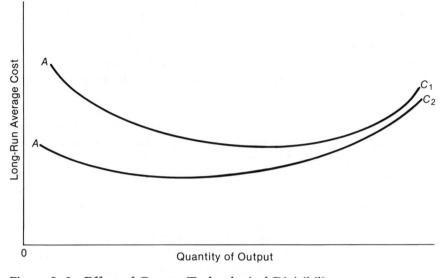

Figure 2–3. Effect of Greater Technological Divisibility on Long-Run Average Costs

Sources of increasing returns to scale were divided into four categories: (1) indivisibility, or unavoidable excess capacity, of some inputs; (2) the inverse relationship between the productivity of some inputs and their cost per unit of productivity; (3) specialization of the production process; and (4) a statistical property of large numbers. We maintain that if these effects are present, the banking industry will exhibit economies of scale at least up to a given volume of output.

Following a brief discussion of the bank's cost (input) characteristics, we have elaborated on the techniques of measuring scale effects. Comparing the Cobb-Douglas, CES, and translog cost functions, we have concluded that the translog cost function is the most suitable for a study of cost characteristics in the banking industry, because it allows the greatest degree of flexibility without requiring any unnecessary theoretical restrictions about the shape of the cost curve. Most important, it allows for the effects of multiproduct operations on costs (otherwise known as economies of scope) and subadditivity on unit and marginal costs. One drawback of the translog, as applied in bank cost studies, is that measurement of the degree of scope economies is not possible in situations in which zero values for some outputs occur, because one cannot take the log of zero. The hybrid translog was suggested as one way to overcome this problem, since it allows for zero output values.

We have also discussed the problem of endogeneity in the measurement of scale and scope economies in the banking industry. Kim has argued that bank cost studies need to correct for the endogeneity problem inherent in bank outputs by solving a system of simultaneous equations, including the translog cost function, a set of cost-share equations, and a set of revenue-share equations (see appendix 2B). Kim attributes the endogeneity problem to a tendency on the part of large banks to provide a wider range of deposit services in order to attract holders of larger deposit balances. Simply put, we propose that larger banks offer a wider range of deposit services than smaller banks because holders of larger deposit balances demand the services. Assuming that consumer sovereignty is applicable to banking (as to any other industries), no endogeneity problem necessarily exists.

Finally, we have discussed potential effects of the recent technological divisibility on bank cost structures. This divisibility should influence cost curves in two ways: (1) because large banks lose their comparative advantage of size with respect to technological indivisibility as technology becomes more and more divisible, the long-run average cost curve should become flatter, ceteris paribus; and (2) since greater divisibility allows small banks to use the new technology cost-effectively, they will be able to introduce products that were previously only available from large banks and, in turn, they possibly could reduce costs because of greater scope economies.

Notes

1. John R. Walker, *Bank Costs for Decision Making* (Boston: BP, 1970), 27.
2. This discussion is adapted from George J. Stigler, *The Theory of Price*, 3rd ed. (New York: Macmillan, 1966), 153–60.
3. A similar phenomenon exists in the generation and transmission of electricity. For example, capital and operating costs of transmission facilities increase approximately in direct proportion to the voltage, whereas transmission capacity increases as the square of voltage, implying that the larger the transmission lines, the cheaper the transmission costs per unit. For further discussion of this effect, see Charles R. Scherer, *Estimating Electric Power Marginal Costs* (Amsterdam: North-Holland, 1977), 80, 81, 207–12.
4. This inventory effect on the cash needs of banks may be formally derived as follows: Consider bank depositors withdrawing cash from their deposit accounts in a perfectly foreseen and steady manner. Assume that over a given period of time, an individual customer withdraws a total of T dollars in a steady stream. Assume, also, that the opportunity cost of holding cash is i dollars per dollar per period. The individual withdraws C dollars from his account evenly throughout the period. The transaction cost of each withdrawal (which includes the opportunity cost of time spent and other costs) is b dollars. Given these assumptions, the number of times the individual withdraws cash can be specified as T/C and the total costs of withdrawals as bT/C. The withdrawal costs must be added to the opportunity costs of holding cash balances to obtain the total costs to the individual of withdrawing cash and holding cash for personal expenditures. The individual's average holding per period is $C/2$, because

each time he withdraws C dollars, he spends it in a steady manner and withdraws another C dollars the moment it is all spent. Since at the beginning of each withdrawal period he has C dollars, and at the end of the period he has zero dollars, his average holding cash balance is $iC/2$. The total cost for the use of cash is thus $K = bT/C + iC/2$. The problem is determining how many times the individual should withdraw cash so that K is minimized. In other words, what is the most efficient value of C.

We find the most economical value of C by taking the first derivative of the foregoing expression with respect to C and setting the resulting value equal to zero, or $K/C = -bT/C^2 + i/2 = 0$. Solving for C yields $\sqrt{2bT/i}$. This result implies that the rational bank customer will demand cash in proportion to the *square root* of the value of his account, or T. Since the size of accounts for larger banks is larger than the size of accounts for smaller banks, the amount of withdrawals per dollar of total deposits is smaller for larger banks. For example, if the average size of deposits in a large bank is \$1,600 but it is only \$400 in a small bank, for equal values of b and i we have $C_L/C_S = 1600/400 = 2$, where C_L is the amount of each withdrawal from the large bank and C_S is that amount for the small bank. Although the average deposit size in the large bank is four times the average deposit size in the small bank, withdrawals are only twice as large for the large bank. This finding implies that large banks do not need to keep proportionately as much cash to meet withdrawals as small banks do. This analysis is drawn from William J. Baumol, "The Transaction Demand for Cash: An Inventory Theoretic Approach," *Quarterly Journal of Economics* 66(November 1952): 545–56.

5. In contrast to this definition of econmies of scale, many authors define economies of scale as situations in which the long-run *average* cost (not the long-run *marginal* cost) falls with the expansion of size. For our purposes, we prefer the definition in this book because it is much easier and less arbitrary to obtain marginal cost than average cost from the estimated parameters. More specifically, all parameter estimates in our empirical analysis will be in terms of the elasticity of total cost with respect to outputs; for example, $(\partial TC/\partial Q) \cdot (Q/TC)$, where TC is total costs and Q reflects output. Marginal cost, $\partial TC/\partial Q$, is simply derived by multiplying the elasticity formula by the TC/Q ratio.

6. Stuart I. Greenbaum, "A Study of Bank Costs," *National Banking Review* 4(June 1967): 415–34.

7. A comparable approach was taken by Powers. See John Anthony Powers, "Branch Versus Unit Banking: Output and Cost Economies," *Southern Economic Journal* 36(October 1969): 153–64.

8. George J. Benston, "Economies of Scale in Financial Institutions," *Journal of Money, Credit, and Banking* 4(May 1972): 321.

9. Thomas W. Gilligan and Michael L. Smirlock, "An Empirical Study of Joint Production and Scale Economies in Commercial Banking." *Journal of Banking and Finance* 8(1984): 67–77.

10. See, for example, George J. Benston, "Economies of Scale and Marginal Costs in Banking Operations," *National Banking Review* 2(June 1965): 507–49.

11. Marc Nerlove, "Returns to Scale in Electricity Supply," in F. Carl Christ, ed., *Measurement in Economics* (Stanford, Calif.: Stanford University Press), 167–98.

12. K.J. Arrow, H.B. Chenery, B. Minhas, and R.M. Solow, "Capital Labor

Substitution and Economic Efficiency," *Review of Economics and Statistics* 43(August 1961): 225–50.

13. H. Uzawa, "Production Functions with Constant Elasticity of Substitution," *Review of Economic Studies* 29(October 1962): 291–99. D.L. McFadden, "Further Results on C.E.S. Production Functions," *Review of Economic Studies* 30(June 1963): 73–83.

14. Laurits R. Christensen, Dale W. Jorgenson, and Lawrence J. Lau, "Transcendental Logarithmic Production Frontiers," *Review of Economics and Statistics* 55(February 1973): 28–45.

15. William Baumol, "On the Proper Tests for Natural Monopoly in a Multiproduct Industry," *American Economic Review* 67(December 1977): 809–22.

16. Melvyn Fuss and Leonard Waverman, "Regulation and the Multiproduct Firm: The Case of Telecommunications in Canada," in Melvyn Fuss and Daniel McFadden, eds., *Production Economics: A Dual Approach to Theory and Application* (New York: North-Holland, 1978), 384.

17. For example, see Randall S. Brown, Douglas W. Caves, and Laurits R. Christensen, "Modelling the Structure of Cost and Production in Multiproduct Firms," *Southern Economic Journal* 46(July 1979): 256–76; James L. Bothwell and Thomas F. Cooley, "Efficiency in the Provision of Health Care: An Analysis of Health Care Organizations," *Southern Economic Journal* 48(April 1982): 970–84; Thomas Gilligan, Michael Smirlock, and William Marshall, "Scale and Scope Economies in the Multi-Product Banking Firm," *Journal of Monetary Economics* 13(1984): 393–405; and Gilligan and Smirlock, "An Empirical Study."

18. Fuss and Waverman "Regulation and the Multiproduct Firm," 281.

19. John C. Panzar and Robert Willig, "Economies of Scope, Product Specific Returns to Scale, and Multiproduct Competitive Industries," Unpublished paper, Bell Laboratories, Murray Hill, N.J., 1978.

20. Robert D. Willig, "Multiproduct Technology and Market Structure," *American Economic Review* 69(May 1979): 346.

21. George Benston, Gerald Hanweck, and David Humphrey, "Scale Economies in Banking: A Restructuring and Reassessment," *Journal of Money, Credit, and Banking* 14(November 1982): 439.

22. Moshe Kim, "Scale Economies in Banking: A Methodological Note," *Journal of Money, Credit, and Banking* 17(February 1985): 96–102.

Appendix 2A: Other Cost Functions

I n this appendix, we briefly touch upon problems with the translog cost function and possible alternative cost functions that may overcome these problems. One problem with the translog methodology is that it does not allow for zero output because the logarithm of zero is undefined. A desirable characteristic of a multiproduct cost function is that it allows for zero values for one or more outputs. To obtain information on the entire industry, it is necessary that firms with zero output for some products be included in the analysis. The zero output problem in the translog is not problematic in bank studies that focus on outputs common to all banks, such as deposits, loans, and securities. To the extent that the bank's outputs are defined in these aggregate terms, the translog cost function is an appropriate methodology. However, if the purpose of the study is to estimate cost functions for disaggregated outputs, such as commercial loans, installment loans, agricultural loans, international loans, and so forth, the translog cost function will not be capable of including in the analysis those banks that do not produce one or more of the outputs.

A function that permits zero values for outputs is the hybrid translog production (or cost) function. The hybrid translog function can be expressed as

$$\ln C = \alpha_0 + \sum_i \alpha_i \ln W_i + \sum_k \beta_k \left[\frac{Q_k^\theta - 1}{\theta} \right] + \frac{1}{2} \sum_i \sum_j \gamma_{ij} \ln W_i \ln W_j$$

$$+ \frac{1}{2} \sum_k \sum_l \delta_{kl} \left[\frac{Q_k^\theta - 1}{\theta} \right] \left[\frac{Q_l^\theta - 1}{\theta} \right]$$

$$+ \sum \sum \rho_{ik} (\ln W_i) \left[\frac{Q_k^\theta - 1}{\theta} \right] \tag{2A.1}$$

where $\gamma_{ij} = \gamma_{ji}$ and $\delta_{kl} = d_{lk}$.

This cost function was suggested by Caves, Christensen, and Tretheway,[1] and separately by Fuss and Waverman, as a generalization of the translog function. Notice that costs will not be zero if an output is zero. The hybrid cost function is a generalization of the translog function, because the expression for output in (2A.1) approaches the logarithm of output as θ approaches zero, or

$$\lim_{\theta \to 0} \frac{[Q_k^\theta - 1]}{\theta} = \ln Q_k \tag{2A.2}$$

Since the duality theorem requires that the cost function be linearly homogeneous in input prices, the following restrictions should be imposed on the price-related parameters:

$$\sum \alpha_i = 1, \qquad \sum \gamma_{ij} = 0, \qquad \sum_i \rho_{ik} = 0 \tag{2A.3}$$

An alternative functional form suggested by Baumol, Panzar, and Willig is the quadratic cost function.[2] This cost function can be expressed as

$$C = g(w)\left[F + \sum_i a_i Q_i + \frac{1}{2}\sum_i \sum_j a_{ij} Q_i Q_j\right] \tag{2A.4}$$

where $F \geq 0$ is the fixed cost parameter and $g(w)$ is a multiplicative price relationship. To our knowledge, this functional form has never been used to estimate the cost structure of banks. For an application of this functional form, see Braunstein and Pulley, who apply the model to the information industries.[3] Also, Mayo has used a quadratic functional form to estimate the cost characteristics of public utilities in the United States.[4]

Notes

1. Douglas W. Caves, Laurits R. Christensen, and Michael W. Tretheway, "Flexible Cost Functions for Multiproduct Firms," *Review of Economics and Statistics* 62(August 1980): 477–81.

2. William Baumol, John Panzar, and Robert Willig, *Contestable Markets and the Theory of Industry Structure* (New York: Harcourt, Brace, Jovanovich, 1982).

3. Y.M. Braunstein and L.B. Pulley, "Flexible Multiproduct Cost Functions: An Empirical Investigation," Brandeis University, Department of Economics, October 1981, mimeographed.

4. John W. Mayo, "Multiproduct Monopoly, Regulation, and Firm Costs," *Southern Economic Journal* 51(July 1984): 208–18.

Appendix 2B: An Alternative Solution to the Simultaneity Problem

F ollowing Fuss and Waverman, Kim expresses the bank's profit maximization behavior as

$$\max \pi = \sum_i q_i Q_i - C(Q_1, \ldots, Q_n; P_1, \ldots, P_m) \qquad (2B.1)$$

subject to the constraint that certain outputs are provided, or

$$Q_i \leq \bar{Q}_i \quad \text{for } i \in T \qquad (2B.2)$$

where q_i is the price of output Q_i and T is the class of exogenously determined outputs. Substituting equation (2B.2) in equation (2B.1) yields

$$\pi = \sum_{i \notin T} q_i Q_i + \sum_i q_i \bar{Q}_i - C(\bar{Q}_1, \ldots, \bar{Q}_T,$$
$$\bar{Q}_{T+1}, \ldots, Q_n; P_1, \ldots, P_m) \qquad (2B.3)$$

The first-order conditions for profit-maximizing behavior are

$$\frac{\partial \pi}{\partial Q_i} = q_i + \bar{Q}_i \frac{\partial q_i}{\partial Q_i} - \frac{\partial C}{\partial Q_i} = 0 \quad \text{for } i = T + 1, \ldots, n \quad (2B.4)$$

which can be interpreted as the familiar condition that marginal revenue (MR) equals marginal cost (MC) at the level of output chosen by the profit-maximizing bank.

Given these results, the following systems of equations are to be estimated: (1) the translog cost function, as in BHH; (2) a set of derived input demand functions; and (3) a set of derived revenue share functions. Consider, for example, the following multiproduct translog cost function:

$$\ln C = \alpha_o + \sum_i \alpha_i \ln Q_i + \sum_j \beta_j \ln P_j + \frac{1}{2}\sum_i \sum_k \delta_{ik} \ln Q_i \ln Q_k$$

$$+ \frac{1}{2}\sum_j \sum_k \gamma_{jk} \ln P_j \ln P_k + \sum_i \sum_j \rho_{ij} \ln Q_i \ln P_j \qquad (2\text{B}.5)$$

Taking the first derivative of equation (2B.5) with respect to P_j, the following set of input demand functions (Shephard's Lemma), or, equivalently, cost-share equations, is obtained:

$$\frac{\partial \ln C}{\partial \ln P_j} = \frac{\partial C}{\partial P_j} \cdot \frac{P_j}{C} \equiv P_j X_j / C \equiv S_j$$

$$= \beta_j + \sum_k \gamma_{jk} \ln P_k + \sum_i \rho_{ij} \ln Q_i \qquad (2\text{B}.6)$$

The primary reason for including the set of cost-share equations is to obtain more efficient parameter estimates for the cost function.[1] The set of revenue-share equations is obtained by taking the first derivative of equation (2B.5) with respect to $\ln Q_i$, where Q_i are the set of endogenous outputs. To ensure that the revenue-share equations meet the profit-maximizing behavior of banks, the MR = MC condition in equation (2B.4) is substituted to obtain

$$\frac{\partial \ln C}{\partial \ln Q_i} \equiv \frac{\partial C}{\partial Q_i} \cdot \frac{Q_i}{C}$$

$$= MC(Q_i / C) = MR(Q_i / C)$$

$$= \left(q_i + Q_i \frac{\partial q_i}{\partial Q_i}\right)(Q_i / C)$$

$$= q_i\left(1 + \frac{1}{\eta_i}\right)(Q_i / C) \qquad (2\text{B}.7)$$

where η_i is the own-price elasticity of the endogenous output. Setting $q_i Q_i / C = R_i$, equation (2B.7) can be rewritten as

$$\frac{\partial \ln C}{\partial \ln Q_i} = R_i\left(1 + \frac{1}{\eta_i}\right) \qquad (2\text{B}.8)$$

where

$$\frac{\partial \ln C}{\partial \ln Q_i} = \alpha_i + \sum_k \delta_{ik} \ln Q_k + \sum_j \rho_{ij} \ln P_j \qquad (2B.9)$$

Substituting equation (2B.9) into equation (2B.8) and rearranging yields the following set of revenue-share equations:

$$R_i = \left(\alpha_i + \sum_k \delta_{ik} \ln Q_k + \sum_j \rho_{ij} \ln P_j \right) \left(1 + \frac{1}{\eta_i} \right)^{-1} \qquad (2B.10)$$

where $k = 1, \ldots, T$ indicates exogenous outputs. The simultaneity problem is resolved when the systems of equations (2B.5), (2B.6), and (2B.10) are simultaneously run using iterative three-stage least squares.[2]

Notes

1. See Laurits R. Christensen and William H. Greene, "Economies of Scale in U.S. Electric Power Generation," *Journal of Political Economy* 84(August 1976): 655–76.

2. For an application of this methodology, see Melvyn Fuss and Leonard Waverman, "Regulation and the Multiproduct Firm: The Case of Telecommunications in Canada," in Melvyn Fuss and Daniel McFadden, eds., *Production Economics: A Dual Approach to Theory and Application* (New York: North-Holland, 1978).

3
Literature on the Cost Economics of Banking

istorically, bank structure in the United States has been heavily regulated at both the state and federal levels. Regulators evaluate and approve (or deny) applications for new bank charters and mergers between existing banks. Product lines, geographic expansion, and limitations on interest rates payable on deposits have constrained bank growth in the past. The deregulation of deposit rate ceilings has dramatically expanded the growth potential of banks, especially since the emergence of a nationwide market for deposit funds. If deregulation of product lines and geographic restraints are assumed to proceed in the years to come, the growth prospects for banks will increase further. The resulting competition should touch off a wave of new bank charters and mergers. Will this wave swamp small banks? Will it contribute to greater operating efficiency in the banking system and, thus, translate into lower costs of bank services for the public? Will larger banks inherit so large a cost advantage that monopoly profits and resource misallocations could occur? These questions are looming larger than ever before because of the pressure of market innovation in the financial system.

In order to assess potential future changes in the structure of the banking industry and their potential implications for the public, banks, government policy, and the economy as a whole, it is worthwhile to consider the significant body of bank cost literature that has accumulated over the last twenty years. This literature was stimulated by past structural changes in the banking industry. In the 1960s, there was concern over the rapid expansion by banks into multioffice operations such as branching and holding company arrangements. The resultant spurt of mergers and acquisitions heightened interest in the cost characteristics of bank production. Because there were potential public policy implications, many studies were undertaken by the research staffs of federal regulators (the Federal Reserve System, Federal Deposit Insurance Corporation, Office of the Comptroller of the Currency, and Federal Home Loan Bank Board), often in collaboration with academic researchers. In this chapter, we review the findings of a number of these studies. Selected results are cited at times to let readers judge for themselves the implications of the evidence. We begin with a brief discussion of early studies and then turn to more technical papers that were published between the mid-1960s and the end of the 1970s. We also review more recent studies—in the 1980s—that are based on the translog cost function. The last section provides a summary in addition to a discussion of potential weaknesses and gaps in the literature.

Before proceeding, we advise that a certain amount of caution be exercised in the generalization of any particular study's findings to all banks over all time periods. Research design invariably requires that limitations be adopted either directly (for example, sample control, data availability, and so forth) or indirectly (for example, assumptions about the bank and its environment, statitistical assumptions inherent in econometric models, and so forth). It is the weight of the entire body of literature that is crucial to gaining a broad understanding of the results and subsequent conclusions. This is the purpose of this chapter, which must be read in its entirety to acquire an appreciation of the answers to our earlier questions.

Early Studies of Bank Costs

Initial attempts to examine bank costs for banks of different size were distinctive in their simplicity. Instead of using econometric methods to represent cost functions, these studies relied on balance sheet and income statement data to calculate financial ratios relating to bank costs and their output. Early studies can be categorized into two groups: (1) studies that measured output in terms of earning assets and (2) studies that used total assets to measure output.

Earning Assets as Output

Alhadeff was the first to document in depth the cost differences between banks of different size.[1] Data from the Federal Reserve Bank of San Francisco for the years 1938–50 were gathered for the 210 banks that existed in California in 1948. Four large branch bank organizations with multicity facilities were segregated from the other banks and designated *unit banks*.[2] Output was measured as the ratio of loans and investments to total assets to reflect the used capacity to total capacity of the bank, a ratio known as the *load factor* in the electric utility industry. With this measure, Alhadeff found that branch banks produced greater output per dollar resources than unit banks did.

Average costs were measured by the ratio of total expenses to loans and investments. In this sense, *earning assets* was being used as the measure of bank output. In general, for eight different size groups, the smallest banks exhibited unit costs twice as large as those of the largest banks. Unit costs were broken down further for wages and salaries, interest on time deposits, and all other expenses. Consistent trends between size and unit costs were uncovered for each of these component expenses. In this regard, there was a tendency for unit costs to become relatively constant in the middle size groups. This evidence suggests that there are increasing returns to scale (or decreasing average costs) in size extremes and constant returns to scale (or constant average costs) for mid-sized banks. Table 3–1 summarizes selected details of Alhadeff's unit cost comparisons among banks of different size.

Alhadeff found that branch banks in California had different product, account size, and loan characteristics when compared to large unit banks. For example, a greater proportion of assets was loaned rather than invested in securities among branch banks compared to large unit banks. In terms of account size, branch banks made larger numbers of small loans than did large unit banks. These differences were cited in an effort to explain higher unit costs among branch banks as compared to large unit banks. Relative efficiency was ruled out as an explanation because of the obvious differences in the business operations of branch and unit banks. After interest costs were removed, branch and unit bank costs were comparable, a conclusion that led Alhadeff to the notion that branch banks gain greater cost benefits from specializing than do large unit banks. Finally, compared to small unit banks, branch banks had lower average unit costs because of lower wages and miscellaneous costs. Unfortunately, small unit banks had larger proportions of small loans than branch banks, disallowing a relative-efficiency conclusion once again.

In a retrospective comment, Alhadeff observed that size and structure (that is, branch versus unit banking) are often so intertwined as to be inseparable. For example, some large unit banks could not be readily classified structurally because of their correspondent ties with smaller banks and therefore were called "pseudo-branch banks" by Alhadeff. By inference, the study of structural effects on scale economies is much more difficult than simple size comparisons. Consequently, comparisons should be conducted by using data from either unit or branch banks to reduce the confounding of size and structural effects.

Subsequent studies by the Federal Reserve Bank of Kansas City[3] and Horvitz[4] produced results that supported those of Alhadeff for the most part. The Kansas City research found bank average costs to be fairly constant for banks with deposits in the $2 million to $50 million range, after which some scale economies were identified as real economies of labor (that is, cost savings attributable to more productive labor) as opposed to pecuniary economies (that is, cost savings relating to low wage rates). Horvitz also noticed similar labor economies among larger banks and argued that larger loans

Table 3–1
Selected Unit Cost Results for Banks of Different Sizes, 1938–50
(percentage)

	1938	1941	1944	1947	1950
1. Total expenses/loans and investments					
a. Smallest unit banks	6.33	5.96	2.14	3.68	4.38
b. Group 6 unit banks[a]	4.01	3.71	1.55	1.69	1.99
2. Wages and salaries/loans and investments					
a. Smallest unit banks	3.22	3.17	1.01	1.84	2.30
b. Group 6 unit banks[a]	1.85	1.60	0.75	0.92	1.02
3. Interest on time deposits/loans and investments					
a. Smallest unit banks	1.28	1.13	0.47	0.32	0.41
b. Group 6 unit banks[a]	1.27	1.04	0.25	0.29	0.29
4. All other expenses/loans and investments					
a. Smallest unit banks	1.83	1.66	0.66	1.51	1.67
b. Group 6 unit banks	0.89	0.86	0.52	0.52	0.66

Source: Adapted from David Alhadeff, Monopoly and Competition in Banking (Berkeley: University of California Press), 78–80, 82.
[a]Group 8 was the largest group of banks reported, but data were missing in many of the years, as they were for group 7. The exact size range of banks in groups was not used, because the ranges varied from year to year, according to Alhadeff.

required less labor per dollar volume (for example, credit checks of large and established applicants take less time). It is interesting that over the period 1940–60, Horvitz observed a narrowing of cost differences between large and small banks.

Because branching and high proportions of time deposits can influence costs, and because these factors were not controlled in his sample, Horvitz obtained data from the Federal Reserve System for 1959 to consider these factors. Table 3–2 shows selected results for the ratio of total operating expenses to loans and investments. As shown in the table, with the exception of branch banks with $5 million to $25 million assets, larger proportions of time deposits raise costs, which is not surprising because interest costs would be higher for time deposits than for demand deposits. We should comment here that this breakdown is likely to implicitly recognize differences in location and (related) output mix. In effect, there are different types of banks that can confound the size results, just as structural form can blur size results (for example, branch banks generally had relatively higher average costs than unit banks). When each column in table 3–2 is viewed separately—thus controlling, at least partially, for type and structure effects—average costs decline with size for all time deposit categories, except for banks with more than 50 percent time deposits. Although it is speculative, it appears that banks utilizing relatively large proportions of time deposits to fund assets may be trading off asset growth and associated market power against cost containment to a greater extent than other banks. Therefore, it is not possible to conclude from this evidence that one type of liability mix is superior to any other in the sense that market competitiveness and cost control may not be perfectly related.

From this rather comprehensive body of data, Horvitz concluded that

Table 3–2
Total Operating Expenses as a Percentage of Loans and Investments, 1959

	Unit Banks			Branch Banks		
Bank Asset Size ($ millions)	<25% Time Deposits	25–50% Time Deposits	>50% Time Deposits	<25% Time Deposits	25–50% Time Deposits	>50% Time Deposits
0–5	3.26	3.47	3.55	—	—	—
5–25	3.24	3.50	3.46	4.20	4.07	3.66
25–100	3.17	3.39	3.49	3.44	3.71	3.82
100–500	2.95	4.01	—	3.29	3.70	4.03
>500	2.31	—	—	2.88	3.53	—

Source: Adapted from Paul M. Horvitz, "Economies of Scale in Banking," in *Private Financial Institutions* (Englewood Cliffs, N.J.: Prentice-Hall, 1962), 28–33.

scale economies in banking are not large and do not outweigh diseconomies relating to branching. In other words, small banks should not feel threatened by the prospect of deregulation of state prohibitions on branch banking. Of course, it is not likely that small banks can compete directly with large banks, but this is generally unnecessary because their loan mixes differ substantially. Also, for small loans at least, small banks are cost efficient producers, which precludes the possibility of a natural monopoly prevailing throughout a large geographic region. These findings and conclusions certainly parallel those of Alhadeff and, as we shall see, establish a precedent that later research appears to consistently reaffirm.

Total Assets as Output

One drawback of using earning assets to measure output is that other assets, such as trust operations, are excluded. This omission would tend to bias the average unit costs of larger banks upward, perhaps veiling a declining cost curve at higher output levels. Studies by Schweiger and McGee[5] and Gramley[6] were not subject to this potential bias because *total assets* was used to normalize expense data. Table 3–3 shows selected results from Schweiger and McGee's analysis of 6,233 Federal Reserve member banks in 1959. As shown there, unit banks' costs in large metropolitan areas located in Standard Metropolitan Statistical Areas (SMSAs) declined gradually with size but then dropped markedly after $200 million in deposits. By comparison, branch banks in this same market had higher costs that did not decline much until at least $200 million in deposits.[7] Costs tended to decrease as the population of the market area declined, which may be related to a reduction in account activity levels (that is, demand for services is lower in less-populated areas). It could also reflect the fact that the output mix of city banks differs from the output mix of rural banks. Whatever the case may be, the results for banks in SMSAs at least confirm the suspicion that costs of large banks were inflated by using earning assets to measure output. Large banks appeared to have a distinct cost advantage per unit of assets over small and medium-sized banks. Additionally, Schweiger and McGee used multiple regression analysis to show that bank costs were higher among banks with greater proportions of time deposits, commercial and industrial loans, and consumer installment loans. This finding highlights the fact the output mix can be an important determinant of bank costs.

Gramley's study examined costs per unit of total assets for 270 Tenth District member banks as of the end of 1959. Statistical analyses of total asset ratios, based on multiple regression runs using fifteen variables, indicated that the following six variables (and their associated directional relationship) were most relevant to costs: (1) bank size (−); (2) total time deposits to total deposits (+); (3) total loans to total assets (+); (4) securities other than U.S.

Table 3–3
Total Operating Expenses as a Percentage of Total Assets, 1959

Bank Deposit Size ($ millions)	Unit Banks				Branch Banks			
	Large Metro Areas in SMSAs	Other Metro Areas Not in SMSAs	Large Towns Not in SMSAs	Small Towns Not in SMSAs	Large Metro Areas in SMSAs	Other Metro Areas in SMSAs	Large Towns Not in SMSAs	Small Towns Not in SMSAs
5–10	2.98	2.92	2.79	2.60	3.10	3.25	3.18	2.92
25–50	2.63	2.54	2.62	—	3.11	2.97	2.81	3.26
50–100	2.67	2.38	—	—	3.12	2.86	2.87	—
100–200	2.54	2.11	—	—	3.09	2.84	—	—
200–500	2.17	1.91	—	—	2.60	2.53	—	—
>500	1.80	—	—	—	2.33	2.86	—	—

Source: Adapted from Irving Schweiger and John McGee, "Chicago Banking: The Structure of Banks and Related Financial Institutions in Chicago and Other Areas," *Journal of Business* 24(July 1961): 320.

government issues to total assets (–); (5) consumer loans to total loans (+); and (6) percentage growth of total assets between 1956 and 1959 (+). For banks of different sizes, cost ratios declined at an increasing rate and did not turn upward for large banks with more than $300 million assets; hence, no U-shaped pattern could be detected.

An interesting aspect of the Gramley study was the observation that perhaps small banks' costs were higher because they simply did not work as hard to control cost. If this were so, the variation of cost ratios would be larger among small banks than among large banks. Table 3–4 shows the results of a test for this hypothesis. The lack of any clear trend led Gramley to infer that *real* economies were responsible for declining unit costs with bank size. He concluded that larger banks can somehow reap cost advantages from labor-saving methods of operation. This conclusion is consistent with that of Schweiger and McGee (and Horvitz to some degree) but differs from that of Alhadeff. Consequently, papers using total assets (as opposed to earning assets) to measure output reveal that scale efficiencies increase with bank size. On a somewhat ominous note, Gramley warned that the period 1956–59 predates the advent of automated accounting and check-clearing techniques (which were beginning to spread at the time of his publication in the early 1960s) and that such capital-intensive innovations may further disturb the balance of relative costs.

Will small banks be able to muster strategies for competing at cost parity with large banks in an automated bank payments system? In the next section, we summarize the findings of studies in the 1960s and 1970s that provide some answers to this question and, in the process, raise many new questions.

Later Studies of Bank Costs

Subsequent research studies in the area of bank costs are distinguished by the introduction of relatively sophisticated econometric methods. These methods have roots in production theory and are based on modeling the cost function, as discussed in chapter 2. For the sake of organization, we have split studies in this section into two parts: (1) studies from the mid to late 1960s and (2) studies in the 1970s. Because of the large number of publications on bank costs in these two periods, coverage will be restricted to widely cited studies.

Studies in the Mid to Late 1960s

Two studies by Benston in 1965 formed the beginnings of a new branch of bank cost literature. These studies marked two major changes in methodology: (1) detailed cost data were obtained from the Functional Cost Analysis (FCA) program of the Federal Reserve System, and (2) marginal cost calculations for specific bank outputs were made. FCA data for small and medium-

Table 3–4
A Size Comparison of the Variation of Bank Costs, 1959

Bank Asset Size ($ millions)	Cost Variation Measure[a]
0–5	15.0
5–10	18.1
10–25	11.4
25–50	15.7
> 50	18.6

Source: Adapted from Lyle E. Gramley, *A Study of Scale Economies in Banking* (Kansas City: Federal Reserve Bank of Kansas City, 1962), 35.

[a]Residuals from the six-variable regression model discussed in the text were used as measures of cost variation—that is, the differences between actual and expected costs.

sized New England member banks for 1950 (eighty-three banks), 1960 (eighty-two banks), and 1961 (eighty banks) were used in both studies. These banks volunteered detailed information on the direct and indirect (administration, business promotions, occupancy, and so forth) costs allocated to particular bank services, including demand deposits, time deposits, mortgage loans, installment loans, business loans, and securities.[8] In one study, Benston investigated the marginal costs of these outputs by using a logarithmic function relating allocated costs to the quantity, quality, mix, growth, and variability of output, in addition to factor prices, bank type, mergers, technology, and other random factors.[9] It is important to note that output was measured in terms of the numbers of accounts instead of the dollar size of accounts, because it was believed that dollars might confuse the cost efficiency in the production of large accounts with the cost efficiency of operations in general. In recognition of the relationship between costs and account size, the *average account size* was added to the regression function.

Table 3–5 summarizes some of the direct-cost results of Benston's study. The elasticity indicates the percentage change in costs per percentage change of output. An elasticity value less (or more) than one indicates economies (or diseconomies) of scale. According to table 3–5, demand deposits exhibited slight economies of scale in 1959, with a trend toward greater economies in 1960 and 1961. Benston attributed this change to the automation of these services—therefore, this evidence supports Gramley's earlier contention that automated banking services could lower costs for larger banks. Services that were not automated, such as time deposits, mortgage loans, installment loans, and business loans, did not follow this downward trend. Regarding diseconomies of business loan production in 1961 (that is, elasticity equal to 1.006), Benston observed that larger banks may offset slight cost inefficiencies by making large loans, which itself enables cost efficiencies.

Table 3-5
Elasticities and Marginal Costs of Basic Banking Services, 1959-61

Bank Services	Elasticities of Cost with Respect to Output[a]			Average Marginal Cost[b]		
	1959	1960	1961	1959	1960	1961
Demand deposits	0.91	0.86	0.79	$21.18	$19.32	$19.14
Time deposits	0.71	0.95	0.88	$1.50	$1.80	$1.94
Mortgage loans	0.85	0.96	0.93	$17.46	$21.63	$23.38
Installment loans	0.76	0.88	0.97	$10.52	$11.70	$14.42
Business loans	0.98	0.92	1.01	$17.77	$20.11	$26.08
Securities	0.94	0.70	0.57	$1.02	$0.28	$0.32

Source: Adapted from George J. Benston, "Economies of Scale and Marginal Costs in Banking Operations," *National Banking Review* 2(June 1965): 507-49.

[a]Output was measured in numbers of accounts, except securities, which were measured in thousands of dollars.

[b]Marginal costs are based on holding other variables in the regression equation constant at their geometric mean values. For business loans, average loan size was allowed to vary. For securities, marginal costs are measured per $1,000 securities.

Because of data problems, the results for securities were less reliable than those for the other outputs; nevertheless, their marginal costs were found to be small. Results for indirect expenses (accounting for over 40 percent of total operating expenses, excluding interest payments) did not reveal any scale economies. Indeed, larger banks appeared to be subject to some occupancy expense diseconomies. From these results, Benston concluded that although economies of scale exist on both sides of the balance sheet, they are not large. In effect, bank size does not, in itself, provide a cost advantage.

A second study by Benston focused on the issue of the relative cost efficiency of branch and unit banks.[10] If entry in banking is regulated, it is important to know which form best serves the public (disregarding differential effects on market power and differences in the bank customer's costs of obtaining desired services).[11] Branch banks have the advantage of becoming large enough to allow managers to specialize more than unit bank managers possibly could. On the downside, branch banks are spread out geographically and require that resources be expended to coordinate the activities of multiple offices. To test for cost differences by bank type, Benston used a logarithmic regression model (as before) and experimented with three different branching variables: (1) number of branch offices, (2) a zero-one dummy, and (3) a matrix of five dummy variables (corresponding to the number of branch offices where the fifth variable denoted five or more branch offices). Since the matrix-dummy approach appeared to work best, reported results were based on it.

Table 3–6
Effect of Branching on Direct Costs of Selected Bank Services, 1959–61

	Net Added Costs (percentages)		
Bank Services	1959	1960	1961
Demand deposits			
1 branch	—[a]	– 14.4	– 19.2
3 branches	—[a]	– 0.1	0.0
> 5 branches	—[a]	17.9	11.8
Time deposits[b]			
1 branch	– 32.1	– 4.5	– 12.2
3 branches	– 13.3	21.7	13.6
8 branches	—[a]	– 4.5	– 12.2
Installment loans			
1 branch	– 3.8	– 5.1	– 4.3
3 branches	11.7	6.1	9.2
8 branches	—[a]	20.2	26.0

Source: Adapted from George J. Benston, "Branch Banking and Economies of Scale," *Journal of Finance* 20(May 1965): 318, 320–21.

[a]None of the branch variables was significant in this year, disallowing comparisons between branch and unit banks.

[b]Direct costs do not include interest expenses. Because branch variables were not very significant, these results may be subject to some degree of error.

Table 3–6 presents some of the findings of the Benston study. Net added costs are defined as the cost of merging unit banks into one branch bank after subtracting the cost benefit gained from larger scale. For example, the 17.9 percent result for demand deposits in 1960 suggests that merging five unit banks into one branch bank would increase the cost of producing the same number of demand deposit accounts by 17.9 percent, after taking into account the benefit of scale on costs.

Note that only banks with three or fewer branches experienced cost benefits. After three branches, the increased costs of managing multiple offices outweighed the benefits of larger size. For time deposits, results were mixed, and the results for installment loans were not unlike those for demand deposits—that is, only small branch banking organizations were more cost-efficient than a unit bank structure. Other bank outputs, including business loans, mortgage loans, and securities, were tested, but no trends were obvious. Further tests of indirect costs revealed that administrative expenses rose gradually as the number of branches increased, as did occupancy expenses (except for a sudden jump from three to four branches).

Benston concluded that as branch offices are added, demand deposit, installment loan, and occupancy expenses (on net) rise. As observed earlier (see note 11), there is some question as to whether or not the higher operating costs of branch (relative to unit) banking are outweighed by public benefits in the form of greater customer convenience. Another conclusion of his findings was that one- and two-branch banking organizations have cost characteristics comparable to those of unit banks; therefore, Benston recommended that future research add small branch banks into the unit bank sample.

Greenbaum reviewed the issues and findings of the literature cited thus far in this chapter (as well as some other studies).[12] A major thesis of his work was that a socially optimal banking structure should maximize productive efficiency, improve allocative neutrality (that is, see to it that bank structure does not disrupt natural flows of savings to investment), avoid exploitation of consumers and sellers of bank inputs, and foster maximum responsiveness of banks to market and technological change. Cost studies are justifiable to the extent that they can tell us if a public policy directed toward promoting competition can attain this optimum. Are scale economies exhausted rapidly enough to enable smaller institutions to compete effectively? Greenbaum concluded, from previous research, that banks with less than $10 million in assets were "grossly inefficient," probably because of high overhead unit costs, lack of sufficient specialization, high transaction costs, and limited diversification. These deficiencies suggested that in the absence of regulatory entry barriers, small banks would be merged out or absorbed by branching organizations. International experience indicated that a consolidated system of fewer than 100 banks would be predicted if entry restrictions were lifted. Further inferences from the literature regarding the efficiency and the allocative and exploitive properties of the present decentralized system compared to a consolidated system led Greenbaum to the belief that more concentration would move banking closer to the social optimum.[13]

Some amount of caution should be taken, however, in extrapolating these inferences to the present. As pointed out by Greenbaum, automation of banking services may well render the findings of past studies obsolete. At that time, the prevalent opinion was that correspondent banking could not sufficiently rectify small bank inefficiencies. But small banks today can use bankers' banks, leasing arrangements, and other cooperative (or third-party) means to provide low-cost technology to their customers. Therefore, circumstances now may be more favorable to small banks than was previously anticipated, and the prospect of a highly concentrated banking system is less certain. It also may be possible for small banks to serve a useful role in achieving the social optimum for the future because of changes in the financial and economic environment.

Further research by Bell and Murphy and Powers in the 1960s contributed significantly to the growing evidence on the cost economics of banking. In a 1967 study, Bell and Murphy related bank service charges to bank cost factors, including scale of operations, the wage rate, and branching structure.[14] They found that a one-dollar increase in the marginal direct cost of processing a demand deposit raised service charges by about 32 percent (estimated from a derivative Cobb-Douglas cost function analysis of FCA data for ninety-two New England banks). This finding supported their belief that bank pricing policies are based on production costs—an association that, in part, justifies the study of bank costs and the goals of fostering a system that tends to lower the long-run average cost curve.

In 1969, Bell and Murphy calculated elasticity estimates for services and cost functions comparable to Benston's for 283 banks. Regression coefficients ranged from 0.86 to 0.96, indicating increasing returns to scale. Notably, "output modifying variables," such as account size, activity, and composition, were found to be significantly related to costs in many instances. On the surface, these results are not surprising, because they simply reflect the fact that all accounts are not equal. Closer inspection, however, shows that they suggest that there may be systematic differences in bank outputs that affect costs.

A likely problem with Bell and Murphy's results is that output is measured by an index that cumulatively accounts for the quantity, size, activity, and composition of a particular bank service. If these account characteristics are correlated, how might this association be removed to avoid estimation bias? (At a more fundamental level, as discussed in chapter 2, our position is that the market competitively prices accounts in such a way that the cost to the bank of one dollar in any account, regardless of its characteristics, is the same.) In Bell and Murphy's study, the coefficient relating to the number of accounts may be biased by intercorrelations of the different account attributes, especially the average account size. If this is so, the 0.90 coefficient for demand deposits reported by Bell and Murphy as an average estimate would be too high for small banks and too low for large banks, since an additional account at a large bank would require much greater size, activity, and variety of composition than it would at a small bank.

Bell and Murphy conducted other tests of the long-standing presumption that large banks gain scale economies from greater specialization of labor than do small banks. In this way, less skilled labor and relatively more capital may be employed by large banks. Tests for changing the labor-skill mix as size increases supported this notion. Tests for differences between branch and unit banks were not significant. Therefore, Bell and Murphy inferred that larger banks do tend to reduce costs by using less-skilled labor.

Once again, we should caution that technological progress may depreciate the relevance of this finding to today's banking world. For example, most bookkeeping duties are now performed by computers, with low marginal costs of operation. However, it is not known to what extent computer technology (and other automated methods) for both large and small banks can be applied to lower average costs per unit of output.

A different view of what constitutes output was proposed separately by Greenbaum and Powers as noted in chapter 2. Powers argued, for example, that if two banks had equal dollar levels of business loans but unequal average yields on these loans, their output would not be the same—that is, the bank with higher yields is providing relatively more service to the community judging by market demand.[15] A weighted sum of outputs was constructed, therefore, where the weights for different assets corresponded to their respective interest rates earned by the bank and the weights for liabilities were taken as the difference between the short-term government securities rate and the particular time deposit rate at the bank. From the 1962 Call Reports of Income and Condition, data for all insured banks in the Seventh District were gathered. Subsamples of banks were formed on the basis of the following stratification criteria: (1) size, (2) the ratio of operating revenue to total output, and (3) the ratio of lending output to total output. The third criterion controls, in part, for differences in service output mix among banks. In general, the size results were mixed, with some strata demonstrating increasing returns to scale, others exhibiting a U-shaped cost pattern, and still others indicating decreasing returns to scale. Branch banks had higher average costs than did unit banks, but in one stratum the reverse was found. Appropriately, Powers concluded that neither branching nor size inherently lends itself to cost advantages worthy of public policy action in its favor.

Studies in the 1970s

In the 1970s, research sought to update and extend previous work on holding companies, technology, and other emerging trends in banking.[16] Table 3–7 contains capsulized summaries of often-cited papers in the 1970s.[17] From this research emerges the consensus that although there are economies of scale in banking, they are not of sufficient magnitude to preclude small and medium-sized banks from viable competition. The conclusions for branch banking are clouded by mixed results. Moreover, although some studies alluded to customer costs of obtaining bank services, they did not directly address such costs, other than service charges paid to cover private bank costs. In 1978, Mullineaux further suggested that the restrictiveness of state branching regulations can influence the branch bank findings. If this is true, resource misallocations in banking may be caused more by the dearth of state and federal regulations than by the failure of some banks to reduce costs of operations.[18]

The possibility that regulation may alter bank cost functions is intriguing. However, its relevance could not be measured to a degree that was meaningful in the 1960s and 1970s studies because data generally spanned the period 1958–71, within which few regulatory changes occurred. During the 1970s, a number of liability-side changes in regulation developed. In 1973, commercial banks were permitted to offer ceiling-free, small-denomination

Table 3-7
Capsule Summaries of Bank Cost Studies in the 1970s

Author	Year	Purpose	Data	Findings	Conclusions
Murphy	1972	Update past studies with 1968 results	FCA data for 1968 on 967 banks	Cobb-Douglas analyses showed coefficients for outputs not significantly different from unity in general	Scale economies were present in 1965 but were undetectable in 1968
Schweitzer	1972	Examine the cost effects of the holding company form of organization	Call Reports of Income and Condition data on Ninth District banks with less than $100 million assets	A logarithmic regression model not too unlike that of Greenbaum revealed U-shaped cost curves with constant returns to scale in the $3 million to $25 million assets range; in the latter range, dummies for holding company affiliation were significant with negative signs	Scale economies in banking are exhausted for the most part after $3.5 million in assets, and diseconomies exist beyond $25 million in assets; also, holding company affiliation tends to reduce costs, as hypothesized
David, Longbrake, and Murphy	1973	Determine the effects of different types of technology on the costs of servicing demand deposits	FCA data for 1968 on 967 banks	Cobb-Douglas–based cost functions were adapted for technology by means of dummies to represent the use of computers; small banks were cost-inefficient regarding computers	Banks with fewer than about 10,600 (or $18 million) in demand deposit accounts should use conventional accounting systems; larger banks can improve operating efficiency by using technology
Kalish and Gilbert	1973	Determine how size and organizational form affect bank efficiency	FCA data for 1968 on 898 banks	Based on a methodology comparable to Greenbaum and Schweitzer, frontier cost curves (i.e., the lowest average cost curve) were estimated; cost curves were U-shaped; unit banks had the lowest operating costs, followed by affiliated banks and branch banks	Banks affiliated with a holding company have greater cost efficiency than branch banks at lower output levels, but the reverse is true at higher output levels; also, U-shaped cost curves imply that efficient production and competition in banking are not conflicting goals of public policy

Table 3–7 (continued)

Author	Year	Purpose	Data	Findings	Conclusions
Longbrake and Haslem	1975	Study effects of bank size and organizational form on the cost of producing demand deposits	FCA data for 1968 on 967 banks	A log-linear model in the spirit of studies done by Bill and Murphy indicated differences in cost function shapes between banks with various legal forms of bank organization	Unit affiliates (as compared to nonaffiliates) have economies of account quantity; all banks had economies of account size; also the number of branch bank offices did not affect the cost of producing demand deposit services
Mullineaux	1975	Test Benston's assumptions that cost equations are identical for branch and unit banks	FCA data for 1970	The Benston cost equation for unit banks and branch banks was estimated, and coefficients were found to differ significantly for three out of five bank outputs	Disaggregated estimates of cost equations should be comparable to utilize the Benston dummy variable approach; further, more research is needed on branching before policy indications can be trusted
Mullineaux	1978	Determine the proper specifications of the commercial bank profit function and estimate the effect of branching regulations on bank profits	FCA data for 1971 on 892 banks and for 1972 on 859 banks	A combination translog/Cobb-Douglas profit function, using net operating income as the dependent variable, yielded evidence of price-setting behavior by banks; profits were positively related to the restrictiveness of states' branching regulations, banks were able to capture additional scale economies by affiliation with a holding company, market structure affected profits, and the Cobb-Douglas function could not be rejected	Banks in branching states had constant returns to scale, while increasing returns were found in unit banking states; imperfect competition exists in the banking industry, suggesting that market structure may influence bank profits, which data tended to confirm

certificates of deposit under the "wild card experiment." Six-month money market certificates (MMCs) with interest rates tied to Treasury bill yields were authorized in 1978 for all depository institutions. Relatively higher interest rate levels in the 1970s increased the awareness of consumers and businesses alike to the interest rates paid and charges levied by banks on deposit accounts. This awareness is best exemplified by the phenomenal success of money market mutual funds (MMMFs). Unable to pay deposit rates comparable to MMMFs because of Regulation Q, banks sought to provide higher implicit returns in the form of a wider array of automated services (for example, direct deposit of payroll checks, telephone bill paying, other automatic bill paying, detailed deposit statements, automatic transfer services, drive-in facilities, and so forth). Thus, the latter part of the 1970s was marked by the growing trend toward increased banking deregulation of interest rates, customer sophistication, and banking innovation.

Changes such as these substantially increased competition in the banking industry. It becomes interesting, therefore, to reexamine questions on economies of scale in banking. Also, in light of heightened competition in the financial services industry, it may be more appropriate now than in the past to consider the relationship between resource misallocations and bank regulations. Although the studies to which we turn next did not necessarily focus on the effect of regulation, their findings have some relevance to this cost issue. More important, they may provide some insight into the true, or competitively determined, cost curve in the partially deregulated banking industry.

Recent Bank Cost Studies

Prior research generally recognized the multiproduct nature of banking but did not deal with the effect that joint production of multiple services might have on bank costs.[19] Previous studies viewed different bank outputs as separable from one another. This view was challenged by Adar, Agmon, and Orgler, who believed that banking firms normally face interdependent cost consequences of output decisions.[20] In more specific terms, the profit function of banks for a particular output, assuming fixed market prices, can generally be stated as follows:

$$\pi = \sum_i P_i Q_i - C(Q_1, Q_2, \ldots, Q_n) \qquad (3.1)$$

where π is profit, P_i is unit price of output i, Q_i is quantity of output i, and $C(Q_1, Q_2, \ldots, Q_n)$ is unit cost of output given the output mix. Profit is maximized when

$$\frac{\partial \pi}{\partial Q_I} = P_i - \frac{\partial C(Q_1, Q_2, \ldots, Q_n)}{\partial Q_i} = 0 \tag{3.2}$$

where the marginal cost, $\partial C(Q_1, Q_2, \ldots, Q_n) / \partial Q_i$, depends on all output levels because costs $C(Q_1, Q_2, \ldots, Q_n)$ are not additive—that is, $C(Q_1) + C(Q_2) + \cdots + C(Q_n) \neq C(Q_1, Q_2, \ldots, Q_n)$. For the multiproduct firm, the latter nonadditivity condition makes it necessary to *jointly* maximize the profits of all outputs simultaneously, which can be written as

$$\max \pi = \sum_i Q_i P_i(Q_1, Q_2, \ldots, Q_n) - \sum_i Q_i C(Q_1, Q_2, \ldots, Q_n)$$

$$\tag{3.3}$$

Jointness in production, as discussed in chapter 2, exists if $\sum_i C_i(Q_i) > C(Q_1, Q_2, \ldots, Q_n)$—that is, the cost of separately producing outputs exceeds their joint production cost. If there is jointness, the bank must find the optimal output mix to maximize profits, given regulatory constraints, that, if changed, could affect this mix, and, in turn, the cost function.

The first study to publish tests for jointness in the production of bank services was by Benston, Berger, Hanweck, and Humphrey (hereafter BBHH).[21] A translog model was fitted to 1978 FCA data for each of the following outputs: demand deposits, time and savings deposits, real estate loans, commercial loans, and installment loans. Output was measured in terms of the number of accounts, where control variables included the average size of accounts, salaries and fringe benefits (price of labor), rental cost per square foot of office space in the bank's market (price of capital), number of branching offices, and holding company affiliation. Costs for each output corresponded to direct and allocated expenses, excluding interest payments. Also, unit bank and branch bank states were analyzed separately.

Table 3–8 gives selected economies of scale results from the BBHH study. As can be seen, scale economies prevailed for all sizes of branch offices except the largest. At the firm level, no apparent scale economies or diseconomies were detected. For states with unit banking, economies of scale were found for banks with less than $50 million deposits, but diseconomies appeared at about $200 million deposits.

BBHH could not generate tests and measures for scope economies from their model because some outputs were zero in the sample. In an attempt to correct this problem, they substituted one unit of output for zero in the sample but obtained uninterpretable results. A test for the presence of cost complementarities was conducted, however. Table 3–9 presents their findings. Values less than one indicate that increased output of one product reduces the marginal cost of the other product with which it is matched, and vice versa. With the exception of time deposits and real estate loans for unit

Table 3–8
Scale Economy Estimates, Using a Translog Cost Function, 1978

Deposit Size ($ millions)	Branch Banking States[a]		Unit Banking States[a]
	Office Level	Firm Level	
0–10	0.84*	0.96	0.78**
25–50	0.92**	1.02	0.93**
75–100	0.90**	1.02	1.00
200–300	0.90*	1.03	1.11*
>400	0.90	1.04	1.11

Source: Adapted from George J. Benston, Allen N. Berger, Gerald A. Hanweck, and David B. Humphrey, "Economies of Scale and Scope in Banking," *Proceedings of a Conference on Bank Structure and Competition,* Federal Reserve Bank of Chicago (May 1983).

[a] Asterisks indicate the level of significance at which estimated elasticities are different from one: *$p < .10$; ** $p < .05$.

Table 3–9
Cost Complementarities between Bank Outputs, Using the Translog Cost Function, 1978

Matched Products	Branch Banking States	Unit Banking States
Demand deposits and real estate loans	– 0.0236	
Time deposits and commercial loans	– 0.0077	– 0.0107
Time deposits and installment loans	– 0.0011	– 0.0001
Commercial loans and real estate loans	– 0.0137	– 0.0011
Demand deposits and time deposits		– 0.0002
Time deposits and real estate loans		– 0.0277
Real estate loans and installment loans		– 0.0154
Commercial loans and installment loans		– 0.0125

Source: Adapted from George J. Benston, Allen N. Berger, Gerald A. Hanweck, and David B. Humphrey, "Economies of Scale and Scope in Banking," *Proceedings of a Conference on Bank Structure and Competition,* Federal Reserve Bank of Chicago (May 1983), 451.

banking states, none of the coefficients were significant at the 10 percent level. The greater number of negative coefficients in unit banking states, compared to branch banking states, suggested to the authors that unit banks might adapt their output mix to counteract regulatory restrictions on bank location. In any event, this evidence does not make a very convincing case for economies of scope in banking. On balance, therefore, the authors concluded that there is a relatively low likelihood of natural monopoly in banking.

Gilligan and Smirlock were next to publish tests related to jointness in banking.[22] Data on more than 2,700 unit state banks were gathered from

Table 3–10
Scale Economies Estimates for Output, Measured in Liability and Asset
Terms, 1973, 1975, and 1977

Deposit Size ($ millions)	Liabilities[a]			Assets[a]		
	1973	1975	1977	1973	1975	1977
0–10	0.97*	0.95*	0.94*	0.98*	0.98*	0.98*
10–25	0.98*	0.98*	0.98*	1.00	0.99	0.99
25–50	1.00	1.05*	1.05*	1.03*	1.02	1.02
50–75	1.06*	1.07*	1.08*	1.05*	1.05*	1.05*
75–100	1.09*	1.10*	1.12*	1.08*	1.08*	1.07*
>100	1.16*	1.15*	1.17*	1.11*	1.11*	1.10*

Source: Adapted from Thomas W. Gilligan and Michael L. Smirlock, "An Empirical Study of Joint Production and Scale Economies in Commercial Banking," *Journal of Banking and Finance* 8(1984): 74.

[a]Asterisks indicate scale elasticities significantly different from one, using a one-tail test at the 0.5 level.

Call Reports of Income and Condition (compiled by the Federal Reserve Bank of Kansas City) for the period 1973–78. Bank output was measured in terms of either liabilities or assets: (1) the dollar amounts of demand deposits and time deposits and (2) the dollar amounts of loans and securities. Costs were proxied by total operating expenses in both cases. A translog cost function was fitted to the data to obtain estimates of scale economies. Table 3–10 gives some of their findings. Both output approaches in all years yielded scale economies for banks with less than $10 million deposits and diseconomies beyond $50 million deposits. A better fit to the data was found for assets than for liabilities, which suggests that scale economies are exhausted by $10 million deposits. These results are consistent, therefore, with those of BBHH.

Although Gilligan and Smirlock did not report estimates of the extent of scope economies due to jointness, they did perform tests for their possible existence. In all years and for both sides of the balance sheet, jointness tests proved strongly positive—that is, bank outputs should not be separately examined as if they were derived from independent production processes. The consistency of the evidence in this study gives at least preliminary support for jointness in bank production.

One potential drawback of the Gilligan and Smirlock study was their assumption that input prices are constant and so do not affect the marginal costs of outputs differently as the level of prices change. Therefore, no input price variables were used in the translog model. A study by Gilligan, Smirlock, and Marshall incorporated input prices (that is, the manufacturing wage rate in the state) into a translog model that related the FCA costs allocated to total deposits and total loans to the number of these accounts.[23]

Separate runs were made for unit state and branch state banks. As in the BBHH study, average account size was used to adjust for the positive association between account number and size, and the price of capital was approximated by the rental cost (per square foot) of bank and office buildings in each of nine U.S. geographic regions. The level of input prices, based on 1978 data, did significantly affect the marginal costs of outputs. Therefore, the previous assumption of separability (or constant input prices) was rejected. Tests for nonjointness were rejected also. Thus, the element of economies of scope was believed to be a potentially important characteristic of bank output. Unfortunately, the results of this study are suspect because the model was not homogeneous with respect to price (that is, they misspecified the input price restrictions).

If possible problems with estimation due to incorrectly imposed model restrictions are ignored, measures of scale economies showed cost benefits of expansion for small banks with less than $25 million deposits but diseconomies for banks beyond $100 million deposits. The authors observed that jointness was not so large as to appreciably bias the scale results, because their results closely paralleled those of others in which jointness was not an issue (for example, Benston, Hanweck, and Humphrey, to be discussed shortly). They reconciled the reality of large banks' existence with their findings regarding diseconomies by noting the possibility that scale economies are traded off against scope economies (which are increasingly captured by expanding product lines). This explanation concurs with that of BBHH, but it puts more faith in the ability of banks to obtain scope economies than the BBHH results would suggest.

Another recent study by Benston, Hanweck, and Humphrey[24] (hereafter BHH) reexamined scale economies in banking using a new output measure called the Divisia multilateral index, which is roughly defined as the weighted average of the number of accounts of various outputs under consideration.[25] Weights were based on the proportionate share of total operating costs attributable to each output. Five outputs were aggregated in this way: demand deposits, time and savings deposits, real estate loans, installment loans, and business loans. A translog model using FCA data covering the period 1975–78 was employed. Factor prices for wages and capital, in addition to homogeneity (dummy) variables for holding company affiliation and state branching status and average account size, were included in the model.

Table 3–11 gives selected scale economy findings using the Divisia index for 1975 and 1978. The scale economy estimates there correspond to the percentage change in total bank operating costs per percentage change in bank output. For unit banking states, the estimates clearly show diseconomies of scale, whereas slight economies of scale were found in branch banking states. These results are opposite from those of Mullineaux, whose 1978 study, summarized in table 3–7, was based on 1971 and 1972 data. BHH attributed

Table 3–11
Scale Economy Estimates, Using Divisia Index, 1975 and 1978

Deposit Size ($ millions)	Branch Banking States[a]		Unit Banking States[a]	
	1975	1978	1975	1978
0–10	0.87*	0.81**	1.00	0.95
25–50	0.95	0.93	1.12**	1.07
75–100	0.94	0.92	1.21**	1.13**
200–300	0.93	0.92	1.32**	1.19**
>400	0.91	0.92	1.46**	1.23**

Source: Adapted from George Benston, Gerald Hanweck, and David Humphrey, "Scale Economies in Banking: A Restructuring and Reassessment," Working Paper No. AEM 8201, University of Rochester, Graduate School of Management (November 1981).

[a] Asterisks indicate the level of significance at which estimated elasticities are different from one: $*p < .10; **p < .05$.

Table 3–12
Scale Economy Estimates for Average Account Size, 1975 and 1978

Deposit Size ($ millions)	Branch Banking States[a]		Unit Banking States[a]	
	1975	1978	1975	1978
0–10	0.11**	−0.05**	−0.16**	−0.19***
25–50	0.29**	0.37**	0.24**	0.19**
75–100	0.35**	0.56**	0.55**	0.47**
200–300	0.42**	0.70**	1.14	0.93
>400	0.72**	0.95**	1.73**	1.02

Source: Adapted from George Benston, Gerald Hanweck, and David Humphrey, "Scale Economies in Banking: A Restructuring and Reassessment," Working Paper No. AEM 8201, University of Rochester, Graduate School of Management (November 1981).

[a] Asterisks indicate the level of significance at which estimated elasticities are different from one: $*p < .10; **p < .05; ***p < .01$.

their results to the fact that branch banks can expand the number of accounts by opening new branches, rather than increasing the burden on a single office, as is required in unit banking states.

Table 3–12 reports some of the BHH estimates of scale economies for different average account sizes. It is obvious that unit banks servicing larger accounts than their branch bank counterparts experienced greater proportionate operating costs. The authors explain this by noting that larger account customers demand more implicit service returns than do smaller customers, and that monitoring costs are higher on larger loans.

Other findings of the BHH study were (1) that holding company affiliation does not affect operating costs; (2) that the cost of adding a branch office increases as bank size increases and exceeds that of an additional unit bank for all sizes; (3) that bank average operating costs tend to be either U-shaped or upward-sloping; and (4) that the minimum, or optimum, cost size is in the range of $10 million to $25 million in deposits.

The BHH study may be interpreted to mean that the rising competition for deposits and technological advances within the banking industry were reducing the minimum efficient plant size. This conclusion stands in sharp contrast to the doom and gloom predictions of researchers in the 1960s on the ability of small banks to adapt to mechanization and the concomitant competition from banks overstepping traditional barriers to entry. As is suggested by BBHH, it is possible that these changes have spurred banks to choose their output mix more carefully in order to minimize their joint costs. Also, more competitive deposit rates might be expected to cause banks that are practicing liability management to more closely control the joint costs of acquiring deposit funds and investing them in appropriate assets (to maximize the net interest margin per unit risk).

Studies by Clark and Nelson round out the recent research progress on bank costs. To describe bank production, Clark used a general functional form of which the log linear model is a special case.[26] Tests using Call Report data for 1,207 unit banks over the years 1972–77, however, did not find the general form results different from the Cobb-Douglas results. Also, results based on different output measures yielded similar downward-sloping cost curves, indicative of only slight scale economies. Estimated output elasticities were significantly less than one but no less than 0.95. These results are consistent with those reported in the 1960s by comparable econometric methods.

Nelson returned to the issue of branching and cost efficiencies but did not retrace the footsteps of prior studies.[27] Instead, a new bank cost function that accounts for customer convenience (by including branch variables) was developed. Costs were measured by total labor and capital costs on the balance sheet to reflect the expenses of financial intermediation. Data from 1979 Call Reports (and other sources) were collected for 431 New York, New Jersey, and Connecticut banks with assets ranging from $3 million to almost $100 billion. Consistent with Benston's 1965 results, average costs declined on the branch level and tended to level out at about $200 million in assets. Counterbalancing these cost gains were bankwide diseconomies as size increased; however, instead of their approximately canceling each other, a net decline in marginal costs was found even for branch banking organizations exceeding the norm in the United States at that time. The prominence of small banks in branch banking states in the face of these pro-size results was reconciled by Nelson as being a consequence of convenience. It was argued that branch size could be increased to reap scale economies, but only at the expense of less customer convenience. Since the total cost to the customer is the sum of explicit costs (related to scale economies) and implicit costs (related to convenience), cost efficiency at the plant level cannot be directly translated into optimal size.

This conclusion implies that banking structure is a function of the ability of different banks to satisfy public needs. Since such needs may vary greatly among different customers, a multisize, multiorganization bank structure is to be expected. Thus, the problem for most banks would logically seem to be the implementation of the appropriate (minimum bank cost and maximum convenience) bank size and type to fit their intended market niches. In a broader sense, this idea can be conceptualized by the notion that banks specialize in different output mixes to meet divergent needs of distinct market segments.

In chapter 1, we mentioned McKinsey & Company's conclusion that deregulation in banking would lead to a new equilibrium industry structure composed of national distributors, low-cost producers, and specialty banks. Therefore, deregulation and market innovation should tend to motivate increased diversity of specialization among banks. In turn, we can expect greater ambiguity in what constitutes an optimal bank size; for example, interst rate deregulation has caused some banks that are oriented toward the retail market to focus on high-net-worth consumers. This kind of shift in output mix toward quality services may well require a different optimal bank size than would an output mix geared toward service quantity—for instance, low minimum balance requirements and free checking to attract small depositors.

It should be clear that deregulation has tended to cause cost curves to be unique for different banks, depending on the particular specialization of outputs and factors of production. Because of competitive markets, banks will seek output-mix and production-factor combinations that have comparable (minimum) marginal costs. Not all combinations will be consistent with minimum costs. Those that do allow minimum cost production are likely to imply different optimal bank sizes. If small banks are not able to manage their output-mix and production-factor combination at costs lower than those of larger banks producing the same combination (or subsets thereof), consolidation of bank resources should occur naturally. In chapter 5, we attempt to group banks by their output mix and compare their cost efficiency after adjusting for factors of production.

Miscellaneous Bank Cost Studies

In this section, we briefly touch upon some peripheral areas of research that nonetheless contribute important clues to the question of scale economies in banking. The following areas are covered: (1) consumer loan costs, (2) social costs of structure restraints, (3) product costs and profitability, and (4) product costs and risk.

Consumer Loan Costs

Consumer loans have typically been subject to usury laws that place a ceiling on interest rates charged by lenders. Laws in the United States allow higher ceilings on small loans because of the obvious inverse relationship between lenders' costs and loan size. Benston performed a formal test of how loan size may affect lenders' costs to see if usury schedules were reasonable and did not unduly lean in favor of some borrowers and against others.[28] Data from three major consumer finance companies with a total of 2,200 offices were collected for both 1969 and 1970. Costs were measured by salaries, other cash expenses (total direct expenses excluding occupancy), or total expenses (excluding overhead, advertising, interest, and losses). Output was proxied by the number of loans made to consumers in 15 different loan-size categories. Homogeneity, input price, and market variables were included to adjust for other factors that could affect output costs. Numerous regression runs yielded the following results: (1) different sized loans do not tend to have different costs of issuance and service, and (2) loans over $1,000 are more expensive to produce than are smaller loans, in terms of total costs. Discussion of these findings with consumer finance executives elicited confirmation that loan size and cost are not inversely related in general. Loan costs for any size loan vary greatly, depending on the loan purpose (for example, extension of credit limit, new loan, or refinancing of a delinquent loan) and eventual servicing requirements.[29]

Social Costs of Structure Restraints

In the previous section, we discussed the effect of customer costs on optimal bank size and organizational form. It was argued that convenience costs and bank production costs interact to provide multiple optimal solutions. By implication, states that legally restrict banks from branching may be imposing a social cost on their constituents. Flannery hypothesized that these social costs could take two forms: (1) technical inefficiency as a consequence of not being able to install the least cost firm structure and (2) price inefficiency that may come about because entry is cheaper in branching states (that is, a new charter is not needed and monopoly rents may be available).[30] To test these hypotheses, a matched sample of 135 bank pairs in unit bank and branch bank states was selected from 1978 FCA data. A translog function relating profits (as measured by pretax net operating income) to input prices for labor and capital—in addition to dummy variables for the legality in the state of branching, multibank holding companies, or MBHCs, and limited-service branches of unit banks—was developed (in line with earlier work by Mullineaux) to test the second hypothesis.[31] Since banks in unit banking states had significantly higher profits than those in branch states, price inefficiency was believed to have enriched bank shareholders at the expense of customers. To test the technical efficiency hypothesis, a translog cost function was constructed in the spirit of BHH.[32] Less cost efficiency was found in states with prohibitions on limited-service branches of unit banks than in states that allow such branches. Therefore, technical inefficiency appears to be present in unit states that do not allow branching of any kind. Flannery concluded that income transfers and deadweight losses attributable to branch restrictions are substantial social costs in the United States.

Product Costs and Profitability

As mentioned in chapter 1, a number of studies have concluded that expense control is the primary determinant of bank profitability. Kwast and Rose challenged this work on the grounds that no theoretical framework linking earnings and costs had been forwarded.[33] No tests of well-formulated hypotheses had been performed. To overcome this problem, Kwast and Rose proposed the application of a statistical (least-cost) accounting technique, developed in another branch of the literature, which related bank earnings to balance sheet structure. A sample of 41 high-profit banks and 39 low-profit banks with assets exceeding $500 million were examined over the period 1970–77 for differences in (1) yields on assets and liabilities and (2) operating costs as determined by statistical cost analyses. When certain market demand and supply conditions were held constant, yield differences between high-and low-profit banks using gross operating income could not be detected. Therefore, pricing efficiency was not believed to be responsible for gross earnings disparities. When net operating income and net income (after taxes) were used as dependent variables, mixed findings were uncovered, with no strong evidence that high-earning banks had different pricing structures. Tests for differences in earnings flows from scale economies also could not be rejected. In sum, the consensus of previous literature, pointing to expense control as the key to profitability, was not supported. Kwast and Rose cited the following as being potentially responsible for differences in bank profitability: (1) regional conditions, (2) portfolio and risk preferences, and (3) management ability.

In defense of prior research, we should comment that the Kwast and Rose study is limited in scope to large banks; therefore, the results cannot be generalized to the entire banking population. Also, the sample sizes are relatively small compared to previous research studies, and although theory and statistical modeling are applied, further testing is needed to verify the results.

Perhaps the most important inference to be drawn from their study is that the relationship between product costs and profitability is a complex one. Maintenance of peak pricing strategy and operating efficiency does not necessarily ensure impressive earnings. Nonetheless, it is our opinion that they are essential ingredients for survival.

Product Costs and Risk

One of the central functions of banks is risk intermediation; that is, banks accept relatively high credit risk on loans and pass a portion of the associated returns along to depositors, who desire low-credit-risk demand and time deposit accounts. The difference in risks and returns between ultimate borrowers and lenders (depositors) represents the bank's position as intermediary in the credit markets. Since resources must be expended by the bank to achieve any particular intermediate position, these factors must be weighed against the associated risks and returns. In line with this reasoning, Baltensperger has presented theoretical arguments for the positive effect of bank risk on operating costs.[34] On a practical level, banks may reduce their average credit risk per loan by collecting more information about borrowers or simply by making smaller loans; however, both of these risk-reducing methods increase operating costs. Moreover, to reduce the risk of cash-outs caused by deposit withdrawals, the bank can carry more cash reserves and capital, both of which have opportunity costs. Of course, from a theoretical standpoint, the bank must negotiate a course somewhere between these two different alternatives. For example, Baltensperger observed that the bank should hold reserves and issue capital to the point at which marginal opportunity costs just equal the marginal costs of a cash-out. The interesting aspect of his analysis is that the probability of a cash problem is shown to be related to bank size. It has been demonstrated that larger banks have a lower variance of deposit withdrawals (because of the larger number of accounts) than do smaller banks (see also note 4 in chapter 2). For the same reason, as bank size increases, the variance of loan repayments declines. Since lower asset and liability risks reduce the adjustment requirements on larger banks, Baltensperger concluded that larger banks have an operating cost advantage over smaller banks.

As noted by Borts in a comment on the Baltensperger paper, the foregoing results were derived using the number of accounts as a size criterion, rather than in dollar terms.[35] Thus, they are most relevant to how numbers of accounts affect operating costs, with bank size held constant. Other comments by Murphy suggested that credit information is more efficiently transformed by small banks compared to large banks; that is, a closer relationship with customers causes the value of each new unit of information for small banks to exceed that of large banks.[36] Therefore, small banks have some inherent characteristics that enable them to possibly offset other risk disadvantages. Despite these criticisms, the Baltensperger paper is significant because it recognizes the central role of risk in the production costs of intermediating financial services.

Summary and Conclusions

Few bank cost studies were conducted before the 1960s. Work by Benston in the 1960s introduced econometric methods (the Cobb-Douglas model) in the analysis of bank costs. A number of cost studies that considered alternative output definitions, samples, and model variables followed. Recent work has changed econometric methods to allow for multiple product output and the potential jointness cost benefits (the translog model). As in past studies, a number of translog model variants have been published. Some studies assumed constant intput prices, and others account for input price variations. Some studies employed FCA data to allow for allocated costs, whereas others resorted to Call Report data, using total unallocated operating costs. Output definitions have also varied. Studies have used numbers of accounts, dollar values, total revenue, account size, weighted average number of accounts, or some combination thereof. The various types of methodologies, output definitions, and data sources notwithstanding, bank cost studies have shared a common thread—small banks were shown to have higher average costs than their larger counterparts.

The study by Alhadeff, for example, indicated that total expenses as a percentage of earning assets in 1950 were 4.38 percent for small banks, as compared to 1.99 percent for larger banks—a difference of about 120 percent. Similar relationships were obtained for 1938, 1941, 1944, and 1947. These results did not take into account the effect of bank structure; however, subsequent studies by Horvitz and others that did take the effect of bank structure into consideration supported Alhadeff's results. In these studies, bank average costs were shown to be generally higher for branch banks than for unit banks.

A main difference between the results of early studies and those of the more recent ones is the size range of banks within which economies of scale were observed. Early studies concluded either that economies of scale are not large enough to pose meaningful threats to small banks or that they are exhausted within a relatively small range of output. For example, in his first study on bank cost, Benston concluded that results for indirect costs (which account for over 40 percent of total operating expenses) did not show any scale economies. In fact, the results indicated that large banks appear to be subject to some occupancy expense diseconomies. Although the study revealed some overall economies of scale on both sides of the balance sheet,

Benston concluded that the economies in banking were not large. In line with Benston's results, Greenbaum reviewed the early literature on bank costs and concluded that economies of scale are generally exhausted within the first $10 million in assets. He therefore concluded that banks with less than $10 million in assets were inefficient, primarily because of high overhead unit costs, high transaction costs, lack of sufficient specialization, and limited diversification. Other early studies also concluded that economies of scale in banking are exhausted at relatively low levels of output. For example, examining the cost effects of the holding company form of organization, Schweitzer concluded that scale economies in banking are exhausted, for the most part, after $3.5 million in assets and that diseconomies exist beyond $25 million in assets.

Although early studies concluded that economies of scale are exhausted at low levels of output, later studies reported mixed results to some extent. For example, BBHH concluded in 1983 (see table 3–8) that scale economies prevailed for all sizes of branch offices except for the largest (those exceeding $400 million in deposits). The same study, however, concluded that scale economies prevailed only within the first $50 million in deposits in unit banking states. Gilligan and Smirlock concluded that there are economies of scale on both sides of the balance sheet and that they are exhausted within the first $25 million in liabilities and $10 million in assets. Diseconomies of scale were found beyond $50 million in liabilities and assets. In another study, BHH used average account sizes as a measure of output and concluded that economies of scale prevail even beyond $400 million in total deposits for banks in branch banking states. Economies of scale for banks in the unit banking states were found up to $100 million in total deposits.

Another distinguishing feature of the later studies is the testing for jointness between two or more bank outputs. In their 1983 article, BBHH developed the first test for jointness between a set of two bank outputs for banks in both branch banking states and unit banking states. The results of the study indicated that economies of scope existed between time deposits and real estate loans (see table 3–9) but that joint production did not reduce costs in general. Gilligan and Smirlock also conducted tests for jointness between bank outputs and found that economies of scope existed between demand and time deposits, as well as between securities and loans. Therefore, no consensus has yet emerged on the issue of jointness in producing bank services.

Two shortfalls of the findings of past research on bank costs are (1) that banks in different markets are lumped together as if they had identical market niches and (2) that although tests of jointness are conducted to verify the existence of economies of scope, the magnitudes of these economies are not measured. The first problem is significant in that the aggregated results of the empirical tests may well not be meaningful to individual kinds of banks serving distinctly different markets. The second problem is important because bank managers need to know the magnitudes of scope economies (or diseconomies) between the combined outputs in order to choose the most appropriate combination of outputs to produce. Unless such information is available, the cost-effectiveness of bank strategy to change output mixes cannot be carefully assessed. In the next two chapters, we attempt to overcome these problems by proposing a new measure of scope economies and by separating banks into different groups according to their output mix.

Notes

1. David Alhadeff, *Monopoly and Competition in Banking* (Berkeley: University of California Press, 1954).

2. Banks with branches in only one city were denoted as unit banks because it was felt that their economic characteristics were much different from those of intercity branch systems.

3. *Monthly Review,* Federal Reserve Bank of Kansas City (February, March, April, December 1961, and February 1962).

4. Paul M. Horvitz, "Economies of Scale in Banking," in *Private Financial Institutions* (Englewood Cliffs, N.J.: Prentice-Hall, 1962), 1–54.

5. Irving Schweiger and John McGee, "Chicago Banking: The Structure of Banks and Related Financial Institutions in Chicago and Other Areas," *Journal of Business* 34(July 1961): 203–366.

6. Lyle E. Gramley, *A Study of Scale Economies in Banking* (Kansas City, Mo.: Federal Reserve Bank of Kansas City, 1962).

7. Higher costs at branch banks does not necessarily mean that their profitability is lower. Work by Horvitz and Shull showed that the loan mix and higher loan-to-asset ratios of branch banks (relative to unit banks) tend to offset the higher costs, resulting in no systematic difference in profitability. See Bernard Shull and Paul M. Horvitz, "Branch Banking and the Structure of Competition," *National Banking Review* 1(December 1964): 143–88.

8. The fact that data were volunteered has raised suspicions that participating banks are not representative of the banking population. The only study to test this potential limitation was by the Heggestad and Mingo. Employing 1970 FCA data and Call Reports of Income and Condition, they found that FCA banks did have lower cost-to-asset ratios than other banks, all else being the same. Other differences led them to conclude that studies using FCA data should select a sample that compares with the rest of the population. See Arnold A. Heggestad and John J. Mingo, "On the Usefulness of Functional Cost Analysis Data," *Journal of Bank Research* 9(Winter 1978): 251–56.

9. George J. Benston, "Economies of Scale and Marginal Costs in Banking Operations," *National Banking Review* 2(June 1965), 507–49.

10. George J. Benston, "Branch Banking and Economies of Scale," *Journal of Finance* 20(May 1965): 312–31.

11. It is possible that branch banking tends to concentrate industry resources more than unit banking and, therefore, could lead to oligopolistic behavior by banks

that would depreciate any cost advantage branching may have. On the other hand, competitive pricing of bank services may be sacrificed to some extent if it is less costly for the public to obtain bank services under a branching structure. Therefore, the cost of bank services net of customer acquisition costs may be affected little (if any) by branch banking. However, if branch banking is clearly less cost-efficient than unit banking, it would seem that its public benefit could be called into question.

12. Stuart I. Greenbaum, "Competition and Efficiency in the Banking System: Empirical Research and Its Policy Implications," *Journal of Political Economy* 75(1967): 461–81.

13. Cited also was another study by Greenbaum, which attempted to improve on the measurement of output by using a weighted average of earning assets, where the contributions of different assets to gross operating income were used as weights. Regression analyses showed the following: (1) the weighted assets output measure was superior to earning assets and total assets; (2) cost curves were U-shaped; (3) economies of scale were large for small banks and were modest over a large range of outputs; and (4) except for small and large output extremes, branch banks operated at lower average costs than did unit banks. See Stuart I. Greenbaum, "A Study of Bank Costs," *National Banking Review* 4(June 1967): 415–34.

14. Frederick W. Bell and Neil B. Murphy, "Bank Service Charges and Costs," *National Banking Review* 4(June 1967): 449–57; and Frederick W. Bell and Neil B. Murphy, "Economies of Scale and Division of Labor in Commercial Lending," *National Banking Review* 6(October 1969): 131–39.

15. See chapter 2 text accompanying notes 6 and 7. J.A. Powers, "Branch Versus Unit Banking: Output and Cost Economies," *Southern Economic Journal* 36(October 1969): 153–64.

16. By the 1970s, the issue of cost economies began to crop up in bank merger cases also. In corporate merger cases (under section 7 of the Clayton Act), the courts have historically ruled against the use of cost efficiencies as a defense for anticompetitive effects. To the contrary, the concept of economies of size has been applied as partial justification for disallowing a merger. Since such economies in banking appear to exist (albeit to a modest degree), a stronger case can be made for controlling concentration in banking. For example, see Raymond Jackson, "The Consideration of Economies in Merger Cases," *Journal of Business* 43(October 1970): 439–47.

17. Neil B. Murphy, "A Reestimation of the Benston-Bell-Murphy Cost Functions for a Larger Sample with Greater Size and Geographic Dispersion," *Journal of Financial and Quantitative Analysis* 7(December 1972): 2097–105; Stuart A. Schweitzer, Economies of Scale and Holding Company Affiliation in Banking," *Southern Economic Journal* 39(1972): 258–66; Donnie L. Daniel, William A. Longbrake, and Neil B. Murphy, "The Effect of Technology on Bank Economies of Scale for Demand Deposits," *Journal of Finance* 28(March 1973): 131–46; Lionel Kalish, III, and R. Alton Gilbert, "An Analysis of Efficiency of Scale and Organizational Form in Commercial Banking," *Journal of Industrial Economics* 21(July 1973): 293–307; William A. Longbrake and John A. Haslem, "Productive Efficiency in Commercial Banking," *Journal of Money, Credit and Banking* 7(August 1975): 317–30; Donald J. Mullineaux, "Economies of Scale of Financial Institutions," *Journal of Monetary Economics* 1(April 1975): 233–40; and, Donald J. Mullineaux, "Economies of Scale and Organizational Efficiency in Banking: A Profit-Function Approach," *Journal of Finance* 33(March 1978): 259–80.

18. Borts made the same comment regarding the bank cost literature in the 1960s. See G.H. Borts, "The Benston Paper, Some Comments," *Journal of Money, Credit and Banking* 4(May 1972): 419–21.

19. Other well-known surveys of the literature are Frederick W. Bell and Neil B. Murphy, *Costs in Commercial Banking: A Quantitative Analysis of Bank Behavior and its Relation to Bank Regulation* (Boston: Federal Reserve Bank of Boston, Research Report No. 41, 1968); and George J. Benston, *Journal of Money, Credit and Banking* 4(May 1972), 312–41.

20. Zvi Adar, Tamir Agmon, and Yair E. Orgler, "Output Mix and Jointness in Production in the Banking Firm," *Journal of Money, Credit and Banking* 7(May 1975): 235–43.

21. George J. Benston, Allen N. Berger, Gerald A. Hanweck, and David B. Humphrey, "Economies of Scale and Scope in Banking," *Proceedings of a Conference on Bank Structure and Competition,* Federal Reserve Bank of Chicago (May 1983), 432–61.

22. Thomas W. Gilligan and Michael L. Smirlock, "An Empirical Study of Joint Production and Scale Economies in Commercial Banking," *Journal of Banking and Finance* 8(1984): 67–77.

23. Thomas Gilligan, Michael Smirlock, and William Marshall, "Scale and Scope Economies in the Multi-Product Banking Firm," *Journal of Monetary Economics* 13(1984): 393–405.

24. George Benston, Gerald Hanweck, and David Humphrey, "Scale Economies in Banking: A Restructuring and Reassessment," *Journal of Money, Credit and Banking* 14(November 1982), 435–56.

25. The Divisia index was originally developed in W. Erwin Diewert, "Exact and Superlative Index Numbers," *Journal of Econometrics* 14(May 1976): 115–45.

26. Jeffrey A. Clark, "Estimation of Economies of Scale in Banking Using a Generalized Functional Form," *Journal of Money, Credit and Banking* 16(February 1984): 53–68.

27. Richard W. Nelson, "Branching, Scale Economies, and Banking Costs," *Journal of Banking and Finance* 9(1985): 177–91.

28. George J. Benston, "Graduated Interest Rate Ceilings and Operating Costs by Size of Small Consumer Cash Loans," *Journal of Finance* 32(June 1977): 695–707.

29. Other studies of consumer finance companies are Jack Zwick, "A Cross-Section Study of Industry Costs and Savings," in John M. Chapman and Robert P. Shay, eds., *The Consumer Finance Industry, Its Costs and Regulation* (New York: Columbia University Press, 1965): 55–86; Ernest A. Nagata, "The Cost Structure of Consumer Finance Small-Loan Operations," *Journal of Finance* 28(December 1973): 1327–37; and Thomas A. Durkin, "Consumer Loan Costs and the Regulatory Basis of Loan Sharking," *Journal of Bank Research* 8(Summer 1977): 108–17.

30. Mark J. Flannery, "The Social Cost of Unit Banking Restrictions," *Journal of Monetary Economics* 13(1984): 237–49.

31. Mullineaux, "Economies of Scale."

32. Benston, Hanweck, and Humphrey, "Scale Economies in Banking."

33. Myron L. Kwast and John T. Rose, "Pricing, Operating Efficiency, and Profitability Among Large Commercial Banks," *Journal of Banking and Finance* 6(1982): 233–54.

34. Ernst Baltensperger, "Costs of Banking Activites—Interactions Between Risk and Operating Costs," *Journal of Money, Credit and Banking* 4(August 1972): 595–611.

35. George Borts, "Costs of Bank Activities: Interactions Between Risk and Operating Costs: A Comment," *Journal of Money, Credit and Banking* 4(August 1972): 612–13.

36. Neil B. Murphy, "Costs of Banking Activities: Interactions Between Risk and Operating Costs: A Comment." *Journal of Money, Credit and Banking* 4(August 1972): 614–15.

4
Recent Empirical Evidence in a Competitive Environment

C hapter 3 detailed past research on bank cost structures. The evidence indicated a consensus that economies of scale in the commercial banking industry exist within a relatively small range of output. Most scale economies are exhausted when bank size reaches about $25 million in deposits. However, since past research is based on FCA data from no later than 1978, it may well be outdated, especially in light of subsequent changes in the financial services industry. In particular, the Depository Institutions Deregulation and Monetary Control Act of 1980 and the Garn-St. Germain Depository Institutions Act of 1982 changed the competitive scope and powers of depository institutions. In addition, because of market innovation, banks and thrifts compete not only with one another to attract deposit balances but also with other financial institutions. In many respects, competition for deposits is becoming national in scope. Furthermore, it is likely that there will be further deregulation in the years ahead. Because of these changes in the financial environment, in addition to the effects of improved technology on the production capability of banks, it is worthwhile to update analyses of the characteristics of bank cost structures by using more recent FCA data.

There are also methodological reasons for readdressing the issue of scale and scope economies in banking. For example, the extent of economies of scope have not been measured reliably in past research. The main reason for this is that the translog cost model does not allow outputs to be set at zero. In this chapter, we propose a new method of calculating scope economies that overcomes this methodological problem. Results reported for various models lend support for this new scope measure. This measure has the added advantage of allowing comparisons of banks of different size to see if size is related to scope.

In this chapter, empirical results are given for translog cost functions by the use of various combinations of outputs and FCA data for 1979 to 1983. Some insight into the effects of recent external and internal changes in the industry on the production costs of banking services may be gained from an examination of the results over time. The next section presents the model design and cost findings for all banks volunteering data in the FCA program. A subsequent section separates banks into subsamples to test for differences in the cost functions of banks located in unit states as opposed to branch states.

Overall Economies of Scale and Scope in the Multiproduct Banking Firm

Over the past decade, commercial banks in the United States have been adjusting to escalating interest expenses. These more variable costs have motivated many banks to conserve on occupancy expenses. More important, banks have been substituting interest returns for service returns that were paid out as side payments to customers when Regulation Q deposit rate ceilings were a binding constraint on acquiring deposits (as well as on maintaining loan accounts). This trend is indicated by the substantial decline in salaries, wages, and fringe benefits as a proportion of total operating expenses. For example, in 1964, this ratio was between 35 percent and 38 percent, on average, for banks in the United States, whereas labor expenses were around 25 percent in 1970 and only 15 percent to 17 percent in 1982.[1] Since 1982, the relative proportion of total operating expenses devoted to employees has stabilized, which would seem to imply that the adjustment process with regard to rising interest costs has taken place for the most part.

In January 1983, the introduction of money market deposit accounts (MMDAs) and Super-NOWs took place, and within six months they had absorbed about $370 billion; however, with the exception of funds attracted from money market mutual funds because of the high introductory rates offered, these accounts were funded from internal deposit sources that were already paying interest (that is, savings accounts, small-denomination time deposits, and large-denomination time deposits). Hence, they did not further alter the internal cost structure of banks in general (even though the interest sensitivity of deposits increased because these accounts were shorter term, on average, compared to the traditional sources of funds).

The period of study chosen here is advantageous because it enables us to assess the potential effects of recent adjustments to rising interest costs on bank cost curves. It also affords an opportunity to examine the cost characteristics of the banking industry in a more competitive environment than did past studies.

Output Measurement

An important aspect of model design is the definition of output. Authors have used a wide variety of proxies for bank output. As discussed in chapter 2, we prefer the use of dollars over number of accounts to measure output for theoretical reasons; that is, in a competitive banking environment, the cost of an additional dollar of both small and large accounts should be the same. Earlier writers have included the average size of deposit accounts to adjust the number of accounts, but this approach has pitfalls. For example, this approach assumes that there is a perfect correlation between the number and the size of accounts. Our research indicates, however, that although there is a high correlation between the number and the size of accounts, it is not perfect. Other authors have reported scale estimates (consistent with this assumption) for different deposit size ranges in terms of dollars. Of course, if number of accounts is the most appropriate measure of output, scale estimates would best be presented for different ranges of number of accounts. To the extent that number and size of accounts are not perfectly correlated, there is some degree of confusion in clearly interpreting the results as reported by those who used number of accounts.

There are other reasons for avoiding the use of number of accounts to measure output. For example, since the number and the average size of accounts are highly correlated, their joint use in a multiple regression context may well lead to a biased estimation of model coefficients (because of multicollinearity). On a more practical level, bankers most likely consider their output in terms of the total dollars of accounts. Naturally, one large account is considered more beneficial than a handful of small accounts, but this preference derives from the fact that large accounts bring in more dollars than do small accounts. Related to this, one way to view output is in terms of market share—a bank goal that is normally measured in terms of total dollars held by the bank relative to competitors. If a greater number of accounts were the objective of the bank, it could simply divide large accounts into many smaller accounts to boost output artificially. This suggests that the number of accounts is not critically related to the objectives of most banks. Therefore, we believe there are theoretical, interpretational, statistical, and practical reasons for measuring bank output in terms of dollars.

Another problem area in the measurement of bank output is specification of outputs themselves. Most earlier studies have considered deposit accounts, loan accounts, and securities investments as outputs, but, there are some critics of this broad approach to output measurement. The general complaint is that deposits are actually an input (rather than an output) in the production of loans and securities. We believe that this criticism is valid but incomplete. Deposits are indeed an input in the process of asset production, but they are distinct from raw materials (such as iron ore in the production of finished metal goods) used in manufacturing industries in that legal ownership rights are not available in the case of deposits. Depositors may immediately withdraw their funds (within certain limits) and cause the bank to collapse. It is possible that a raw materials supplier providing trade credit to a manufacturing firm may call the short-term debt due; however, contractual terms in trade credit would normally prevent this circumstance. In our opinion, the nonownership (and associated riskiness) of deposits sets them apart as a unique input in the production of assets.

Consequently, we propose that banking involves a two-stage production process. The first stage is devoted to acquiring funds, including primarily deposits plus various nondeposit sources of funds. The second stage of the production process utilizes the output of the first stage as an input. In its role as financial intermediary, the bank coordinates the joint production of both liabilities and assets. In effect, the bank as a firm is a vertically integrated company that obtains cost benefits from internalizing the production of its own inputs (deposits). With this perspective in mind, we chose to measure output in three different ways: (1) the stage one production of deposits (which dominate the sources of funds), (2) the stage two production of loans and securities, and (3) the vertically integrated production of deposits and loans. In this way, it is possible to observe the cost characteristics of different aspects of the total production process in banking.

In line with this conceptual framework for bank output, the following translog cost models were estimated:

Model I:

$$\ln C_1 = \alpha_0 + \alpha_1 \ln DD + \alpha_2 \ln TD + \frac{1}{2}\delta_{11}(\ln DD)^2 + \frac{1}{2}\delta_{22}(\ln TD)^2$$

$$+ \delta_{12}(\ln DD)(\ln TD) + \beta_1 \ln W + \beta_2 \ln R + \frac{1}{2}\gamma_{11}(\ln W)^2$$

$$+ \frac{1}{2}\gamma_{22}(\ln R)^2 + \gamma_{12}(\ln W)(\ln R) + \rho_{11}(\ln W)(\ln DD)$$

$$+ \rho_{12}(\ln W)(\ln TD) + \rho_{21}(\ln R)(\ln DD)$$

$$+ \rho_{22}(\ln R)(\ln TD) + \mu \qquad (4.1)$$

Model II:

$$\ln C_2 = \alpha_0 + \alpha_1 \ln SEC + \alpha_2 \ln LOAN + \frac{1}{2}\delta_{11}(\ln SEC)^2$$

$$+ \frac{1}{2}\delta_{22}(\ln LOAN)^2 + \delta_{12}(\ln SEC)(\ln LOAN) + \beta_1 \ln W + \beta_2 \ln R$$

$$+ \frac{1}{2}\gamma_{11}(\ln W)^2 + \frac{1}{2}\gamma_{22}(\ln R)^2 + \gamma_{12}(\ln W)(\ln R)$$

$$+ \rho_{11}(\ln W)(\ln SEC) + \rho_{12}(\ln W)(\ln LOAN)$$

$$+ \rho_{21}(\ln R)(\ln SEC) + \rho_{22}(\ln R)(\ln LOAN) + \mu \tag{4.2}$$

Model III:

$$\ln C_3 = \alpha_0 + \alpha_1 \ln LOAN + \alpha_2 \ln DEP + \frac{1}{2}\delta_{11}(\ln LOAN)^2$$

$$+ \frac{1}{2}\delta_{22}(\ln DEP)^2 + \delta_{12}(\ln LOAN)(\ln DEP) + \beta_1 \ln W$$

$$+ \beta_2 \ln R + \frac{1}{2}\gamma_{11}(\ln W)^2 + \frac{1}{2}\gamma_{22}(\ln R)^2$$

$$+ \gamma_{12}(\ln W)(\ln R) + \rho_{11}(\ln W)(\ln LOAN)$$

$$+ \rho_{12}(\ln W)(\ln DEP) + \rho_{21}(\ln R)(\ln LOAN)$$

$$+ \rho_{22}(\ln R)(\ln DEP) + \mu \tag{4.3}$$

where C_i's are the allocated costs for the specific outputs appearing in each regression model. The input prices are (1) the average wage rate, W, computed as the total wage bill of bank i divided by the number of bank i's employees; and (2) the opportunity cost of capital, R, computed as the rate of return on bank i's U.S. Treasury securities. Use of the second input price calculation differs from past studies that used rental cost, but it is preferred because, as the minimum rate of return, this measure would be highly correlated with the true opportunity cost of capital. The output notation coincides to the following accounts: (1) DD, demand deposits; (2) TD, time deposits; (3) SEC, total securities; (4) LOAN, total loans; and (5) DEP, the sum of demand and time deposits.

The models were run on SAS (a well-known statistical package). Initial runs suggested that better estimates of model parameters could be obtained by discarding outliers. This procedure sacrifices some information in order to gain more accurate estimates of model parameters. We opted in favor of this procedure, because these estimates are used to derive the scale and scope estimates that are ultimately sought. Without accurate parameter estimation, the scale and scope findings may well be meaningless. We defined outliers as those banks with ratios of cost divided by the outputs in each model that are greater than two standard deviations from the mean ratio. The following sample sizes were obtained (the number of observations dropped from the study for the foregoing reasons are in parentheses):

Year	Model I	Model II	Model III
1979	669(47)	664(52)	672(44)
1980	604(49)	597(56)	582(71)
1981	616(47)	618(45)	593(70)
1982	590(55)	574(71)	567(78)
1983	623(53)	629(47)	603(73)

Empirical Results

Tables 4–1, 4–2, and 4–3 give the estimated parameters (and associated *t*-tests for significance) and overall statistical results for models I, II, and III, respectively. Notice that the R^2 values (indicating the percentage of the variance of costs associated with the variance of the predictor variables) are relatively high and stable, ranging from a low of 88 percent to a high of 91 percent. The *F*-statistics of all models are statistically significant at the .00001 percent level, which confirms the goodness of fit for all models. When the overall results for the different models are compared, both sides of the balance sheet, whether taken separately or jointly, have about the same level of association to allocated costs. Hence, all three models appear to be fairly well fitted to the data.

The significance of the models' coefficients (shown by the *t*-statistics in parentheses below the coefficients) varied from model to model and from year to year. For example, in 1979, models I and III had a number of highly significant coefficients, but model II had no significant coefficients. In 1980 and 1982, few coefficients in any of the models were significant, whereas in 1981 and 1983, there were many significant coefficients among the three models. These results are not unlike those found in studies published in the past; that is, the overall significance of the models and the variability of the significance of coefficients over time and across models parallel the findings of previous studies. Differences between models can be attributed to a number of factors, including differences in the samples from year to year, changes in the financial environment over time, errors in the measurement of data items in the FCA reports, and the possibility of errors in the specification of the cost functions.

Estimates of Economies of Scale and Scope

The coefficients reported in tables 4–1, 4–2, and 4–3 were used to calculate overall economies of scale and scope for each model and year. Table 4–4

Table 4–1
Estimates of Multiproduct Cost Functions, 1979 and 1980[a]

Coefficients	1979			1980		
	Model I (Demand and Time Deposits)	Model II (Securities and Loans)	Model III (Loans and Deposits)	Model I (Demand and Time Deposits)	Model II (Securities and Loans)	Model III (Loans and Deposits)
α_0	62.45 (2.94***)	−30.72 (−.67)	82.40 (3.56***)	11.51 (−.58)	7.01 (.33)	28.41 (1.39)
α_1	1.84 (1.23)	−.73 (−.38)	−.95 (−.40)	1.75 (1.42)	−1.74 (−1.18)	2.30 (1.07)
α_2	−3.53 (−2.06**)	−1.09 (−.57)	−1.76 (−.67)	−1.29 (−.95)	1.58 (1.08)	−3.52 (−1.45)
δ_{11}	−.02 (−.40)	−.01 (−.08)	−.01 (−.12)	−.01 (−.25)	−.07 (−.97)	−.06 (−.51)
δ_{22}	.14 (1.89*)	.00 (−.06)	.11 (.72)	.12 (1.95*)	−.03 (−.48)	−.05 (−.34)
δ_{12}	−.02 (−.34)	.03 (.48)	−.01 (−.04)	−.03 (−.51)	.07 (1.14)	.10 (.69)
β_1	−6.98 (−2.81***)	8.65 (1.18)	−8.79 (−3.22***)	2.04 (.85)	−.26 (−.10)	−2.04 (−.84)
β_2	7.98 (−3.22***)	−7.65 (−1.05)	9.79 (3.59***)	−1.04 (−.43)	1.26 (.49)	3.04 (1.26)
γ_{11}	.43 (3.24***)	−.91 (−1.52)	.49 (3.34***)	−.08 (−.61)	.03 (.21)	.07 (.54)
γ_{22}	.43 (3.24***)	−.91 (−1.52)	.49 (3.34***)	−.08 (−.61)	.03 (.21)	.07 (.54)
γ_{12}	−.43 (−3.24***)	91 (1.52)	−.49 (−3.34***)	.08 (.61)	−.03 (−.21)	−.07 (−.54)
ρ_{11}	.01 (.16)	−.04 (−.26)	−.13 (−.74)	.01 (.19)	−.15 (−1.13)	.21 (1.36)
ρ_{21}	−.01 (−.16)	.04 (.26)	.13 (.74)	−.01 (−.19)	.15 (1.31)	−.21 (−1.36)
ρ_{12}	.13 (1.01)	.11 (.75)	.04 (.22)	−.01 (−.08)	−.12 (−1.13)	0.29 (1.66*)
ρ_{22}	−.13 (−1.01)	−.11 (−.75)	−.04 (−.22)	.01 (.08)	.12 (1.13)	−.29 (−1.66*)
R^2	.91	.89	.91	.91	.88	.91
F	815***	576***	713***	666***	501***	607***
N	699	664	672	604	597	582

[a]Asterisks indicate significance of the following levels: $*p < .10$; $**p < .05$; $***p < .01$.

gives the overall scale estimates (and scope estimates, to be discussed shortly) for six different bank size groups over the period 1979–83. Scale estimates significantly less (or more) than one indicate increasing (or decreasing) returns to scale, and no significant difference from one is coincident with constant returns to scale.

Table 4–2
Estimates of Multiproduct Cost Functions, 1981 and 1982[a]

	1981			1982		
Coefficients	Model I (Demand and Time Deposits)	Model II (Securities and Loans)	Model III (Loans and Deposits)	Model I (Demand and Time Deposits)	Model II (Securities and Loans)	Model III (Loans and Deposits)
α_0	8.73 (.71)	−12.42 (−1.20)	7.58 (.58)	2.90 (.11)	−17.98 (−.63)	5.24 (.19)
α_1	2.36 (2.22**)	−2.38 (−1.93*)	−.57 (−.37)	.01 (.01)	−1.60 (1.02)	.44 (.23)
α_2	−4.66 (−3.65***)	1.65 (1.55)	−1.32 (−.70)	−1.89 (−1.19)	.18 (.12)	−2.71 (−1.23)
δ_{11}	−.08 (−1.53)	−.11 (−1.68*)	−.16 (−1.26)	−.06 (−.95)	−.03 (−.47)	−.01 (−.18)
δ_{22}	.16 (3.98***)	−.09 (−1.51)	−.26 (−1.58)	.09 (1.14)	−.01 (−.10)	.01 (.07)
δ_{12}	−.00 (−.03)	.12 (2.04**)	.24 (1.67*)	.02 (.34)	.03 (.63)	.03 (.33)
β_1	2.75 (2.23**)	3.91 (3.39***)	2.36 (1.81*)	3.04 (.74)	5.70 (1.29)	3.28 (.80)
β_2	−1.75 (−1.42)	−2.91 (−2.52**)	−1.36 (−1.04)	−2.04 (−.50)	−4.70 (−1.07)	−2.28 (−.55)
γ_{11}	−.42 (−3.78***)	−.40 (−3.14***)	−.42 (−3.69***)	−.39 (−1.16)	−.64 (−1.73*)	−.49 (−1.43)
γ_{22}	−.42 (−3.78***)	−.40 (−3.14***)	−.42 (−3.69***)	−.39 (−1.16)	−.64 (−1.73*)	−.49 (−1.43)
γ_{12}	.42 (3.78***)	.40 (3.14***)	.42 (3.69***)	.39 (1.16)	.64 (1.73*)	.49 (1.43)
ρ_{11}	.02 (.23)	−.19 (−1.84*)	.04 (.39)	−.12 (−1.04)	−.14 (−1.16)	.03 (.24)
ρ_{21}	−.02 (−.23)	.19 (1.84*)	−.04 (−.39)	.12 (1.04)	.14 (1.16)	−.03 (−.24)
ρ_{12}	.17 (1.66*)	−.12 (−1.28)	.21 (1.45)	−.00 (−.01)	.00 (.02)	.20 (1.21)
ρ_{22}	−.17 (−1.66*)	.12 (1.28)	−.21 (−1.45)	.00 (.01)	.00 (−.02)	−.20 (−1.21)
R^2	.90	.88	.90	.90	.89	.90
F	582***	511***	569***	609***	524***	589***
N	616	618	593	590	574	567

[a]Asterisks indicate significance of the following levels: $*p < .10$; $**p < .05$; $***p < .01$.

The scale results shown in table 4–4 suggest that bank cost curves were U-shaped in general. That is, significant economies of scale were present at output levels below $50 million in deposits in most models over time, and significant diseconomies of scale normally occurred beyond $50 million to $100 million in deposits, with the exception that in 1983, no significant disecono-

Table 4–3
Estimates of Multiproduct Cost Functions, 1983[a]

Coefficients	Model I (Demand and Time Deposits)	Model II (Securities and Loans)	Model III (Loans and Deposits)
α_0	−13.04 (−.38)	−31.94 (−.80)	−34.24 (−.91)
α_1	−1.21 (−.93)	−.93 (−.58)	−3.55 (−1.89*)
α_2	−.85 (−.68)	−.61 (−.41)	2.23 (1.07)
δ_{11}	.15 (4.70***)	.07 (1.19)	−.06 (−.91)
δ_{22}	.12 (4.46***)	.02 (.40)	−.19 (−2.33*)
δ_{12}	−.10 (−4.13***)	−.04 (−.92)	.14 (1.91*)
β_1	5.88 (1.09)	8.28 (1.30)	8.25 (1.37)
β_2	−4.88 (−.90)	−7.28 (−1.14)	−7.25 (−1.20)
γ_{11}	−.68 (−1.51)	−.93 (−1.76*)	−.88 (−1.78*)
γ_{22}	−.68 (−1.51)	−.93 (−1.76*)	−.88 (−1.78*)
γ_{12}	.68 (1.51)	.93 (1.76*)	.88 (1.78*)
ρ_{11}	−.08 (−.84)	−.05 (−.38)	−.21 (−1.37)
ρ_{21}	.08 (.84)	.05 (.38)	.21 (1.37)
ρ_{12}	.07 (.72)	.15 (1.23)	−.04 (−.25)
ρ_{22}	−.07 (−.72)	−.15 (−1.23)	.04 (−.25)
R^2	.90	.88	.91
F	610***	491***	655***
N	623	629	603

[a]Asterisks indicate significance of the following levels: *$p < .10$; **$p < .05$; ***$p < .01$.

mies appeared in models I and II (that is, these cost curves were flat). Indeed, in 1983, significant scale economies were not exhausted until about $400 million in deposits for securities and loans (model II). Of course, this trend can be explained partially by the increase in the nominal price level over time, but the rate of inflation in 1982 and 1983 was relatively low, which would imply that the sudden appearance of scale economies at higher output levels

Table 4–4
Estimates of Overall Scale and Scope Economies, 1979–83 (Evaluated Using the Geometric Mean of Each Size Group)

Bank Deposit Size ($ millions)	Model I (Demand and Time Deposits)		Model II (Securities and Loans)		Model III (Loans and Deposits)	
	Scale[a]	Scope	Scale[a]	Scope	Scale[a]	Scope
A. 1979						
0–25	.93***	.32	.90***	.00	.91***	.07
25–50	.98	.29	.93***	.28	.97*	.30
50–100	1.02**	.33	.96***	.27	1.02*	.31
100–200	1.07***	.20	1.00	.19	1.08***	.25
200–400	1.10***	.27	1.06**	.19	1.15***	.32
>400	1.15***	.20	1.11***	.41	1.21***	.59
B. 1980						
0–25	.96	.25	.91***	–.03	.93**	–.11
25–50	1.00	.31	.95***	.19	.99	.46
50–100	1.04***	.23	.98*	.25	1.04***	.44
100–200	1.06***	.20	1.01	.02	1.09***	.34
200–400	1.08***	.23	1.05*	.17	1.15***	.42
>400	1.11***	.30	1.10**	.37	1.21***	.50

C. 1981

0–25	.90***	.48	.89***	.14	.93**	.30
25–50	.98	.35	.93***	.20	.98	.38
50–100	1.03**	.25	.95***	.19	1.01	.34
100–200	1.07***	.19	.98	−.01	1.05***	.30
200–400	1.13***	.14	1.02	.26	1.10***	.39
>400	1.20***	−.27	1.06*	−.27	1.17***	.34

D. 1982

0–25	.92***	.24	.93**	.21	.92**	.17
25–50	.97	.38	.95***	.21	.97*	.43
50–100	1.03**	.30	.98*	.08	1.02	.33
100–200	1.07***	.30	1.00	−.05	1.06***	.25
200–400	1.13***	.20	1.03*	.25	1.12***	.48
>400	1.17***	.28	1.07*	.27	1.18***	.40

E. 1983

0–25	.91**	.14	.94*	.29	.96	.07
25–50	.97	.13	.94**	.15	.96*	.27
50–100	1.01	.14	.94**	.18	.98	.34
100–200	1.06***	−.05	.94***	.05	1.00	.18
200–400	1.10***	.10	.96**	.11	1.00	.21
>400	1.17***	−.00	.95	.03	1.04	.16

aAsterisks indicate significance at the following levels: *p < .10; **p < .05; ***p < .01.

in 1983 was caused by other factors. One explanation is that the changing financial environment forced larger banks to become more cost-efficient than they had been. Another explanation is that computers, telecommunications, and automated equipment may have had a cost-reducing effect on production costs at higher output levels. Since technology would most likely have its greatest effect on demand and time deposits — but the cost curve for these outputs did not change much in 1983 — we can infer that recent changes affecting the banking industry were most likely responsible for the flattening of the cost curves for securities and loans as well as those for deposits and loans.

In comparing the results for different models, the evidence suggests that scale economies were exhausted more rapidly in stage one (model I) of the production process than in stage two (model II). It also appears that scale economies in the joint production of loans and deposits, or vertical integration (represented by model III), were exhausted at about the same output levels as in the production of deposits (model I) but at lower output levels than in the production of assets (model II). Economies of scale were exhausted in the following deposit range: (1) model I — $50 million to $100 million throughout the period 1979–83; (2) model II — $100 million to $200 million throughout the period 1979–82 and over $400 million in 1983; and (3) model III — $50 million to $100 million throughout the period 1979–83.

The intermediary role banks have of jointly acquiring deposits and making loans does not require that they expand to a very large size to reap most of the cost benefits associated with scale. In the production of securities and loans alone, however, large size is more likely to be important in reducing the costs of operations. It is important to note that evidence suggests that banks offering competitive interest rates to attract new deposits and expand their output can expect to face not only a larger interest expense but also (at some point) an increase in operations expenses per dollar deposited.

Before turning to the scope results, we need to discuss its measurement. As discussed in chapter 2, a two-step process is needed to test for the existence of economies of scope. First, a nonjointness restriction is imposed on the cost function. Second, the results of the restricted model are compared to results of the unrestricted model. A log-likelihood ratio can then be calculated to test for jointness that has a chi-square distribution. Unfortunately, however, the nonjointness test is severely limited when the translog functional form is used. As is well known, the translog cost function is approximated from a Taylor series expansion of

$$\ln C = \ln G(\ln p, \, \mathrm{H}(\ln Q)) \tag{4.4}$$

about the point, $p_i = 1, Q_k = 1$ for all $i, k,$ and as such it is not amenable to a global test of nonjointness. In other words, a test that may fail to reject nonjointness is limited only to the point of expansion; tests based on other points of the translog function could, however, reject the nonjointness hypothesis.[2]

To find the *degree* of scope economies (SC) for two outputs, for example, the following ratio can be calculated:

$$SC = \frac{[C(Q_1, 0) + (C(0, Q_1) - C(Q_1, Q_2)]}{C(Q_1, Q_2)} \qquad (4.5)$$

As previously discussed, the translog does not allow the calculation of costs when an output is zero. To remedy this problem some researchers have attempted to calculate equation (4.5) by substitution $\theta = 0.001$ where $Q_i = 0$. Although this procedure is conceptually appealing, researchers using this approach have found that SC is extraordinarily large and essentially uninterpretable, which is consistent with our experience. We believe that the cause of the unreasonable results is that when output is set far outside the range of outputs used to fit the translog model, the predicted values are extrapolated far beyond the limits of the model, causing far-fetched estimates of SC.

Another way to get around the zero-output problem and derive a measure of the degree of scope economies (not previously suggested in the literature) is to substitute the *minimum* quantity of output produced by banks in their respective size groups for the zero level of output in equation (4.5). To do this, we define Q_1^m and Q_2^m as the minimum quantities of Q_1 and Q_2, respectively, for a given size group, where the minimum value is the smallest amount of Q_i produced by a bank in the size group. Also, we define the increase in total costs for Q_1, Q_2, and Q_1 and Q_2 combined due to an increase in output level equal to ΔQ_1 and ΔQ_2 as, respectively,

$$\Delta C_1 = C(Q_1^m + \Delta Q_1, Q_2^m) - C(Q_1^m, Q_2^m) \qquad (4.6a)$$

$$\Delta C_2 = C(Q_1^m, Q_2^m + \Delta Q_2) - C(Q_1^m, Q_2^m) \qquad (4.6b)$$

$$\Delta C_{1,2} = C(Q_1^m + \Delta Q_1, Q_2^m + \Delta Q_2) - C(Q_1^m, Q_2^m) \qquad (4.6c)$$

The degree of scope economies using minimum output levels can be defined now as

$$SC^m = \frac{\Delta C_1 + \Delta C_2 - \Delta C_{1,2}}{\Delta C_{1,2}} \qquad (4.7)$$

This measure avoids the pitfall of extrapolating costs far beyond the relevant range of output for a given size group, because it corresponds more closely with the range of output that banks produce. It also is a measure of scope economies that is more realistic in studying key bank services (deposits, loans, and securities), because all banks offer these services. Our measure asks the following question: What are the scope economies associated with expanding output by jointly producing bank services in an output mix that approximates the average for a bank size group relative to those associated with expanding output by producing each output (one at a time) separate from any other output, from the minimum output level to the average output level. If we assume that banks act to maximize scope economies as they expand their total output and we hold all else the same, our new measure of scope therefore captures the extent of the cost savings that may be available from joint production in a dynamic sense.

The following results were obtained from the log-likelihood ratio tests for jointness:

Models	1979	1980	1981	1982	1983
I. Demand and time deposits	.78	.49	2.51	.01	.43
II. Securities and loans	.07	.48	1.07	22.31***	.08
III. Loans and deposits	.10	.57	.10	.04	.56

As shown, all of the tests are not significant, with the exception of the test for securities and loans in 1982 (significant at the .001 level). These results would seem to imply that cost complementaries do not exist in banking. However, as discussed above the nonjointness test based on the translog cost function is only a local test and as such does not necessarily imply a lack of global jointness. Second, the jointness results may also depend on the assumption that there are no important variables missing from the regression equation. From previous research studies on bank costs, it is known that the branching status of the state within which the bank resides can influence the cost curve. To see if this was partly affecting the results, a dummy variable was introduced into the models for the branching status of each bank's state (this tests for a difference in the intercept terms). In all years and models, the dummy variable was significant at the .0001 level. Therefore, the next part of this section will present detailed analyses of both unit states and branch states. Before moving on, however, we should note that table 4–4 displays the scope estimates calculated from equation (4.7) for the six translog models over the period 1979–83. The most obvious result is that SC^m is positive in almost all instances. Despite the general insignificance of the jointness tests, the large number of positive scope measures suggests that cost complementaries are present in key banking services; that is, expanding output by jointly producing bank services is less costly than expanding output by increasing each output one at a time.

Scale and Scope Results for Unit and Branch States

Branch banks normally can be expected to have lower fixed, or start-up, expenses than unit banks have. Since they are more retail-oriented in terms of marketing strategy, branch banks can also be expected to have lower account sizes than unit banks have. Unit banks located in states that permit branch banking would be subject to greater competition for retail deposits, therefore, than those in strictly unit banking states. According to our earlier arguments in chapter 2 concerning the use of dollars (rather than numbers) of accounts to measure output, the equilibrium cost of large and small accounts in branch banking states would be different from those in unit banking states because of the asymmetric competitive pressures. In branch banking states (as well as unit banking states), competition causes the cost of a dollar in small and large accounts to equilibrate to the same amount in both unit banks and branch banks. Consequently, the relevant cost comparison is not between unit and branch banks but between unit banking and branch banking states. The question that needs to be addressed, therefore, is whether the branch banking form of organizational structure significantly alters the cost function of banks relative to the unit banking structural form.

Although FCA data were available for the entire period 1979–83, only 1970, 1980, and 1982 data listed state locations for banks. Thus, data limitations prevented branch state versus unit state analyses for1981 and 1983. To compare cost functions in these two types of banking states, separate translog functions were run and *F*-tests for differences in coefficients were performed.[3] As before, observations with ratios of cost to output for each model that were more than two standard deviations from the mean ratio were dropped from the analyses as outliers.

Tables 4–5, 4–6, and 4–7 give the results for branch and unit state cost functions and their comparisons. There appear to be major differences between the cost characteristics of branch bank and unit bank states. In 1979, all three models had a number of significant differences, supporting the separate analyses of unit and branch states so common in previous bank cost studies. The findings for 1980 and 1982 were much less supportive of this approach. In both 1980 and 1982, only model II (based on securities and loans) revealed any significant differences in states' coefficients (and these were few in number). Thus, the evidence indicates that the organizational structure of the state can be quite significant in the estimation of translog cost functions at times (but not always). The irregularity of the significance of the branching status of the state implies that it should be considered a potentially important factor influencing cost curves in banking. We should add that further tests for significant differences between states that permit one-bank holding companies versus multibank holding companies were performed, but few differences were found.

Table 4–5
Estimates of Multiproduct Cost Functions, 1979: Unit Bank States versus Branch Bank States[a,b]

Coefficients	Model I			Model II			Model III		
	Unit	Branch	F-Test[c]	Unit	Branch	F-Test[c]	Unit	Branch	F-Test[c]
α_0	128.50 (3.18***)	-56.20 (-1.20)	8.67***	-85.38 (-1.22)	36.89 (.61)	1.79	116.05 (2.88***)	-28.19 (-.52)	4.50**
α_1	-1.79 (-.66)	-1.12 (-.65)	.04	-.77 (-.26)	-1.70 (-.70)	.05	.10 (.02)	-3.11 (-.98)	.43
α_2	-2.07 (-.60)	.57 (.31)	.52	-2.18 (-.73)	-.43 (-.17)	.21	-3.38 (-.76)	.32 (.09)	.45
δ_{11}	-.52 (-3.35***)	.07 (1.08)	14.32***	.16 (1.51)	-.10 (-1.23)	3.89**	.21 (.94)	-.08 (-.49)	1.14
δ_{22}	-.25 (-1.35)	.14 (1.87*)	4.52**	.20 (1.78*)	-.12 (-1.26)	4.87**	.42 (1.52)	-.05 (-.27)	2.05
δ_{12}	.38 (2.39**)	-.09 (-1.36)	8.76***	-.18 (-1.78*)	.13 (1.53)	5.64**	-.31 (-1.31)	.10 (.61)	2.14
β_1	-15.14 (-3.38***)	10.94 (1.47)	8.19***	19.25 (1.70*)	-2.37 (-.24)	2.15	-13.59 (-2.99***)	9.67 (1.12)	5.52**
β_2	16.14 (3.61***)	-9.94 (-1.33)	8.19***	-18.25 (-1.61)	3.37 (.34)	2.15	14.59 (3.21***)	-8.67 (-1.00)	5.52**

γ_{11}	.74 (3.71***)	−.99 (−1.66*)	6.43**	−1.99 (−2.10**)	−.05 (−.07)	2.53	.65 (3.16***)	−1.07 (−1.54)	5.37**
γ_{22}	.74 (3.71***)	−.99 (−1.66)	6.43**	−1.99 (−2.10**)	−.05 (−.07)	2.53	.65 (3.16***)	−1.07 (−1.54)	5.37**
γ_{12}	−.74 (−3.71***)	.99 (1.66*)	6.43**	1.99 (2.10**)	.05 (.07)	2.53	−.65 (−3.16***)	1.07 (1.54)	5.37**
ρ_{11}	−.37 (−1.66*)	−.19 (−1.39)	.51	−.10 (−.45)	−.12 (−.61)	.00	−.19 (−.61)	−.25 (−1.01)	.02
ρ_{21}	.37 (1.66*)	.19 (1.39)	.51	.10 (.45)	.12 (.61)	.00	.19 (.61)	.25 (1.01)	.02
ρ_{12}	.02 (.08)	−.10 (−.70)	.18	.19 (.84)	.08 (.44)	.13	.15 (.45)	−.04 (−.18)	.23
ρ_{22}	−.02 (−.08)	.10 (.70)	.18	−.19 (−.84)	−.08 (−.44)	.13	−.15 (−.45)	.04 (.18)	.23
R^2	.87	.95		.85	.92		.88	.93	
F	205***	819***		164***	470***		204***	593***	
N	280***	411***		271	394		272	393	

[a]Asterisks indicate significance at the following levels $*p < .10$; $**p < .05$; $***p < .01$.

[b]Models I, II, and III include input prices and correspond to the following output combinations: I—demand deposits and time deposits; II—total securities and total loans; III—total loans and total deposits.

[c]The F-statistic test for significant differences between coefficients in the unit bank versus branch bank cost equations.

Table 4-6
Estimates of Multiproduct Cost Functions, 1980: Unit Bank States versus Branch Bank States[a,b]

Coefficients	Model I			Model II			Model III		
	Unit	Branch	F-Test[c]	Unit	Branch	F-Test[c]	Unit	Branch	F-Test[c]
α_0	-19.19 (-.53)	7.17 (.32)	.43	18.28 (.55)	19.40 (.73)	.00	26.77 (.75)	48.35 (1.95*)	.25
α_1	.17 (.06)	1.73 (1.05)	.28	-3.93 (-1.41)	-1.28 (-.59)	.58	3.98 (.95)	1.31 (.45)	.29
α_2	-.09 (-.03)	-1.87 (-1.03)	.29	3.39 (1.40)	.18 (.08)	.94	-4.29 (-.82)	-3.45 (-1.11)	.01
δ_{11}	-.21 (-1.79*)	-.01 (-.14)	2.69*	.17 (1.42)	-.24 (-2.70***)	7.84***	.16 (.67)	-.14 (-.91)	1.21
δ_{22}	.14 (.79)	.05 (.82)	.27	.16 (1.79)	-.17 (-1.86*)	4.72**	.09 (.28)	-.17 (-.88)	.53
δ_{12}	.03 (.24)	-.00 (-.06)	.07	-.16 (-1.49)	.22 (2.65***)	8.13***	-.14 (-.55)	.20 (1.15)	1.27
β_1	3.58 (.81)	-.11 (-.04)	.56	-1.60 (-.38)	-1.11 (-.32)	.01	-3.28 (-.81)	-3.98 (-1.21)	.01
β_2	-2.58 (-.58)	1.11 (.40)	.56	2.60 (.62)	2.11 (.61)	.01	4.28 (1.06)	4.98 (1.51)	.01

γ_{11}	-.34 (-1.32)	-.01 (-.09)	1.13	.01 (.05)	-.02 (-.12)	.01	.07 (.28)	.12 (.57)	.02
γ_{22}	-.34 (-1.34)	-.01 (-.09)	1.13	.01 (.05)	-.02 (-.12)	.01	.07 (.28)	.12 (.57)	.02
γ_{12}	.34 (1.34)	.01 (.09)	1.13	-.01 (-.05)	.02 (.12)	.01	-.07 (-.28)	-.12 (-.57)	.02
ρ_{11}	-.30 (-1.46)	.06 (.45)	2.41	-.33 (-1.46)	-.14 (-.83)	.42	.31 (.97)	.17 (.76)	.13
ρ_{21}	.30 (1.46)	-.06 (-.45)	2.41	.33 (1.46)	.14 (.83)	.42	-.31 (-.97)	-.17 (-.76)	.13
ρ_{12}	-.22 (-1.01)	.10 (.70)	1.64	-.21 (-1.11)	-.02 (-.12)	.51	.47 (1.24)	.33 (1.39)	.10
ρ_{22}	.22 (1.01)	-.10 (-.70)	1.64	.21 (1.11)	.02 (.12)	.51	-.47 (-1.24)	-.33 (-1.39)	.10
R^2	.86	.94		.84	.91		.86	.93	
F	147***	655***		126***	415***		141***	500***	
N	230	374		223	374		222	360	

[a] Asterisks indicate significance at the following levels $*p < .10$; $**p < .05$; $***p < .01$.

[b] Models I, II, and III include input prices and correspond to the following output combinations: I—demand deposits and time deposits; II—total securities and total loans; III—total loans and total deposits.

[c] The *F*-statistic test for significant differences between coefficients in the unit bank versus branch bank cost equations.

Table 4–7
Estimates of Multiproduct Cost Functions, 1982: Unit Bank States versus Branch Bank States[a,b]

Coefficients	Model I			Model II			Model III		
	Unit	Branch	F-Test[c]	Unit	Branch	F-Test[c]	Unit	Branch	F-Test[c]
α_0	-19.38 (-.40)	1.90 (.06)	.15	-54.17 (-1.14)	15.75 (.46)	1.47	-34.12 (-.72)	23.28 (.71)	1.04
α_1	1.14 (.41)	-1.07 (-.61)	.50	-4.48 (-1.64*)	1.32 (.68)	3.10*	.23 (.07)	1.56 (.64)	.11
α_2	-2.20 (-.68)	-.38 (-.22)	.27	2.96 (1.27)	-2.43 (-1.38)	3.49*	-2.41 (-.56)	-3.10 (-1.14)	.01
δ_{11}	.05 (.42)	-.07 (-.87)	.75	.21 (1.98**)	-.22 (-2.44**)	9.68***	.15 (.86)	-.03 (-.23)	.72
δ_{22}	.24 (1.48)	-.01 (-.07)	1.93	.06 (.63)	-.03 (-.48)	.65	.22 (.89)	-.13 (-.77)	1.44
δ_{12}	-.13 (-1.04)	.06 (.71)	1.73	-.14 (-1.46)	.12 (1.65*)	4.82**	-.19 (-.94)	.10 (.71)	1.45
β_1	5.51 (.80)	2.53 (.52)	.13	12.04 (1.74*)	-.62 (-.11)	2.12	9.77 (1.49)	-.82 (-.16)	1.69
β_2	-4.51 (-.66)	-1.53 (-.32)	.13	-11.04 (-1.59)	1.62 (.30)	2.12	-8.77 (-1.34)	1.82 (.36)	1.69

	Model I			Model II			Model III		
γ_{11}	-.61 (-1.06)	-.38 (-.95)	.12	-1.26 (-2.15**)	-.16 (-.35)	2.23	-1.17 (-2.13**)	-.13 (-.32)	2.32
γ_{22}	-.61 (-1.06)	-.38 (-.95)	.12	-1.16 (-2.15**)	-.16 (-.35)	2.23	-1.17 (-2.13**)	-.13 (-.32)	2.32
γ_{12}	.61 (1.06)	.38 (.95)	.12	1.16 (2.15**)	.16 (.35)	2.23	1.17 (2.13**)	.13 (.32)	2.32
ρ_{11}	-.09 (-.45)	-.17 (-1.24)	.09	-.27 (-1.28)	-.05 (-.32)	.68	-.08 (-.33)	.21 (1.09)	.90
ρ_{21}	.09 (.45)	.17 (1.24)	.09	.27 (1.28)	.05 (.32)	.68	.08 (.33)	-.21 (-1.09)	.90
ρ_{12}	.04 (.16)	-.02 (-.19)	.06	-.06 (-.35)	.13 (.96)	.76	.18 (.56)	.37 (1.70*)	.25
ρ_{22}	-.04 (-.16)	.02 (.19)	.06	.06 (.35)	-.13 (-.95)	.76	-.18 (-.56)	-.37 (-1.70*)	.25
R^2	.85	.94		.86	.92		.87	.93	
F	141***	549***		150***	428***		158***	473***	
N	230	350		222	354		221	337	

[a] Asterisks indicate significance at the following levels $*p < .10$; $**p < .05$; $***p < .01$.

[b] Models I, II, and III include input prices and correspond to the following output combinations: I—demand deposits and time deposits; II—total securities and total loans; III—total loans and total deposits.

[c] The F-statistic test for significant differences between coefficients in the unit bank versus branch bank cost equations.

The overall F-statistics and R^2 values for the models indicate that the models fitted the data quite well. Notice the relatively higher R^2 values and overall F-statistics in all models and years for branch state models compared to unit state models. Dollar outputs were more closely associated with costs in branch banking states than in unit banking states. If it is true that branch banking stimulates greater competition for account dollars, a closer relationship between costs and outputs would be anticipated, because the cost of small and large accounts would be more likely to be pushed to a single equilibrium dollar cost. We have no direct test of this interpretation, but assuming that branching does increase competition, the results in tables 4–5 to 4–7 are at least consistent with our argument that costs are dependent on output in dollar terms.

Economies of scale and scope were calculated for all models for banks in unit banking and branch banking states. Table 4–8 shows the scale estimates. The most distinguishing feature of the scale results shown is that unit state banks had cost curves that were flat and branch state banks had U-shaped or upward-sloping cost curves in general. In unit states, models I and III did not exhibit either economies or diseconomies, with only one exception—model III in 1979. Model II (based on securities and loans) indicated that there were economies of scale up to about $200 million in deposits, after which the cost curve flattens out. In branch states, all three models in 1979 had U-shaped cost curves, with minimum costs occurring in the range of $50 million to $200 million in deposits. In 1980, model III is U-shaped, but models I and II are flat up to $100 million in deposits and upward-sloping thereafter. Finally, in 1982, model III also takes on an upward-sloping appearance, model I retains the upward-sloping shape (with diseconomies setting in at about $100 million in deposits), and model II flattens out (with no economies or diseconomies of scale present). These marked differences in the shapes of bank cost curves between unit and branch states further substantiate the need to recognize these two subpopulations in cost analyses.

Why have such differences in cost trends emerged? As was found in earlier studies, smaller branch organizations enjoy cost efficiencies as output is expanded, but as the number of branches (and therefore output) increases, diseconomies attributable to decentralized operations appear to occur. Unit banks, by contrast, are not exposed to these kinds of inefficiencies. More important, the differences in cost curves may be attributable to the historical pricing strategies used by these two types of organizational structures. Traditionally, branch banks have used service facilities to pay out implicit returns to depositors, whereas unit banks have used explicit side payments (such as appliances) to entice depositors. These added returns were important in a deposit market constrained by Regulation Q deposit rate ceilings. Of course, as deposit rates were gradually deregulated during the analysis period, the need for resorting to office facilities and appliances to attract deposits dimin-

Table 4–8

Estimates of Scale Economies over Time: Unit Bank States versus Branch Bank States[a,b]

Bank Deposit Size ($Millions)	Model I		Model II		Model III	
	Unit	Branch	Unit	Branch	Unit	Branch
A. 1979						
0–25	1.03	.97**	.91**	.92**	1.01	.90***
25–50	.99	.99	.92***	.94***	.99	.96**
50–100	.98	1.00	.92***	.96***	.95*	1.01
100–200	.98	1.02	.94*	.98	1.00	1.05**
200–400	.96	1.04	.96	1.03	.98	1.14***
>400	.98	1.06*	1.00	1.07*	1.00	1.20***
B. 1980						
0–25	1.02	.96	.91*	.95	1.03	.93*
25–50	1.00	.99	.91**	.98	1.00	.99
50–100	.99	1.02	.90***	1.00	.96	1.03**
100–200	.95	1.04**	.91**	1.02*	.95	1.08***
200–400	.88*	1.06**	.92	1.06*	.93	1.15***
>400	.81*	1.08**	.93	1.10**	.92	1.22***
C. 1982						
0–25	.95	.97	.92	1.02	.98	.97
25–50	.97	.98	.93**	.99	.98	.98
50–100	.99	1.02	.93**	.99	.98	1.01
100–200	.98	1.04***	.93*	.99	.97	1.04**
200–400	.96	1.08***	.92	.99	.96	1.08***
>400	.93	1.11***	.88	1.02	.94	1.14***

[a]Asterisks indicate significance at the following levels: $*p < .10$; $**p < .05$; $***p < .01$.

[b]All estimates are based on the corresponding models with input prices: model I—demand deposits and time deposits; model II—securities and total loans; model III—total loans and total deposits.

ished. This may explain the decision by some branch banks in the last few years to trim their office facilities, as well as the decline in the prevalence of appliance (and related) deals on the part of unit banks. The current strategy used by most banks for attracting deposits is simply to pay the required rate of interest, and in cases where implicit returns are paid out, automated equipment is being used to provide convenience to customers. The use of technology in banking does not appear to be creating cost inefficiencies in small banks, however. According to table 4–8, banks with deposits of less than $50 million were not experiencing any cost gains from increased output on either side of the balance sheet. Therefore, the results indirectly suggest that technology is not indivisible and that large size is not needed in order to efficiently provide banking services (see chapter 6 for a more in-depth discussion of technology).

It is interesting that the cost curve with model II in 1982 for branch banks was flat, as was the case for most of the unit state cost curves. It is possible that the switch to more explicit pricing of services by branch banks is responsible for this trend. The substitution of automated equipment for labor may also be partially responsible for this flattening cost curve trend in branch states. If automation does tend to flatten the cost curve, we may expect to see the cost curves associated with models I and III flatten more in the years to come, unless the technology differs greatly in the different stages of the production process of a bank.

The major implication of a flat cost curve to the banking industry as a whole is that many different sizes of banks should be able to coexist. Casual observation of the number and varied sizes of banks today is consistent with this result. Between 1980 and 1986, approximately 1,800 new banks were chartered in the United States; this supports our finding (in part at least) that small banks can operate cost-efficiently.

As was pointed out in chapter 1, the cost characteristics of the production process in an industry are among the primary determinants of its structure. In this regard, if there are substantial scope economies in the joint production of outputs, the structure of the industry can be affected. In this case, the existence of jointness could imply a cost advantage for large banks if larger banks enjoyed greater cost complementaries than small banks.

The following are the log-likelihood ratio tests for jointness for the different models over time in branch and unit states:

Models	1979	1980	1982
Unit banking states			
I. Demand and time deposits	.21	.21	.13
II. Securities and loans	.03	NC	.87
III. Loans and deposits	29.56***	31.21***	44.92***
Branch banking states			
I. Demand and time deposits	.07	.58	.25
II. Securities and loans	.04	.00	.21
III. Loans and deposits	54.15***	54.21***	72.14***

(One of the runs did not converge, disallowing the calculation of error sums of squares with the restricted model, which is denoted NC.) It is clear that jointness exists in the combination of stages one and two of the production process but not in either of the stages alone. Thus, by vertically integrating the production of deposits and the production of loans, banks tend to lower the cost of producing either output separately. Although this evidence supports the notion of cost complementarities in banking, it says nothing about the extent of cost savings possible from this type of joint production, nor does it lend insight into the possibility that large banks may benefit more than small banks from joint production.

Table 4–9 gives the estimates of scope economies based on our previously defined measure. Even in models that did not have significant jointness tests (models I and II) the scope measure was normally quite positive. The estimates shown in table 4–9 can be interpreted as follows: an estimate of .20 would indicate that a bank's production costs are 20 percent lower if it increases output using an optimal mix of any particular combination of outputs, as compared to increasing the bank's total output by increasing each of

Table 4–9
Estimates of Scope Economies over Time: Unit Bank States versus Branch Bank States[a]

Bank Deposit Size ($Millions)	Model I		Model II		Model III	
	Unit	Branch	Unit	Branch	Unit	Branch
A. 1979						
0–25	.06	.31	.26	.00	.39	− .93
25–50	.23	.35	.42	.27	.54	.50
50–100	.29	.43	.46	.26	.60	.49
100–200	.28	.32	.40	.17	.62	.38
200–400	.31	.43	.37	.33	.67	.47
>400	.64	.33	.72	.40	.80	.57
B. 1980						
0–25	.22	.13	.37	− .25	.15	− .18
25–50	.45	.30	.42	.08	.55	.45
50–100	.29	.25	.51	.19	.58	.43
100–200	.41	.27	.43	− .09	.59	.26
200–400	.42	.22	.44	.09	.59	.36
>400	.90	.30	.78	.35	.82	.46
C. 1982						
0–25	.33	.35	.59	.07	.33	.28
25–50	.48	.37	.51	.21	.51	.46
50–100	.42	.32	.24	.12	.40	.45
100–200	.52	.37	.43	− .12	.55	.23
200–400	.52	.22	.37	.28	.54	.50
>400	.86	.31	.82	.29	.84	.39

[a]Asterisks indicate significance at the following levels: $*p < .10$; $**p < .05$; $***p < .01$.
[b]All estimates are based on the corresponding models with input prices: model I—demand deposits and time deposits; model II—securities and total loans; model III—total loans and total deposits.

the bank's products one at a time (from the minimum level for banks of about the same size). Therefore, the results shown in table 4–9 imply that output should be expanded by increasing all outputs simultaneously, rather than separately from one another. It is the sharing of inputs across outputs that yields cost savings in expanding outputs.

Another important result of the scope estimates shown in table 4–9 is that large banks do not appear to be at a cost advantage compared to small banks in terms of joint production. In general, the scope estimates do not systematically vary according to size. There is a tendency for the unit state banks with deposits greater than $400 million to have higher scope estimates, but we believe that this is due to relatively large differences between the minimum and average levels of output in the over $400 million deposits sample (that is, this large difference can cause extrapolation of results beyond a reasonable range, which is the same kind of problem we cited concerning the calculation of scope by earlier researchers). Moreover, branch states banks with more than $400 million in deposits had scope measures that compared with smaller size groups, suggesting that size is not directly related to scope. When we compare unit and branch states, however, the results do appear to imply that unit banks have somewhat higher scope economies than do branch banks—a trend that is fairly obvious across size groups, models, and years.

Summary and Conclusions

This chapter has presented updated findings on economies of scale and scope in the banking industry covering the period 1979–83. Considering all banks as a whole, cost curves were U-shaped in most cases and, although jointness tests were normally insignificant, there was scope evidence that cost complementarities were present in increasing output by expanding outputs jointly, as opposed to one at a time. A dummy variable test for the potential influence of the branch status of the state in which the bank resides was significant, suggesting that banks in branch states should be analyzed separately from banks in unit states.

Different translog cost functions were estimated for unit and branch states, and F-tests for significant differences in comparable models' coefficients were conducted. The F-tests revealed erratic differences between comparable models. Since some models exhibited substantial differences, it was concluded that branch status is a potentially important influence on the cost curve. Subsequent scale estimates for the models supported this distinction, since unit states had cost curves that were almost always flat (with no economies or diseconomies of scale), whereas branch states had cost curves that were either U-shaped or upward-sloping. There did appear to be a trend in branch states for cost curves to flatten out over time. We interpreted this trend as a consequence of the deregulation of interest rates in recent years, which has caused branch banks to substitute explicit payments of returns (by means of higher interest payments) for implicit payments of returns (by means of branch office facilities). It is possible that greater use of technology is also responsible for part of this trend.

From these scale findings, it was concluded that bank size is not a primary determinant of cost efficiency in banking. These findings are not sufficient to conclude that small banks are at no cost disadvantage relative to large banks, because it is possible that large banks can reap relatively greater scope benefits than small banks can from the joint production of multiple bank services. Tests for jointness indicated that cost complementarities are present in the simultaneous production of loans and deposits, but not in the joint production either of demand and time deposits or of securities and loans. We concluded from this that there are substantial economies of vertical integration in a bank's role as financial intermediary and less cost savings to be gained in either stage one (that is, acquisition of deposits) or stage two (that is, the administration of assets) of the production process of banks. We may conclude, further, that banks should have a competitive advantage over financial service companies that produce only deposit services (such as money market mutual funds and nonbank banks set up by holding companies to acquire deposits across state lines and thereby avoid interstate banking restrictions) or only loan services (such as loan production offices of bank holding companies and mortgage banking firms that originate and service loans that they sell in the secondary market).

The result on the extent of economies of scope in branch and unit states yielded two conclusions. First, on average, banks can reduce the cost of expansion by about 30 percent to 50 percent by increasing outputs at the same time, as opposed to increasing each output separately, one at a time. Second, large banks do not have a cost advantage over small banks with respect to expanding outputs jointly. From the scale findings, we can therefore conclude that the cost characteristics of the banking industry do not favor any particular size of bank.

The main inference to be drawn from this chapter is that many different sizes of banks should be able to coexist in the future. Of course, this inference assumes that all else is held equal. In instances in which this assumption does not hold, it is necessary to consider other factors that may affect the competitive balance. For example, small banks in urban locations probably are not on equal footing with large urban banks, because the large banks have greater marketing ability and perhaps greater access to capital. Also, there is an underlying assumption that banks will seek distinct market niches in an attempt to avoid too much overlap with other banks in their trade area. So long as banks seek to serve the diverse needs of the public, the evidence in this chapter indicates that there is no production cost reason to believe that small or large banks will not be able to supply services at cost-efficient prices. Those banks that do not manage their resources in a cost-efficient manner will experience difficulties with earnings and will probably seek to exit the industry eventually (through merger with another bank or acquisition by a holding company).

Although considerable media attention has been given in recent years to the prediction that a major consolidation movement in the United States is due because of the present (and anticipated future) trend toward interstate banking, little factual evidence has been forwarded to support such a position. Surely interstate banking will induce evolution within the structure of the banking system; however, it is not at all clear, from the empirical analyses presented in this chapter, that a large-scale consolidation of resources in the banking industry will occur. With greater geographic powers of expansion (and perhaps new product lines), there should be more opportunities than ever before to explore and develop market niches. It is possible that the number of banks in the United States could actually increase under these circumstances. Indeed, in the 1920s, there were approximately 30,000 banks in the United States (the number declined to about 24,000 in that decade because of the rising competition from thrifts, insurance companies, and other financial service companies) compared to 15,000 today—a difference that was caused by the failure of banks in the Great Depression of the 1930s and the subsequent maintenance, by regulatory control, of a relatively constant number of banks over a period of about fifty years. Since today's economic system is far more developed than the economic system of the early 1900s, there is probably substantial room for many more sellers of banking services than exist at present. Of late, part of the void is being filled by thrift institutions, which are able to offer limited commercial deposit and lending services under the Garn bill of 1982. Perhaps other financial institutions will also enter the market in the years to come because of the development of a nationwide market for deposits and loans. In this regard, a number of retail-oriented firms are entering traditionally banking-related markets. For these firms (and other financial service sellers) the evidence here indirectly implies the same conclusions as those discussed for banks alone. A wide variety of sellers of many different sizes should be able to survive and prosper, as determined by their particular market niches. Also, inefficient producers will be faced with the choice between collapse or free exit through the sale of their firms.

Notes

1. See James Kolari and Asghar Zardkoohi, "Small Banks in a Changing Financial Environment." Study prepared for the U.S. Small Business Administration under grant contract no. SBA–8564–04–84, May 1986.

2. A proof that the translog cost function is incapable of providing a global nonjointness test can be derived as follows. Nonjointness is given by the condition

$$\partial^2 C / \partial Y_i \partial Y_j = 0 \text{ for all } i \neq j \tag{4N.1}$$

where C is cost and Y is an output.

For the translog function

$$\ln C = \alpha_0 = \sum_i \alpha_i \ln Y_i = \sum_h \beta_h \ln P_h = \frac{1}{2} \sum_i \sum_j \alpha_{ij} \ln Y_i \ln Y_j$$

$$+ \frac{1}{2} \sum_h \sum_k \beta_{hk} \ln P_h \ln P_k = \sum_i \sum_h \gamma_{ih} \ln Y_i \ln P_h \tag{4N.2}$$

the nonjointness restriction is derived as follows:

$$\partial C / \partial Y_i = (\partial C / \partial \ln C)(\partial \ln C / \partial \ln Y_i)(\partial \ln Y_i / \partial Y_i) = C / Y_i$$

$$(\alpha_i + \frac{1}{2} \sum_j \alpha_{ij} \ln Y_j + \sum_h \gamma_{ih} \ln P_h) \tag{4N.3}$$

From equation (4N.3), we have

$$\partial^2 C / \partial Y_i \partial Y_j = (1 / Y_i)(\partial C / \partial Y_j)(\alpha_j + \frac{1}{2} \sum_j \alpha_{ij} \ln Y_j$$

$$+ \sum_h \gamma_{ih} \ln P_h) + (\frac{1}{2} \alpha_{ij})(C / Y_i Y_j) \tag{4N.4}$$

Substituting equation (4N.3) in equation (4N.4) and evaluating equation (4N.4) at $Y_i = Y_j = P_h = 1$, we obtain

$$C / Y_i Y_j [(\alpha_j)(\alpha_i) + \alpha_{ij}] = 0 \tag{4N.5}$$

since $C / Y_i Y_j \neq 0$ for all values of $(Y_i, Y_j) \neq 0$, equation (4N.5) implies

$$\alpha_j \alpha_i = - \alpha_{ij} \tag{4N.6}$$

Equation (4N.6) is the restriction that must be imposed to test for nonjointness. Since equation (4N.6) holds only at $Y_i = Y_j = P_h = 1$, the nonjointness test using the translog cost function is a local test.

3. For details on the calculation of the *F*-test, see *SAS User's Guide: Statistics* (Cary, N.C.: SAS Institute, 1982), 47–48.

5
The Cost Economics of Banks with Different Product Mixes

One potential shortcoming of past research is the practice of treating all banks as one homogeneous group. In reality, banks have a tendency to cluster around specific market niches that are distinct from other markets. International banks, for example, enter markets that are almost completely different from those of domestic banks. Similarly, agricultural banks serve markets that are distinct from those served by urban banks. Agricultural loans tend to be different from consumer loans, *ceteris paribus,* in product characteristics such as riskiness, maturity, timing of payments, and so forth. Moreover, deposit and withdrawal patterns for agricultural banks tend to fluctuate seasonally and more radically than those for other banks. We hypothesize, therefore, that differences in product mix influence bank cost structures, including economies of scale and scope characteristics.

In this chapter, we explore the possibility that banks grouped by different product mixes have distinctive cost functions. If this notion is supported by the data, banks should be segregated not only by the branch status of their state but also by their product mix (or market niche). In the next section, we discuss our approach to grouping banks by output mix. We then present empirical results for cost models developed for each (derived) group of banks.

Clustering Banks into Groups by Product Mix

Empirical results based on aggregating all banks into unit states and branch states may well be irrelevant to individual banks that serve different market niches. An agricultural banker may find that the information that scale economies are generally exhausted at $100 million in deposits for all banks in branch states is too general to be meaningful to his particular operations. Economies of scale for agricultural banks in branch states may be exhausted at levels below or above $100 million in deposits.

In order to group banks by their product mix, because no standard grouping of banks is known to exist, a multivariate statistical technique known as *cluster analysis* was used. Cluster analysis allows an ad hoc grouping of observations according to their profiles by specific criterion traits selected by the researcher. In this case, we sought to group banks by the mix of assets and liabilities on their balance sheets. Ideally, each bank in a particular group (or cluster) would have an output mix like that of all other banks in its group but unlike those of other banks in other groups.

In order to group banks by their output mix, we employed the FAST-CLUS procedure in SAS.[1] This procedure is a partitioning technique that separates clusters into disjoint clusters; the researcher specifies the number of clusters to be derived. The method by which FASTCLUS determines closeness of observations in forming clusters is a Euclidean distance that measures interobservation similarity as

$$d_{ij} = [\sum_{t=1}^{r} (x_{it} - x_{jt})]^{1/2} \qquad (5.1)$$

where x_{it} and x_{jt} are the values of observations i and j for the variable x, and r is the number of variables (or traits) characterizing each observation. In the process of clustering, the desired number of clusters is first entered (denoted as k, for example). FASTCLUS proceeds by optimally selecting one observation (called a *seed*) for each cluster[2] and then assigning the remaining observations to the cluster with the nearest seed.[3] In other words, FASTCLUS continues assigning observations to the various clusters until d_{ij} is minimized (and further reassignment would only increase d_{ij}).

Perhaps the most crucial aspect in performing a cluster analysis is defining the criterion variables that will be used to form clusters. We opted to convert the entire balance sheet of each bank into an exhaustive set of outputs expressed on a proportionate basis in order to avoid arbitrary selection of outputs. Eight ratios described the asset side and four ratios were calculated from the liability side: (1) agricultural loans/total assets, (2) commercial loans/total assets, (3) real estate mortgage loans/total assets, (4) installment loans/total assets, (5) cash/total assets, (6) securities and related investments/total assets,[4] (7) credit card loans/total assets, (8) other assets/total assets, (9) demand deposits/total liabilities plus capital, (10) time deposits/total liabilities plus capital, (11) other liabilities/total liabilities plus capital,[5] and (12) capital accounts/total liabilities plus capital. The sum of the balance sheet ratios equals unity. Since one of the ratios on each side of the balance sheet is a linear combination of the other ratios, we deleted the ratios *other assets/total assets* and *capital accounts/total liabilities plus capital* from the cluster runs.

One problem encountered in the use of cluster analysis was the generally disruptive effects on the results of a small number of outliers. Outliers formed specialty groups with too few observations to allow cost function analyses. Because of the potentially distortive effects of outliers on the formation of more common clusters of banks, we ran a preliminary cluster analysis by specifying fifteen clusters, which is large in relation to the number of variables and observations. After outliers were removed from the data, further cluster runs were done by gradually reducing the number of clusters. Our goal was to identify distinguishable groups with noticeable differences in the mean value of each variable across groups. As confirmation of any given year's results, we sought to find groups with similar ratio (or asset and liability) profiles across successive years in the sample period 1979–83. When five clusters were requested, relatively consistent patterns began to appear. As the number of clusters was reduced to three or two bank groups, no clear and consistent patterns could be discerned from year to year. Although four clusters yielded fairly consistent patterns, five clusters were believed to be most interpretable for our aforementioned goal.

The final run, with five clusters, exhibited three readily identifiable bank groups and two other groups that are less clearly defined. Table 5–1 shows the mean value results for the ratio variables over time. In every year, group 1 is associated with a relatively high proportion of agricultural loans. Banks in group 1 had about 20 percent or more of their asset bases devoted to agricultural loans, but other groups had no more than 2 percent in this area. We will therefore refer to group 1 as *farm banks.* Groups 2 and 4 differ from other bank groups in their relatively high proportion of commercial and industrial loans. Notice, however, that group 4 funds its assets with relatively high proportions of other liabilities (or borrowed money), which distinguishes it from group 2, which uses a balanced mix of demand deposits, time deposits, and other liabilities. We interpret group 2 as *city banks,* whereas group 4 is *wholesale banks* in general. Groups 3 and 5 are not so easily identified. Neither group concentrated in any lending activity; instead, they tended to have substantially higher proportions of securities investments. On the liability side of the balance sheet, the two groups obtained a large fraction of their funds in the form of time deposits. If there is any difference between groups 3 and 5, it is that one group had higher proportions of time deposits and simultaneously lower proportions of other liabilities than the other group. Because these differences were not overwhelming, we decided to lump groups 3 and 5 into a fourth group, which we refer to as *retail banks.* Hence, the four types of banks that the cluster analysis tentatively identified (based on output mix) are (1) farm banks, (2) city banks, (3) wholesale banks, and (4) retail banks.

Table 5–1
Cluster Means for Variables as a Proportion of Total Assets, 1979–83[a]

Clusters	Agriculture Loans	Commercial Loans	Real Estate Loans	Installment Loans	Cash	Securities	Credit Cards	Demand Deposits	Time Deposits	Other Liabilities
A. 1979										
1	.25	.13	.00	.09	.08	.27	.01	.25	.59	.01
2	.02	.21	.00	.18	.10	.26	.01	.34	.43	.14
3	.02	.14	.01	.12	.09	.44	.00	.30	.46	.14
4	.02	.31	.00	.11	.12	.28	.01	.33	.30	.29
5	.02	.16	.00	.15	.07	.31	.00	.23	.61	.08
B. 1980										
1	.24	.13	.00	.09	.08	.29	.00	.22	.60	.10
2	.01	.27	.00	.15	.09	.28	.00	.26	.51	.14
3	.01	.15	.01	.14	.09	.39	.01	.31	.46	.15
4	.01	.27	.00	.11	.12	.31	.01	.35	.29	.28
5	.02	.13	.00	.14	.07	.35	.00	.20	.64	.08

C. 1981										
1	.20	.15	.00	.07	.07	.33	.00	.22	.59	.10
2	.01	.27	.00	.14	.08	.31	.00	.26	.51	.15
3	.01	.14	.00	.14	.08	.41	.01	.30	.44	.16
4	.01	.27	.00	.10	.11	.33	.01	.33	.28	.31
5	.01	.12	.01	.12	.06	.39	.00	.19	.65	.08
D. 1982										
1	.22	.13	.00	.08	.06	.35	.00	.21	.59	.12
2	.01	.22	.00	.11	.06	.36	.01	.24	.53	.15
3	.01	.12	.00	.10	.05	.48	.00	.20	.61	.10
4	.01	.31	.00	.09	.09	.34	.01	.29	.30	.33
5	.01	.17	.00	.19	.09	.34	.01	.35	.41	.15
E. 1983										
1	.21	.11	.00	.07	.04	.41	.00	.22	.61	.08
2	.01	.18	.00	.11	.06	.42	.00	.27	.53	.12
3	.01	.08	.04	.09	.03	.40	.00	.12	.74	.07
4	.02	.30	.00	.10	.08	.33	.01	.35	.33	.24
5	.00	.01	.00	.58	.02	.30	.01	.10	.82	.02

[a]Based on SAS FASTCLUS procedure, using FCA data.

Cost Analyses of Bank Groups

The sample sizes for the different bank groups in each year were as follows;[6]

Group	1979	1980	1981	1982	1983
1 (farm banks)	60	46	47	35	41
2 (city banks)	181	122	121	184	320
3 (wholesale banks)	96	80	84	99	100
4 (retail banks)	354	348	354	264	157

For the purpose of empirical analysis, the farm bank samples are too small to be further divided according to the branching status of the states. Dividing farm banks into branch and unit states would yield observations of less than twenty, which is too small to produce reliable statistical results. Accordingly, we ran the regressions on the overall samples for each group. A second reason for not dividing the farm bank samples according to the branching status of states is that the dummy variable distinguishing the two types of states in some regressions proved to be insignificant. For the sake of consistency and meaningful comparison between the bank groups, we decided to treat the remaining groups without distinguishing between the state types.

Regression Results

The three models we discussed in chapter 4 as equations 4.1, 4.2, and 4.3 were used to examine the cost characteristics of the four bank groups. The models were run separately for each group of banks and for each of the successive years in the sample period 1979–83. Therefore, sixty regressions were run in to collect information on the cost characteristics of the four bank groups for the three models and five sample years. We also compared the regression results across groups. This analysis yielded ninety sets of comparisons among the bank groups; these are reported in the appendix to this chapter.

Tables 5A–1 through 5A–5 in the appendix display parameter estimates for Model I (demand and time deposits) as well as the results of the F-tests between each pair of bank groups. The F-statistics indicate that the overall goodness of fit of each model (as applied to any given bank group) is statistically significant at the .01 level. Furthermore, except for the farm bank group, the R^2 statistics (which show the percentage variations in the logarithm of operating costs due to variations in the explanatory variables) were relatively high at about 90 percent. By comparison, R^2 for the farm group was 77 percent. However, parameter coefficients were not generally significant for the different models in the sample years 1979 and 1982. Caution should be exercised, therefore, in interpreting results for these two years.

Appendix tables 5A–6 through 5A–10 give the regression results for model II (securities and loans) over the five-year sample period. Once again, in 1979, the coefficients were not significant in general, except for group 3, wholesale banks, which showed significant coefficients on the squares of input prices and their interaction. In other years, the parameters were relatively more significant. For all years, though, the overall F-statistics and R^2 values were quite high, which indicates a strong relationship between bank costs and outputs (and associated inputs).

Appendix tables 5A–11 through 5A–15 document the statistical results for model III (loans and deposits) over time. These results mostly parallel those for model II.

Finally, the F-test results of pairwise comparisons between the regression coefficients of the cost models of different bank groups, shown in the appendix, tend to support our hypothesis that output mix affects the cost characteristics of banks. Although the significance of the F-tests varies over time and model comparisons, the frequency of significant results suggests that output mix is an important determinant of the cost function in banking.

Economies of Scale for Different Bank Groups

In this section we present our findings on scale economies across bank groups for each of the three models over the sample period 1979–83. As discussed in chapter 2, a finding of economies of scale alone does not necessarily imply the existence of a natural monopoly. To have a natural monopoly in a multiproduct industry, it is necessary to show both economies of scale within the relevant range of demand and economies of scope between products. Tables 5–2, 5–3, and 5–4 present our economies-of-scale findings for the four bank groups over the period 1979–83 for models I, II, and III, respectively.

Model I. Table 5–2 gives the results for model I (demand and time deposits). As can be seen, the scale estimates are generally different across the groups. Group 1 (farm) banks normally show no significant economies or diseconomies of scale for the three models over the five years. In other words, our results indicate flat average cost curves for farm banks.

The scale results for group 2, which we have labeled *city banks* because

Table 5–2
Estimates of Scale Economies for Different Bank Groups, 1979–83: Model I (Demand and Time Deposits)

Bank Deposit Size (millions)	Group 1	Group 2	Group 3	Group 4
A. 1979				
0–25	.82	.84***	.63***	.96
25–50	1.01	.94***	.78***	.99
50–100	1.17	1.02	.89***	1.01
100–200	NA	1.08	1.01	1.03
200–400	NA	1.19**	1.13**	1.05
>400	NA	1.25***	1.23***	1.07
B. 1980				
0–25	1.09	1.00	.76**	.98
25–50	.95	1.01	.88*	1.00
50–100	.90	1.07**	.94	1.03
100–200	.93	1.10**	1.00	1.04
200–400	NA	1.17**	1.10	1.06
>400	NA	1.25**	1.14	1.07
C. 1981				
0–25	1.03	.89	.50**	.90**
25–50	.99	.99	.70**	.97
50–100	1.01	1.07*	.83***	1.01
100–200	1.02	1.10**	.95***	1.07***
200–400	NA	1.17***	1.08	1.11***
>400	NA	1.24**	1.27**	1.17***
D. 1982				
0–25	.97	1.00	.70**	.92*
25–50	.92	1.01	.84**	.98
50–100	.91	1.05*	.95*	1.02
100–200	.86	1.07**	1.04	1.07***
200–400	NA	1.09**	1.11**	1.13***
>400	NA	1.13**	1.26**	1.17***
E. 1983				
0–25	.97	.87**	.74***	.92
25–50	.72***	.93***	.89**	.95
50–100	.83***	1.00	1.00	.97
100–200	.90	1.05**	1.13	.98
200–400	NA	1.11***	1.24***	1.00
>400	NA	1.18***	1.36***	1.05

[a]Asterisks indicate significance at the following levels: *$p < .10$; **$p < .05$; ***$p < .01$

Table 5–3
Estimates of Scale Economies for Different Bank Groups, 1979–83: Model II
(Securities and Loans)

Bank Deposit Size ($ millions)	Group 1	Group 2	Group 3	Group 4
A. 1979				
0–25	.78	.73***	.76**	.89***
25–50	.96	.87***	.83**	.94***
50–100	1.12	.91***	.89**	.98
100–200	NA	1.05	.91*	1.00
200–400	NA	1.13**	1.00	1.06*
>400	NA	1.25***	1.05	1.11**
B. 1980				
0–25	.82	.81**	.75**	.93**
25–50	.78	.93	.85***	.97*
50–100	.81**	.99	.90**	1.00
100–200	.85	1.08	.95	1.02
200–400	NA	1.21**	1.00	1.07*
>400	NA	1.27**	1.03	1.12**
C. 1981				
0–25	.98	.67***	.79**	.92**
25–50	.92	.85***	.87**	.94***
50–100	.93	.93*	.92**	.94***
100–200	.95	1.04	.96	.95**
200–400	NA	1.15**	1.02	.96
>400	NA	1.32***	1.05	.99
D. 1982				
0–25	1.23	.92*	.54***	.89**
25–50	1.03	.92*	.66***	.94**
50–100	.85	.96	.83***	.98
100–200	.88	.99	1.00	1.02
200–400	NA	1.04	1.16**	1.06
>400	NA	1.12*	1.28***	1.13*
E. 1983				
0–25	1.00	.95	.59***	.83**
25–50	.99	.96	.73***	.86**
50–100	1.05	.97	.87***	.86***
100–200	1.07	.98	1.01	.86***
200–400	NA	.99	1.10**	.90***
>400	NA	1.00	1.19**	.88***

[a]Asterisks indicate significance at the following levels: *p < .10; **p < .05; ***p < .01.

Table 5–4
Estimates of Scale Economies for Different Bank Groups, 1979–83: Model III (Deposits and Loans)

Bank Deposit Size ($ millions)	Group 1	Group 2	Group 3	Group 4
A. 1979				
0–25	.77*	.76***	.64***	.91***
25–50	.94	.89***	.78***	.97**
50–100	1.07	.97	.88***	1.00
100–200	NA	1.06*	1.02	1.04*
200–400	NA	1.18***	1.11**	1.09**
>400	NA	1.28***	1.21**	1.14***
B. 1980				
0–25	.96	.94	.69***	.93**
25–50	.95	1.02	.83***	.98
50–100	.96	1.02	.93***	1.02
100–200	1.00	1.06	1.03	1.06**
200–400	NA	1.17	1.15**	1.11***
>400	NA	1.23	1.22**	1.16***
C. 1981				
0–25	1.03	.81**	.48***	.89***
25–50	.99	.92*	.77***	.94**
50–100	.99	1.00	.90**	.97*
100–200	.98	1.06	1.02	1.01
200–400	NA	1.21***	1.16***	1.05
>400	NA	1.33***	1.31***	1.13**
D. 1982				
0–25	1.19	.96	.75**	.86***
25–50	1.05	.98	.86**	.93**
50–100	.88	1.01	.95	.99
100–200	.83	1.04*	1.04	1.05*
200–400	NA	1.08**	1.12***	1.12**
>400	NA	1.13**	1.23***	1.19***
E. 1983				
0–25	1.15	.90**	.72***	.87**
25–50	.96	.95*	.86***	.89***
50–100	.97	.99	.98	.90**
100–200	.86	1.03*	1.07**	.91***
200–400	NA	1.07**	1.16***	.92***
>400	NA	1.13**	1.30***	.95

[a]Asterisks indicate significance at the following levels: *$p < .10$; **$p < .05$; ***$p < .01$.

of their relatively high business lending and nondeposit borrowing, revealed patterns that are different from those of farm banks. Banks in this group generally showed either U-shaped cost curves or upward-sloping cost curves, where constant returns to scale prevailed at low levels of output and diseconomies of scale appeared at higher levels of output. In 1979 and 1983, group 2 banks showed strong economies of scale up to about $50 million in deposits and diseconomies beyond $100 million in deposits. The results were different, however, for 1980, 1981, and 1982, in which constant returns to scale existed up to $50 million in deposits and diseconomies of scale prevailed for output levels beyond $50 million in deposits.

Group 3 (wholesale) banks appeared to have different cost structures from group 2 (city) banks in that economies of scale for group 3 were exhausted at higher levels of output. For example, in 1979, 1981, and 1982, results for group 3 in table 5–2 indicate that economies of scale prevailed up to about $200 million in deposits. Another difference between group 2 and group 3 banks is that economies and diseconomies of scale were of relatively greater magnitude for group 3 banks. In other works, group 2 banks have less U-shaped cost curves than group 3 banks.

Group 4 (retail) banks are distinguishable from the other three groups in that economies of scale (when present) were exhausted more rapidly. For example, in 1981 and 1982, retail banks showed small economies of scale, which disappeared at about $25 million in deposits. In these years, diseconomies of scale prevailed up to about $100 million in deposits. Group 4 banks demonstrated no economies or diseconomies in 1979, 1980, and 1983 (that is, flat cost curves).

Model II. Table 5–3 shows the results for model II, in which outputs are securities and loans. Group 1 (farm) banks exhibited no significant economies or diseconomies of scale in general. This result is consistent with the results for demand and time deposits.

Group 2 (city) banks normally had U-shaped cost curves, except in 1983, when the curve was flat. Another finding is that economies of scale for this group were exhausted at different levels of output over the sample years. For example, in 1979, economies of scale for model II prevailed up to about $100 million in deposits, whereas they were exhausted rapidly in 1980 at about $25 million in deposits.

Group 3 (wholesale) banks had more consistent results over time. Economies of scale were exhausted, in general, at around $100 million in deposits, and except for 1980 and 1981, wholesale banks had U-shaped cost curves. In

1980 and 1981, cost curves appeared to be L-shaped, since scale economies were achieved at lower output levels, followed by constant returns to scale.

Group 4 (retail) banks also indicated some inconsistencies from year to year. One inconsistency is that economies of scale persisted at all levels of output in 1983, whereas in the previous four years economies of scale were exhausted at some level of output; that is, in 1979, 1980, and 1982, economies of scale were exhausted at about $50 million in deposits, whereas in 1981 they were exhausted at about $200 million in deposits.

Model III. Table 5–4 displays the results for model III. Group 1 (farm) banks consistently showed no economies or diseconomies of scale. Group 2 (city) banks had U-shaped cost curves in 1979, 1981, and 1983. In these years, economies of scale were exhausted at about $50 million in deposits. No economies or diseconomies were indicated in 1980; in 1982, no significant economies were found but diseconomies of scale occurred at about $100 million in deposits. Group 3 (wholesale) banks had U-shaped cost curves over the sample period, with economies of scale exhausted at about $100 million in deposits and diseconomies occurring at about $200 million in deposits in 1979 to 1981. In 1982 and 1983, economies of scale were exhausted at about $50 million in deposits. Except for 1983, group 4 (retail) banks also had U-shaped cost curves, but once again there was no consistency in the level of output at which economies were exhausted over the years. In 1979 and 1982, economies were exhausted at about $50 million in deposits, whereas in 1980 and 1981, they were exhausted at about $25 million in deposits and $100 million in deposits, respectively. In 1983, economies were exhausted at around $400 million in deposits for retail banks.

In sum, models for different bank groups consistently showed different cost curves. This finding is noteworthy because it supports the notion that treating all banks as a uniform group can mitigate the interpretability of statistical results on the cost structure of banks. In turn, their practical value to bankers, regulators, and other interested parties could be diminished.

Economies of Scope for Different Bank Groups

Different types of producers (for example, farm banks versus city banks) may have different scope-economies characteristics. For example, a farm bank may be expected to have little or no cost sharing between securities and loans because it is far more concerned with providing credit to farmers (and the rest of the community) than with providing securities portfolio services. However, the securities services can be significant in cities because of the purchase of large quantities of municipal bonds by banks to fund public facilities in high demand. Therefore, a city bank may need to spread operations costs across loan and securities services more than a farm bank would. Furthermore, it is possible that the scope economies of some types of banks are related to their size. In the case of the city bank, for instance, it may be that larger output levels are needed to fully utilize fixed expenses, which must be incurred to attract downtown business clientele. Sharing costs could be especially important to the city bank in this respect and, indeed, may be the underlying motivation for expanding output.

For these reasons, we tested each of our group classifications of banks (by output mix) for jointness. Tests were performed for all three models for

Table 5–5
Jointness Tests for the Three Models, 1979–83[a]

Year	Group 1	Group 2	Group 3	Group 4
Model I: Demand and Time Deposits				
1979	.26	.02	.21	.04
1980	.38	.38	.10	.30
1981	.12	.58	.03	.16
1982	.00	.00	.06	.02
1983	.02	.01	.02	.08
Model II: Securities and Loans				
1979	.16	.00	.01	.01
1980	.47	.42	.01	.55
1981	.01	.02	.27	.06
1982	.04	.02	.72	.11
1983	.57	.08	.02	.72
Model III: Total Deposits and Loans				
1979	NC	.00	.00	.04
1980	.09	.00	.00	.00
1981	.00	.10	.03	.28
1982	.02	.12	.00	.00
1983	1.23	.07	.26	1.09

[a]The likelihood ratio tests are all insignificant at reasonable levels of significance. If no convergence on model parameters was possible when imposing the nonjointness restrictions, the notation NC is shown.

the entire period 1979–83. As we shall see, these tests are subject to some amount of question in the current context. The measures of scope economies were calculated on the basis of our equation (4.6), discussed in chapter 4. These calculations suggest that banks in general gain substantial cost savings from joint production and that differences do exist between banks of different output mix and size.

Table 5–5 shows the results for the jointness tests for the different bank groups. The tests are insignificant from a statistical standpoint. We do not place much faith in these tests, however, because as was discussed above the translog form does not exhibit global nonjointness.

Tables 5–6, 5–7, and 5–8 present the scope findings for demand and time deposits, securities and loans, and loans and deposits, respectively, based on our measure of the *extent* of scope economies. Once again, our measure indicates the percentage cost gains of increasing outputs from their minimum levels to their average output levels simultaneously, as compared to increasing each output one at a time (or separately from the other outputs). Overall, the weight of the evidence suggests that scope economies are substantial in all stages of the production process in banking (that is, stage one acquisition of deposits, stage two administration of assets, and the vertical integration of these two stages).

Table 5–6 shows that expanding output by jointly increasing demand and time deposits (rather than by increasing them separately from one another) normally allows a cost savings of 30 percent to 70 percent. For farm banks, there is a general trend toward greater scope economies as size is increased. In a comparison of the different bank groups, the retail banks appeared to have lower scope benefits than the other groups in most years. No other trends are readily identifiable.

These same patterns emerge from the scope findings for securities and loans, as shown in table 5–7. Also, banks with over $400 million in deposits tended to have higher scope estimates than did smaller banks in 1979 and 1980, but not thereafter.

Table 5–8 contains the scope results for loans and deposits. One trend that seems fairly obvious is that the farm banks had relatively high scope economies. Also, smaller farm banks gained more than larger farm banks in terms of cost savings from vertical integration.

The scope measures in tables 5–6 through 5–8 suggest a few cost traits that are specific to different types of bank service producers. Farm banks, in particular, appear to have some unique cost characteristics. Larger farm banks enjoy greater scope benefits than smaller farm banks in the production of either demand and time deposits or securities and loans, but the opposite is true for deposits and loans. Of course, small farm banks would normally ser-

Table 5-6
Estimates of Scope Economies for Different Bank Groups, 1979-83: Model I
(Demand and Time Deposits)

Bank Deposit Size ($ millions)	Group 1	Group 2	Group 3	Group 4
A. 1979				
0-25	.64	.46	.82	.16
25-50	.69	.64	.76	.40
50-100	.72	.65	.65	.49
100-200	NA	.62	.57	.41
200-400	NA	.61	.51	.62
>400	NA	.59	.64	.51
B. 1980				
0-25	.61	.61	.87	.13
25-50	.79	.53	.67	.35
50-100	.81	.36	.56	.34
100-200	.85	.62	.57	.39
200-400	NA	.64	.56	.53
>400	NA	1.00	.72	.42
C. 1981				
0-25	1.46	.57	1.00	.47
25-50	.94	.56	.97	.41
50-100	.96	.55	.81	.34
100-200	.78	.72	.72	.33
200-400	NA	.60	.66	.43
>400	NA	.41	.57	.09
D. 1982				
0-25	.20	.37	.86	.26
25-50	.71	.48	.78	.42
50-100	.48	.46	.72	.39
100-200	.88	.46	.54	.42
200-400	NA	.52	.52	.51
>400	NA	.14	.49	.47
E. 1983				
0-25	-.38	.22	.74	.38
25-50	.54	.35	.67	.49
50-100	.48	.35	.63	.45
100-200	.62	.41	.49	.32
200-400	NA	.54	.60	.44
>400	NA	.42	.55	.27

Table 5–7
Estimates of Scope Economies for Different Bank Groups, 1979–83: Model II (Securities and Loans)

Bank Deposit Size ($ millions)	Group 1	Group 2	Group 3	Group 4
A. 1979				
0– 25	.67	.86	.74	.03
25– 50	.68	.62	.70	.33
50–100	.69	.62	.62	.38
100–200	NA	.57	.62	.31
200–400	NA	.58	.61	.42
>400	NA	.74	.74	.66
B. 1980				
0– 25	.38	.62	.45	.02
25– 50	.64	.59	.53	.32
50–100	.60	.56	.59	.36
100–200	.77	.55	.46	.25
200–400	NA	.49	.22	.43
> 400	NA	.82	.58	.63
C. 1981				
0– 25	.61	.33	.45	.29
25– 50	.71	.57	.41	.32
50–100	.77	.48	.50	.33
100–200	.84	.35	.39	.29
200–400	NA	.51	.07	.46
>400	NA	.06	.34	.34
D. 1982				
0– 25	– .35	.38	1.19	.31
25– 50	.14	.63	.49	.36
50–100	.54	.53	.61	.23
100–200	.93	.58	.44	.00
200–400	NA	.45	.08	.46
>400	NA	.29	.30	.58
E. 1983				
0– 25	.59	.20	1.65	.37
25– 50	.64	.35	.63	.21
50–100	.71	.42	.70	.31
100–200	.72	.46	.46	.14
200–400	NA	.59	.44	.21
>400	NA	.54	.36	.05

Table 5–8
Estimates of Scope Economies for Different Bank Groups, 1979–83: Model III (Deposits and Loans)

Bank Deposit Size ($ millions)	Group 1	Group 2	Group 3	Group 4
A. 1979				
0– 25	1.63	1.13	.67	– .19
25– 50	.94	.94	.75	.50
50–100	.88	.91	.77	.52
100–200	NA	.94	.74	.45
200–400	NA	.82	.80	.53
>400	NA	.80	.81	.69
B. 1980				
0– 25	1.79	.66	.60	.05
25– 50	.97	.68	.75	.53
50–100	.97	.70	.74	.51
100–200	.90	.71	.75	.39
200–400	NA	.66	.73	.56
>400	NA	1.00	.83	.60
C. 1981				
0– 25	1.66	1.25	1.00	.49
25– 50	1.02	.87	.67	.60
50–100	.92	.85	.63	.53
100–200	.87	.84	.61	.47
200–400	NA	.77	.28	.54
>400	NA	.65	.52	.59
D. 1982				
0– 25	.00	.36	.71	.50
25– 50	.62	.67	.58	.62
50–100	.57	.67	.66	.57
100–200	.96	.73	.61	.53
200–400	NA	.69	.32	.64
>400	NA	.45	.46	.63
E. 1983				
0– 25	1.36	.27	1.46	.38
25– 50	1.04	.43	.62	.41
50–100	.79	.50	.69	.54
100–200	.82	.61	.65	.36
200–400	NA	.64	.79	.42
>400	NA	.52	.95	.30

vice both the deposit and loan needs of farm operators and associated agribusiness firms. This close relationship with the customer explains the high scope economies found among small farm banks. As farm banks expand, they would naturally become more dependent on time deposits, as opposed to demand deposits, to fund their asset base. Therefore, cost sharing would become more relevant as deposit size increased for farm banks. This explanation is also applicable to securities and loans (that is, securities purchases are so modest for small farm banks that cost sharing is simply not so relevant a concern as it is for large farm banks).

The retail bank group was somewhat different from the other bank groups in that the scope estimates were relatively lower in many cases. In the cluster analyses, banks in this group were identified as having substantially higher proportions of securities than other banks. By implication, securities activities tend to decrease the ability to obtain scope economies as output is expanded. This may be explained by the fact that securities operations require specialized personnel, equipment, and other resources that do not allow much cost sharing with other outputs.

The other two bank groups, city and wholesale banks, did not exhibit any distinct scope patterns. These banks were marked by their proportionately larger holdings of commercial and industrial loans than other banks. The scope estimates made clear that cost savings were available to these "commercial" banks in the joint production of key financial services. Also, as with other bank groups, the scope estimates for loans and deposits (model III) exceeded those for either demand and time deposits (model I) or securities and loans (model II) in most cases. Thus, as we found in chapter 4 for unit and branch states, the vertical integration of deposit and loan production stages enables banks to realize their greatest scope gains.

Summary and Conclusions

This chapter has explored the hypothesis that banks with different output mixes have different cost characteristics. The statistical method of cluster analysis was employed to group banks in terms of underlying patterns in the asset and deposit structures of their balance sheets. Four groups of banks tended to be formed consistently over the period 1979–83. Briefly, their labels and relative descriptions are as follows:

Group 1 (farm banks) — high proportions of agricultural loans;

Group 2 (city banks)—high proportions of commercial and industrial loans and other liabilities;

Group 3 (wholesale banks)—high proportions of commercial and industrial loans and a balanced mix of sources of funds;

Group 4 (retail banks)—high proportions of time deposits and, especially, securities.

The next stage of the analysis was to estimate translog cost functions for each bank group. The models verify that the dependent (cost) and independent (output and input price) variables were related significantly to one another. Tests for differences between the estimated coefficients of various cost models for the different bank groups yielded numerous significant results. Hence, as hypothesized, there is evidence that the output mixes of banks can affect their cost function.

The scale estimates further confirmed this result. Group 1 (farm) banks consistently showed flat cost curves, indicating the existence of neither economies nor diseconomies of scale. Banks in groups 2, 3, and 4 generally had U-shaped cost curves, although in some years, the curves were either L-shaped or upward-sloping.

The tests for product jointness were insignificant, but because of the nature of the test and the likelihood that banks in each of the four groups under study would tend to have a common size range, this test may not be a reliable indicator of jointness. We decided, therefore, to rely more upon the scope estimates, which did reflect fairly substantial cost complementarities for all of the bank groups. Comparisons among bank groups suggested that farm banks have unique cost characteristics compared to other banks. Unlike the situation with any other bank group, scope economies increased in the joint production of both demand and time deposits and securities and loans as deposit size increased, with the reverse being true for loans and deposits. Therefore, size is related to scope for this group of banks. Other scope findings were (1) that retail banks with larger securities investments than other banks appeared to have lower scope economies than other banks, and (2) that all bank groups obtained greater scope economies from vertical integration (that is, producing loans and deposits) than in either stage one (demand and time deposits) or stage two (securities and loans) of the production process.

As discussed in chapter 2, the existence of natural monopoly in a multiproduct industry depends on whether the industry simultaneously exhibits both economies of scale and economies of scope. Consequently, a necessary but not sufficient condition for natural monopoly is a demonstration of economies of scale. In this respect, the findings presented in this chapter reject the notion that the banking industry exhibits natural monopoly characteristics. Almost invariably, the economies-of-scale findings for each group, model, and sample year indicated cost curves that were flat, L-shaped, U-shaped, or upward-sloping. In the absence of scale economies at relatively high output levels, the existence of scope economies is moot, at least with reference to the question of natural monopoly in the banking industry. However, the conclusion that natural monopoly conditions were not found in the period 1979–83 may be somewhat reassuring from a public policy standpoint (for example, extreme concentration of bank resources is not a likely outcome of the interstate banking movement underway at the present time). The scope findings indicated that joint production of key banking services can reduce costs considerably in comparison to separate production; therefore, to the extent that large banks can find ways to improve their scale efficiency in the future, the banking industry could become more prone to dominance by large banks.

Notes

1. See *SAS User's Guide: Statistics* (Cary, N.C.: SAS Institute, 1982), 417–22.

2. To select the initial seeds, FASTCLUS first chooses the first k observations as the temporary k seeds. Using a two-stage process, it then determines whether or not the temporary seeds should be replaced by any other observations:

Stage 1. Using the Euclidian distance formula (5.1), FASTCLUS measures the distance between the current observation j and the nearest seed i, or d_{ij}. If d_{ij} exceeds the distance between the two closest seeds, the seed i that is closest to the current observation j is replaced by j. If an observation fails to qualify as a new seed, stage 2 is invoked.

Stage 2. Stage 2 is similar to stage 1, except that the distance between the current observation and the nearest seed is measured to the second nearest observation — that is, if the shortest distance between the current observation j to all seeds other than the nearest one exceeds the shortest distance between the nearest seed and all other seeds, the nearest seed is replaced by the current observation j.

3. The "nearest centroid sorting" method assigns each observation to the nearest seed. Each time an observation is assigned to its closest seed, the seed is updated (by the SAS option DRIFT) to reflect the mean of the current cluster. One iteration is completed when all observations are assigned. The investigator may assign as many iterations as desired. Iterations continue either until the assigned number of iterations is reached or when the maximum distance by which any seed has changed is less than a small default value computed by FASTCLUS.

4. Related investments are federal funds sold, other liquidity loans, and trading account securities.

5. Other liabilities are federal funds purchased, borrowed money, time deposits over $100,000, and other nondeposit liabilities.

6. Sample sizes differed somewhat across models in each sample year because of data availability. The sample sizes reported in the text relate to model I (demand and time deposits).

Appendix 5A:
Estimates of Multiproduct Cost Functions and Statistical Differences across Groups, by Model and Year

Table 5A-1
1979, Model I (Demand and Time Deposits)ᵃ

Coefficients	Group 1 (Farm Banks)	Group 2 (City Banks)	Group 3 (Wholesale Banks)	Group 4 (Retail Banks)	F-Test between Groups 1 & 2	F-Test between Groups 1 & 3	F-Test between Groups 1 & 4	F-Test between Groups 2 & 3	F-Test between Groups 2 & 4	F-Test between Groups 3 & 4
α_0	41.63 (.37)	22.13 (.37)	-114.45 (-1.27)	-6.22 (-.10)	.03	1.15	.15	1.75	.10	1.09
α_1	-17.29 (-1.25)	1.28 (.28)	5.22 (.93)	1.41 (.46)	1.90	2.15	1.98	.32	.00	.41
α_2	13.58 (1.01)	-6.25 (-1.47)	-8.77 (-1.49)	-1.22 (-.38)	2.32	2.21	1.30	.13	.87	1.47
δ_{11}	.71 (.92)	.14 (.47)	.25 (.82)	.01 (.06)	.56	.28	.91	.08	.15	.60
δ_{22}	-.17 (-.18)	.20 (.78)	.43 (1.18)	.09 (.62)	.16	.32	.08	.29	.14	.91
δ_{12}	-.13 (-.16)	-.12 (-.44)	-.26 (-.81)	-.03 (-.25)	.00	.02	.02	.12	.08	.50
β_1	-2.36 (-.24)	4.29 (.43)	25.18 (1.76*)	1.81 (.19)	.23	2.49	.10	1.55	.03	2.05
β_2	3.36 (.34)	-3.29 (-.33)	-24.18 (1.69*)	-.81 (-.08)	.23	2.49	.10	1.55	.03	2.05

γ_{11}	.24 (.65)	−.84 (−.93)	−2.25 (−1.84*)	−.16 (−.21)	1.18	3.92*	.22	.94	.32	2.38
γ_{22}	.24 (.65)	−.84 (−.93)	−2.25 (−1.84*)	−.16 (−.21)	1.18	3.92*	.22	.94	.32	2.38
γ_{12}	−.24 (−.65)	.84 (.93)	2.25 (1.84*)	.16 (.21)	1.18	3.92*	.22	.94	.32	2.38
ρ_{11}	−.75 (−.84)	.07 (.18)	.39 (.81)	.03 (.11)	.82	1.21	.80	.28	.01	.54
ρ_{21}	.75 (.84)	−.07 (−.18)	−.39 (−.81)	−.03 (−.11)	.82	1.21	.80	.28	.01	.54
ρ_{12}	−.70 (−.82)	.43 (1.20)	.52 (1.10)	.05 (.19)	1.72	1.50	.81	.03	.75	.92
ρ_{22}	.70 (.82)	−.43 (−1.20)	−.52 (−1.10)	−.05 (−.19)	1.72	1.50	.81	.03	.75	.92
R^2	.77	.92	.91	.90						
F	18.79***	224.36***	93.47***	355.64***						
N	60	181	96	354						

[a]Asterisks indicate significance at the following levels *p < .10; **p < .05; ***p < .01.

Table 5A-2
1980, Model I (Demand and Time Deposits)[a]

Coefficients	Group 1 (Farm Banks)	Group 2 (City Banks)	Group 3 (Wholesale Banks)	Group 4 (Retail Banks)	F-Test between Groups 1 & 2	F-Test between Groups 1 & 3	F-Test between Groups 1 & 4	F-Test between Groups 2 & 3	F-Test between Groups 2 & 4	F-Test between Groups 3 & 4
α_0	-75.59 (-.66)	-205.40 (-3.04***)	-113.18 (-.86)	-8.09 (-.31)	1.06	.05	.35	.44	6.62***	.74
α_1	-17.33 (-1.19)	9.44 (1.28)	5.49 (.87)	3.75 (1.90*)	3.05*	1.89	2.19	.16	.49	.08
α_2	23.12 (1.73*)	-10.36 (-1.44)	-3.93 (-.65)	-2.29 (-1.14)	5.49**	3.12*	3.76*	.46	1.03	.08
δ_{11}	1.09 (1.12)	-.29 (-.60)	.16 (.42)	.03 (.25)	1.84	.73	1.26	.51	.37	.13
δ_{22}	.19 (.19)	.25 (.48)	.14 (.46)	.08 (.68)	.00	.00	.01	.03	.09	.04
δ_{12}	-.72 (-.78)	.05 (.11)	-.09 (-.29)	-.04 (-.37)	.63	.37	.57	.06	.03	.03
β_1	3.45 (.31)	36.91 (3.78***)	17.24 (.79)	.18 (.06)	5.41**	.32	.08	.78	11.37***	.71
β_2	-2.45 (-.22)	-35.91 (-3.68***)	-16.24 (-.74)	.82 (.26)	5.41**	.32	.08	.78	11.37***	.71

γ_{11}	.08 (.17)	-3.16 (-4.18***)	-1.07 (-.57)	.12 (.61)	12.98***	.37	.01	1.27	15.54***	.49
γ_{22}	.08 (.17)	-3.16 (-4.18***)	-1.07 (-.57)	.12 (.61)	12.98***	.37	.01	1.27	15.54***	.49
γ_{12}	-.08 (-.17)	3.16 (4.18***)	1.07 (.57)	-.12 (-.61)	12.98***	.37	.01	1.27	15.54***	.49
ρ_{11}	-1.08 (-.90)	.40 (.79)	.49 (.85)	.23 (1.50)	1.49	1.29	1.26	.02	.09	.22
ρ_{21}	1.08 (.90)	-.40 (-.79)	-.49 (-.85)	-.23 (-1.50)	1.49	1.29	1.26	.02	.09	.22
ρ_{12}	-1.23 (-1.16)	.46 (.89)	.28 (.50)	.16 (1.01)	2.33	1.46	1.78	.06	.28	.05
ρ_{22}	1.23 (1.16)	-.46 (-.89)	-.28 (-.50)	-.16 (-1.01)	2.33	1.46	1.78	.06	.28	.05
R^2	.85	.89	.92	.90						
F	23.12***	102.21***	88.24***	356.84***						
N	46	122	80	348						

[a]Asterisks indicate significance at the following levels *$p < .10$; **$p < .05$; ***$p < .01$.

Table 5A–3
1981, Model I (Demand and Time Deposits)ᵃ

Coefficients	Group 1 (Farm Banks)	Group 2 (City Banks)	Group 3 (Wholesale Banks)	Group 4 (Retail Banks)	F-Test between Groups 1 & 2	F-Test between Groups 1 & 3	F-Test between Groups 1 & 4	F-Test between Groups 2 & 3	F-Test between Groups 2 & 4	F-Test between Groups 3 & 4
α_0	-72.61 (-.58)	-156.95 (-2.14**)	3.58 (.09)	3.38 (.21)	.28	.25	.33	3.61*	5.39**	.00
α_1	-5.43 (-.63)	11.35 (1.58)	2.26 (.34)	1.74 (.83)	1.94	.41	.60	.87	1.94	.01
α_2	10.74 (1.18)	-12.71 (-1.85*)	-5.37 (-.74)	-3.74 (-1.94*)	3.65*	1.62	2.25	.55	1.86	.06
δ_{11}	2.90 (2.79***)	-.30 (-.35)	.52 (1.10)	.07 (.66)	4.92**	3.32*	6.76***	.69	.22	1.11
δ_{22}	2.08 (1.99*)	.18 (.22)	.95 (1.75*)	.15 (2.60***)	1.79	.72	3.14*	.62	.001	2.88*
δ_{12}	-2.51 (-2.50**)	.11 (.13)	-.63 (-1.28)	-.08 (-.93)	3.57*	2.21	5.41**	.58	.06	1.62
β_1	4.69 (.26)	29.81 (2.67***)	4.74 (1.15)	3.20 (2.03**)	1.18	.00	.01	4.29**	6.66***	.16
β_2	-3.69 (-.21)	-28.81 (-2.59**)	-3.74 (-.91)	-2.20 (-1.39)	1.18	.00	.01	4.29**	6.66***	.16

γ_{11}	.06 (.05)	-2.59 (-2.84***)	-.36 (-1.15)	-.46 (-3.23***)	2.21	.07	.13	5.13**	6.33***	.10
γ_{22}	.06 (.05)	-2.59 (-2.84***)	-.36 (-1.15)	-.46 (-3.23***)	2.21	.07	.13	5.13**	6.33***	.10
γ_{12}	-.06 (-.05)	2.59 (2.84***)	.36 (1.15)	.46 (3.23***)	2.21	.07	.13	5.13**	6.33***	.10
ρ_{11}	-.22 (-.32)	.63 (1.18)	-.003 (-.01)	.07 (.41)	.82	.05	.15	.61	1.20	.01
ρ_{21}	.22 (.32)	-.63 (-1.18)	.003 (.01)	-.07 (-.41)	.82	.05	.15	.61	1.20	.01
ρ_{12}	-.49 (-.68)	.69 (1.32)	.01 (.02)	.22 (1.45)	1.50	.23	.86	.70	.87	.14
ρ_{22}	.49 (.68)	-.69 (-1.32)	-.01 (-.02)	-.22 (-1.45)	1.50	.23	.86	.70	.87	.14
R^2	.88	.88	.87	.89						
F	31.69***	90.92***	57.65***	325.41***						
N	47	121	84	354						

[a] Asterisks indicate significance at the following levels $*p < .10$; $**p < .05$; $***p < .01$.

Table 5A–4
1982, Model I (Demand and Time Deposits)[a]

Coefficients	Group 1 (Farm Banks)	Group 2 (City Banks)	Group 3 (Wholesale Banks)	Group 4 (Retail Banks)	F-Test between Groups 1 & 2	F-Test between Groups 1 & 3	F-Test between Groups 1 & 4	F-Test between Groups 2 & 3	F-Test between Groups 2 & 4	F-Test between Groups 3 & 4
α_0	-158.06 (-1.21)	-13.16 (-.28)	-12.87 (-.15)	55.17 (1.17)	1.04	.71	2.34	.00	1.07	.58
α_1	.64 (.03)	-1.20 (-.21)	3.77 (.51)	.65 (.29)	.01	.01	.00	.29	.09	.20
α_2	1.97 (.10)	1.48 (.26)	-7.16 (-.94)	-3.15 (-1.51)	.00	.15	.07	.88	.60	.32
δ_{11}	-1.08 (-.95)	-.24 (-.42)	.07 (.16)	.09 (.77)	.42	.69	1.05	.18	.34	.00
δ_{22}	-.55 (-.48)	-.01 (-.02)	.39 (.85)	.10 (.92)	.17	.44	.31	.28	.04	.47
δ_{12}	.79 (.74)	.14 (.25)	-.15 (-.37)	-.06 (-.54)	.27	.52	.62	.17	.12	.06
β_1	24.39 (1.88*)	2.29 (.33)	7.82 (.53)	-4.85 (-.66)	2.18	.64	3.86	.13	.50	.70
β_2	-23.39 (-1.81*)	-1.29 (-.19)	-6.82 (-.46)	5.85 (.80)	2.18	.64	3.86	.13	.50	.70

γ_{11}	-1.92 (-2.01*)	-.12 (-.21)	-.79 (-.57)	.17 (.28)	2.48	.42	3.38	.23	.12	.49
γ_{22}	-1.92 (-2.01*)	-.12 (-.21)	-.79 (-.57)	.17 (.28)	2.48	.42	3.38	.23	.12	.49
γ_{12}	1.92 (2.01*)	.12 (.21)	.79 (.57)	-.17 (-.28)	2.48	.42	3.38	.23	.12	.49
ρ_{11}	-.35 (-.30)	-.29 (-.66)	.14 (.24)	.03 (.16)	.00	.11	.10	.38	.46	.04
ρ_{21}	.35 (.30)	.29 (.66)	-.14 (-.24)	-.03 (-.16)	.00	.11	.10	.38	.46	.04
ρ_{12}	-.43 (-.39)	-.29 (-.65)	.27 (.46)	.22 (1.23)	.01	.25	.33	.62	1.15	.01
ρ_{22}	.43 (.39)	.29 (.65)	-.27 (-.46)	-.22 (-1.23)	.01	.25	.33	.62	1.15	.01
R^2	.85	.89	.89	.90						
F	16.41***	160.79***	77.30***	256.66***						
N	35	184	99	264						

[a]Asterisks indicate significance at the following levels: *p < .10; **p < .05; ***p < .01.

Table 5A-5
1983, Model I (Demand and Time Deposits)[a]

Coefficients	Group 1 (Farm Banks)	Group 2 (City Banks)	Group 3 (Wholesale Banks)	Group 4 (Retail Banks)	F-Test between Groups 1 & 2	F-Test between Groups 1 & 3	F-Test between Groups 1 & 4	F-Test between Groups 2 & 3	F-Test between Groups 2 & 4	F-Test between Groups 3 & 4
α_0	-253.57 (-1.76*)	13.57 (.28)	-204.09 (-2.75***)	13.95 (.17)	2.67	.10	2.81*	5.23**	.00	3.96**
α_1	-4.25 (-.29)	-3.02 (-.77)	-1.42 (-.30)	1.89 (.58)	.01	.04	.19	.06	.88	.33
α_2	20.47 (1.54)	1.08 (.29)	-1.87 (-.43)	-3.05 (-1.08)	1.71	2.70	3.31*	.24	.76	.05
δ_{11}	-2.61 (-2.25**)	-.30 (-1.39)	.61 (2.16**)	.11 (1.04)	3.28*	7.74***	6.05**	5.82**	2.96*	2.76*
δ_{22}	-1.35 (-1.20)	-.25 (-1.16)	.39 (1.69*)	.14 (1.31)	.80	2.44	1.92	3.72*	2.65	1.01
δ_{12}	1.95 (1.75*)	.32 (1.53)	-.42 (-1.73*)	-.11 (-1.10)	1.78	4.57**	3.75*	4.81**	3.52*	1.40
β_1	19.61 (1.03)	1.24 (.16)	38.99 (3.34***)	.30 (.02)	.70	.79	.76	6.31**	.00	5.09**
β_2	-18.61 (-.98)	-.24 (-.03)	-37.99 (-3.26***)	.70 (.06)	.70	.79	.76	6.31**	.00	5.09**

γ_{11}	.27 (.17)	-.23 (-.35)	-3.33 (-3.44***)	-.19 (-.19)	.07	3.81*	.06	6.18**	.00	5.01**
γ_{22}	.27 (.17)	-.23 (-.35)	-3.33 (-3.44***)	-.19 (-.19)	.07	3.81*	.06	6.18**	.00	5.01**
γ_{12}	-.27 (-.17)	.23 (.35)	3.33 (3.44***)	.19 (.19)	.07	3.81*	.06	6.18**	.00	5.01**
ρ_{11}	-1.07 (-.87)	-.26 (-.84)	.12 (.32)	.11 (.42)	.35	.90	.97	.56	.80	.00
ρ_{21}	1.07 (.87)	.26 (.84)	-.12 (-.32)	-.11 (-.42)	.35	.90	.97	.56	.80	.00
ρ_{12}	-2.32 (-1.94*)	-.14 (-.50)	.24 (.69)	.25 (1.07)	2.71	4.49**	4.92**	.65	1.07	.00
ρ_{22}	2.32 (1.94*)	.14 (.50)	-.24 (-.69)	-.25 (-1.07)	2.71	4.49**	4.92**	.65	1.07	.00
R^2	.88	.88	.94	.92						
F	26.79***	258.76***	159.01***	182.75***						
N	41	320	100	157						

[a] Asterisks indicate significance at the following levels: *$p < .10$; **$p < .05$; ***$p < .01$.

Table 5A–6
1979, Model II (Securities and Loans)[a]

Coefficients	Group 1 (Farm Banks)	Group 2 (City Banks)	Group 3 (Wholesale Banks)	Group 4 (Retail Banks)	F-Test between Groups 1 & 2	F-Test between Groups 1 & 3	F-Test between Groups 1 & 4	F-Test between Groups 2 & 3	F-Test between Groups 2 & 4	F-Test between Groups 3 & 4
α_0	-322.14 (-1.19)	-33.06 (-.49)	-210.51 (-1.70*)	26.46 (.38)	1.43	.15	2.02	1.77	.37	3.13*
α_1	16.72 (1.28)	-.18 (-.04)	-2.37 (-.36)	.78 (.26)	1.86	1.76	1.82	.07	.03	.21
α_2	-10.35 (-.79)	-3.21 (-.63)	1.36 (.21)	-.95 (-.30)	.32	.66	.62	.32	.14	.11
δ_{11}	.14 (.17)	.59 (1.96*)	.05 (.22)	-.02 (-.20)	.34	.01	.05	2.03	3.41*	.09
δ_{22}	.61 (1.26)	.26 (.81)	.36 (1.06)	.06 (.46)	.44	.19	1.56	.05	.32	.80
δ_{12}	-.30 (-.58)	-.36 (-1.21)	-.16 (-.62)	.01 (.12)	.01	.06	.46	.26	1.31	.43
β_1	46.39 (1.23)	11.05 (.97)	37.32 (1.81*)	-3.26 (-.30)	1.04	.05	2.03	1.40	.81	3.44*
β_2	-45.39 (-1.20)	-10.05 (-.88)	-36.32 (-1.76*)	4.26 (.39)	1.04	.05	2.03	1.40	.81	3.44*

γ_{11}	-2.97 (-1.08)	-1.17 (-1.17)	-3.09 (-1.79*)	.28 (.33)	.49	.00	1.63	1.04	1.17	3.46*
γ_{22}	-2.97 (-1.08)	-1.17 (-1.17)	-3.09 (-1.79*)	.28 (.33)	.49	.00	1.63	1.04	1.17	3.46*
γ_{12}	2.97 (1.08)	1.17 (1.17)	3.09 (1.79*)	-.28 (-.33)	.49	.00	1.63	1.04	1.17	3.46*
ρ_{11}	1.14 (1.47)	.27 (.62)	-.38 (-.65)	.04 (.15)	1.18	2.52	2.38	.86	.21	.50
ρ_{21}	-1.14 (-1.47)	-.27 (-.62)	.38 (.65)	-.04 (-.15)	1.18	2.52	2.38	.86	.21	.50
ρ_{12}	.49 (.63)	.47 (1.09)	-.35 (-.59)	.05 (.19)	.00	.75	.37	1.34	.69	.43
ρ_{22}	-.49 (-.63)	-.47 (-1.09)	.35 (.59)	-.05 (-.19)	.00	.75	.37	1.34	.69	.43
R^2	.68	.90	.90	.88						
F	10.92***	157.25***	75.47***	282.81***						
N	55	169	88	343						

[a] Asterisks indicate significance at the following levels: *$p < .10$; **$p < .05$; ***$p < .01$.

Table 5A–7
1980, Model II (Securities and Loans)[a]

Coefficients	Group 1 (Farm Banks)	Group 2 (City Banks)	Group 3 (Wholesale Banks)	Group 4 (Retail Banks)	F-Test between Groups 1 & 2	F-Test between Groups 1 & 3	F-Test between Groups 1 & 4	F-Test between Groups 2 & 3	F-Test between Groups 2 & 4	F-Test between Groups 3 & 4
α_0	51.99 (.38)	−190.79 (−2.53**)	−34.33 (−.27)	40.64 (1.40)	2.90*	.20	.01	1.24	7.76	.47
α_1	−17.21 (−1.35)	−7.15 (−1.32)	−.35 (−.06)	4.36 (1.72*)	.66	1.27	3.62*	.67	3.49	.65
α_2	16.51 (1.34)	3.38 (.61)	−.28 (−.04)	−4.60 (−1.58)	1.18	1.25	3.63*	.16	1.54	.41
δ_{11}	.18 (.23)	−.13 (−.32)	.00 (.02)	−.10 (−.79)	.15	.04	.16	.07	.01	.22
δ_{22}	−.65 (−.85)	−.53 (−1.19)	−.03 (−.11)	.12 (.96)	.02	.50	1.32	.72	1.88	.29
δ_{12}	.26 (.38)	.39 (.97)	.05 (.20)	.01 (.10)	.03	.08	.17	.45	.77	.02
β_1	−7.24 (−.52)	37.90 (3.50***)	7.14 (.33)	−5.93 (−1.63)	7.48***	.31	.01	1.89	13.90***	.52
β_2	8.24 (.60)	−36.90 (−3.41***)	−6.14 (−.29)	6.93 (1.91*)	7.48***	.31	.01	1.89	13.90***	.52

γ_{11}	.56 (.97)	-3.45 (-4.15***)	-.57 (-.30)	.50 (2.12**)	15.81***	.34	.01	2.32	19.65***	.46
γ_{22}	.56 (.97)	-3.45 (-4.15***)	-.57 (-.30)	.50 (2.12**)	15.81***	.34	.01	2.32	19.65***	.46
γ_{12}	-.56 (-.97)	3.45 (4.15***)	.57 (.30)	-.50 (-2.12**)	15.81***	.34	.01	2.32	19.65***	.46
ρ_{11}	-.83 (-.93)	-.20 (-.53)	.03 (.06)	.24 (1.14)	.54	.60	1.77	.12	.97	.15
ρ_{21}	.83 (.93)	.20 (.53)	-.03 (-.06)	-.24 (-1.14)	.54	.60	1.77	.12	.97	.15
ρ_{12}	-.76 (-.92)	.02 (.06)	.07 (.10)	.27 (1.21)	.90	.56	1.87	.00	.28	.11
ρ_{22}	.76 (.92)	-.02 (-.06)	-.07 (-.10)	-.27 (-1.21)	.90	.56	1.87	.00	.28	.11
R^2	.78	.87	.88	.90						
F	12.60***	80.15***	66.72***	326.34***						
N	41	120	89	337						

[a]Asterisks indicate significance at the following levels: $*p < .10$; $**p < .05$; $***p < .01$.

Table 5A–8
1981, Model II (Securities and Loans)[a]

Coefficients	Group 1 (Farm Banks)	Group 2 (City Banks)	Group 3 (Wholesale Banks)	Group 4 (Retail Banks)	F-Test between Groups 1 & 2	F-Test between Groups 1 & 3	F-Test between Groups 1 & 4	F-Test between Groups 2 & 3	F-Test between Groups 2 & 4	F-Test between Groups 3 & 4
α_0	-228.38 (-1.54)	-35.05 (-.43)	-6.22 (-.21)	-1.68 (-.10)	1.25	2.24	2.86*	.11	.20	.02
α_1	-1.53 (-.18)	-.08 (-.01)	-5.62 (-1.26)	1.04 (.51)	.02	.19	.11	.54	.04	2.07
α_2	5.27 (.56)	-1.69 (-.26)	3.99 (1.09)	-2.26 (-.95)	.36	.02	.74	.60	.01	2.24
δ_{11}	.20 (.29)	-.53 (-.92)	-.14 (-.66)	-.05 (-.47)	.64	.22	.15	.43	.85	.17
δ_{22}	.80 (.99)	-.87 (-1.46)	-.14 (-.85)	.04 (.33)	2.71	1.37	1.10	1.43	2.77*	.85
δ_{12}	-.51 (-.80)	.79 (1.38)	.16 (.92)	.01 (.13)	2.24	1.07	.81	1.13	2.23	.61
β_1	34.08 (1.57)	9.44 (.76)	4.08 (1.27)	2.65 (1.58)	.94	1.95	2.60	.18	.37	.17
β_2	-33.08 (-1.53)	-8.44 (-.68)	-3.08 (-.96)	-1.65 (-.99)	.94	1.95	2.60	.18	.37	.17

γ_{11}	−2.53 (−1.46)	−.75 (−.75)	−.49 (−1.72*)	−.40 (−2.52**)	.76	1.39	1.85	.06	.15	.09
γ_{22}	−2.53 (−1.46)	−.75 (−.75)	−.49 (−1.72*)	−.40 (−2.52**)	.76	1.39	1.85	.06	.15	.09
γ_{12}	2.53 (1.46)	.75 (.75)	.49 (1.72*)	.40 (2.52**)	.76	1.39	1.85	.06	.15	.09
ρ_{11}	−.57 (−.89)	.38 (.77)	−.45 (−1.22)	.03 (.17)	1.34	.03	1.00	1.82	.55	1.55
ρ_{21}	.57 (.89)	−.38 (−.77)	.45 (1.22)	−.03 (−.17)	1.34	.03	1.00	1.82	.55	1.55
ρ_{12}	−.79 (−1.29)	.37 (.73)	−.31 (−.98)	.19 (.99)	2.08	.50	2.84	1.31	.13	2.00
ρ_{22}	.79 (1.29)	−.37 (−.73)	.31 (.98)	−.19 (−.99)	2.08	.50	2.84	1.31	.13	2.00
R^2	.80	.84	.90	.88						
F	15.24***	64.73***	92.20***	276.24***						
N	43	116	97	352						

[a]Asterisks indicate significance at the following levels: *p < .10; **p < .05; ***p < .01.

Table 5A–9
1982, Model II (Securities and Loans)[a]

Coefficients	Group 1 (Farm Banks)	Group 2 (City Banks)	Group 3 (Wholesale Banks)	Group 4 (Retail Banks)	F-Test between Groups 1 & 2	F-Test between Groups 1 & 3	F-Test between Groups 1 & 4	F-Test between Groups 2 & 3	F-Test between Groups 2 & 4	F-Test between Groups 3 & 4
α_0	-134.65 (-1.22)	13.74 (.28)	-43.94 (-.51)	1.09 (.02)	1.09	.35	.87	.33	.03	.19
α_1	3.51 (.33)	-1.31 (-.27)	-16.04 (-3.51***)	1.56 (.73)	.12	2.16	.02	4.91**	.29	11.81***
α_2	.79 (.07)	-.72 (-.15)	7.69 (1.77*)	-2.19 (-.96)	.01	.24	.04	1.64	.07	3.94**
δ_{11}	-2.38 (-2.12**)	-.07 (-.24)	-.40 (-2.15**)	-.02 (-.23)	2.74*	2.20	2.88*	.82	.03	3.21*
δ_{22}	-1.20 (-1.15)	.00 (.01)	-.51 (-2.40**)	.04 (.48)	.85	.31	.93	1.66	.01	5.55**
δ_{12}	1.70 (1.68)	.06 (.21)	.57 (3.06***)	.02 (.25)	1.68	.89	1.80	1.95	.02	7.04***
β_1	17.79 (1.53)	1.14 (.15)	20.15 (1.38)	1.21 (.14)	1.10	.01	.99	1.32	.00	1.22
β_2	-16.79 (-1.44)	-.14 (-.02)	-19.15 (-1.31)	-.21 (-.03)	1.10	.01	.99	1.32	.00	1.22

γ_{11}	−1.47 (−1.76*)	−.28 (−.44)	−2.26 (−1.69*)	−.11 (−.15)	1.00	.24	1.19	1.76	.03	1.96
γ_{22}	−1.47 (−1.76*)	−.28 (−.44)	−2.26 (−1.69*)	−.11 (−.15)	1.00	.24	1.19	1.76	.03	1.96
γ_{12}	1.47 (1.76*)	.28 (.44)	2.26 (1.69*)	.11 (.15)	1.00	.24	1.19	1.76	.03	1.96
ρ_{11}	−.64 (−.81)	−.14 (−.35)	−1.10 (−2.90***)	.11 (.64)	.24	.22	.58	3.20*	.34	8.14***
ρ_{21}	.64 (.81)	.14 (.35)	1.10 (2.90***)	−.11 (−.64)	.24	.22	.58	3.20*	.34	8.14***
ρ_{12}	−.65 (−.82)	.04 (.09)	−.66 (−1.91*)	.16 (.91)	.44	.00	.66	1.78	.08	4.34**
ρ_{22}	.65 (.82)	−.04 (−.09)	.66 (1.91*)	−.16 (−.91)	.44	.00	.66	1.78	.08	4.34**
R^2	.91	.88	.89	.87						
F	26.16***	138.09***	83.69***	190.24***						
N	33	180	98	256						

[a] Asterisks indicate significance at the following levels: $*p < .10$; $**p < .05$; $***p < .01$.

Table 5A–10
1983, Model II (Securities and Loans)[a]

Coefficients	Group 1 (Farm Banks)	Group 2 (City Banks)	Group 3 (Wholesale Banks)	Group 4 (Retail Banks)	F-Test between Groups 1 & 2	F-Test between Groups 1 & 3	F-Test between Groups 1 & 4	F-Test between Groups 2 & 3	F-Test between Groups 2 & 4	F-Test between Groups 3 & 4
α_0	-152.42 (-.92)	-96.03 (-1.44)	27.48 (.25)	11.76 (.17)	.11	.83	.84	.97	1.27	.01
α_1	26.63 (1.60)	1.93 (.72)	-1.23 (-.24)	-6.65 (-2.51**)	2.51	2.63	3.91**	.33	5.24**	.90
α_2	-22.48 (-1.45)	-2.20 (-.85)	-4.32 (-1.08)	4.79 (1.78*)	1.92	1.31	2.98*	.21	3.60*	3.55*
δ_{11}	.47 (.74)	-.12 (-.94)	.21 (1.05)	.08 (.75)	.97	.16	.37	2.06	1.45	.34
δ_{22}	.60 (.82)	-.15 (-1.39)	.10 (.56)	-.04 (-.44)	1.21	.45	.75	1.51	.74	.46
δ_{12}	-.51 (-.84)	.14 (1.27)	-.08 (-.46)	-.02 (-.23)	1.29	.47	.64	1.24	1.38	.11
β_1	20.40 (.89)	16.93 (1.58)	4.17 (.24)	2.01 (.18)	.02	.32	.52	.42	.96	.01
β_2	-19.40 (-.84)	-15.93 (-1.48)	-3.17 (-.18)	-1.01 (-.09*)	.02	.32	.52	.42	.96	.01

γ_{11}	-1.25 (-.62)	-1.47 (-1.66*)	-.75 (-.54)	-.47 (-.52)	.01	.04	.12	.21	.64	.03
γ_{22}	-1.25 (-.62)	-1.47 (-1.66*)	-.75 (-.54)	-.47 (-.52)	.01	.04	.12	.21	.64	.03
γ_{12}	1.25 (.62)	1.47 (1.66*)	.75 (.54)	.47 (.52)	.01	.04	.12	.21	.64	.03
ρ_{11}	2.12 (1.68)	.17 (.75)	.08 (.18)	-.48 (-2.21**)	2.68	2.42	4.14	.04	4.34**	1.41
ρ_{21}	-2.12 (-1.68)	-.17 (-.75)	-.08 (-.18)	.48 (2.21**)	2.68	2.42	4.14	.04	4.34**	1.41
ρ_{12}	1.82 (1.59)	.26 (1.21)	.39 (1.21)	-.27 (-1.15)	2.09	1.47	3.20	.13	2.84*	2.72
ρ_{22}	-1.82 (-1.59)	-.26 (-1.21)	-.39 (-1.21)	.27 (1.15)	2.09	1.47	3.20	.13	2.84*	2.72
R^2	.86	.88	.90	.86						
F	19.15***	249.82***	97.10***	114.46***						
N	37	304	107	176						

[a]Asterisks indicate significance at the following levels: *$p < .10$; **$p < .05$; ***$p < .01$.

Table 5A–11
1979, Model III (Loans and Deposits)[a]

Coefficients	Group 1 (Farm Banks)	Group 2 (City Banks)	Group 3 (Wholesale Banks)	Group 4 (Retail Banks)	F-Test between Groups 1 & 2	F-Test between Groups 1 & 3	F-Test between Groups 1 & 4	F-Test between Groups 2 & 3	F-Test between Groups 2 & 4	F-Test between Groups 3 & 4
α_0	-31.69 (-.25)	-8.42 (-.15)	-111.13 (-1.33)	-7.30 (-.12)	.22	.09	.21	1.09	.00	1.01
α_1	-14.62 (-.69)	-3.09 (-.50)	-1.89 (-.19)	-2.75 (-.69)	1.40	1.14	1.43	.01	.00	.01
α_2	16.05 (.66)	-1.13 (-.18)	-1.16 (-.11)	1.90 (.46)	1.95	1.43	1.52	.00	.15	.07
δ_{11}	2.42 (1.31)	.67 (1.28)	.07 (.11)	-.21 (-.89)	.09	.23	2.04	.52	2.15	.17
δ_{22}	2.23 (.93)	.86 (1.59)	.57 (.94)	-.21 (-.88)	2.62	1.25	.05	.13	2.99	1.49
δ_{12}	-2.25 (-1.09)	-.70 (-1.34)	-.24 (-.39)	.24 (1.06)	—[b]	—[b]	—[b]	.32	2.50	.55
β_1	3.53 (.31)	8.32 (.87)	24.06 (1.85*)	3.30 (.34)	.02	1.04	.05	1.01	.13	1.69
β_2	-2.53 (-.22)	-7.32 (-.77)	-23.06 (-1.77*)	-2.30 (-.24)	.02	1.04	.05	1.01	.13	1.69

γ_{11}	.16 (.40)	-.99 (-1.16)	-2.09 (-1.92*)	-.33 (-.44)	1.15	3.27*	.20	.67	.31	1.80
γ_{22}	.16 (.40)	-.99 (-1.16)	-2.09 (-1.92*)	-.33 (-.44)	1.15	3.27*	.20	.67	.31	1.80
γ_{12}	-.16 (-.40)	.99 (1.16)	2.09 (1.92*)	.33 (.44)	1.15	3.27*	.20	.67	.31	1.80
ρ_{11}	-1.12 (-.84)	-.35 (-.69)	-.43 (-.50)	-.19 (-.62)	.76	.45	1.04	.01	.07	.07
ρ_{21}	1.12 (.84)	.35 (.69)	.43 (.50)	.19 (.62)	.76	.45	1.04	.01	.07	.07
ρ_{12}	-1.38 (-.92)	-.11 (-.21)	-.34 (-.36)	-.13 (-.40)	1.45	.74	1.46	.05	.00	.05
ρ_{22}	1.38 (.92)	.11 (.21)	.34 (.36)	.13 (.40)	1.45	.74	1.46	.05	.00	.05
R^2	.77	.92	.93	.91						
F	19.11***	219.08***	117.13***	371.85***						
N	59	172	91	342						

[a] Asterisks indicate significance at the following levels: *p < .10; **p < .05; ***p < .01.
[b] Least-squares solutions for the parameters are not unique.

Table 5A–12
1980, Model III (Loans and Deposits)[a]

Coefficients	Group 1 (Farm Banks)	Group 2 (City Banks)	Group 3 (Wholesale Banks)	Group 4 (Retail Banks)	F-Test between Groups 1 & 2	F-Test between Groups 1 & 3	F-Test between Groups 1 & 4	F-Test between Groups 2 & 3	F-Test between Groups 2 & 4	F-Test between Groups 3 & 4
α_0	-25.18 (-.21)	-160.13 (-2.64***)	-31.92 (-.29)	22.39 (.84)	1.18	.00	.24	1.20	5.69	.23
α_1	15.81 (.74)	.69 (.09)	1.31 (.12)	-.59 (-.15)	.28	.17	.32	.00	.02	.03
α_2	-13.13 (-.56)	-4.54 (-.61)	-1.93 (-.17)	.55 (.14)	.02	.05	.14	.04	.27	.04
δ_{11}	1.69 (.69)	.59 (.58)	-.05 (-.09)	.07 (.30)	.36	.01	.15	.27	.00	.04
δ_{22}	2.03 (.77)	.51 (.55)	.31 (.49)	-.05 (-.21)	.13	.06	.06	.03	.05	.28
δ_{12}	-1.82 (-.75)	-.51 (-.54)	-.05 (-.10)	.02 (.10)	—b	—b	—b	.15	—b	.02
β_1	1.79 (.17)	33.44 (3.96***)	6.90 (.38)	-2.96 (-.92)	6.02**	.05	.26	2.08	11.92***	.29
β_2	-.79 (-.07)	-32.44 (-3.84***)	-5.90 (-.33)	3.96 (1.23)	6.02**	.05	.26	2.08	11.92***	.29

γ_{11}	.06 (.14)	-3.23 (-5.19***)	-.35 (-.23)	.28 (1.42)	18.10***	.05	.33	3.64*	20.78***	.17
γ_{22}	.06 (.14)	-3.23 (-5.19***)	-.35 (-.23)	.28 (1.42)	18.10***	.05	.33	3.64*	20.78***	.17
γ_{12}	-.06 (-.14)	3.23 (5.19***)	.35 (.23)	-.28 (-1.42)	18.10***	.05	.33	3.64*	20.78***	.17
ρ_{11}	.90 (.61)	.11 (.18)	-.05 (-.05)	.05 (.16)	.18	.18	.20	.02	.00	.01
ρ_{21}	-.90 (-.61)	-.11 (-.18)	.05 (.05)	-.05 (-.16)	.18	.18	.20	.02	.00	.01
ρ_{12}	.76 (.50)	.41 (.72)	-.15 (-.16)	.05 (.17)	.01	.16	.11	.30	.22	.04
ρ_{22}	-.76 (-.50)	-.41 (-.72)	.15 (.16)	-.05 (-.17)	.01	.16	.11	.30	.22	.04
R^2	.83	.90	.93	.90						
F	19.62***	116.10***	109.81***	319.87***						
N	46	120	79	329						

[a]Asterisks indicate significance at the following levels: *$p < .10$; **$p < .05$; ***$p < .01$.
[b]Least-squares solutions for the parameters are not unique.

Table 5A–13
1981, Model III (Loans and Deposits)[a]

Coefficients	Group 1 (Farm Banks)	Group 2 (City Banks)	Group 3 (Wholesale Banks)	Group 4 (Retail Banks)	F-Test between Groups 1 & 2	F-Test between Groups 1 & 3	F-Test between Groups 1 & 4	F-Test between Groups 2 & 3	F-Test between Groups 2 & 4	F-Test between Groups 3 & 4
α_0	-200.29 (-1.48)	-62.38 (-.94)	-12.03 (-.34)	10.33 (.59)	.89	2.14	2.50	.46	1.06	.30
α_1	6.96 (.47)	-8.29 (-1.03)	-5.19 (-.91)	-5.93 (-1.69*)	.28	.15	.20	.10	.33	.01
α_2	-1.39 (-.08)	4.79 (.60)	2.25 (.36)	3.84 (1.11)	.01	.06	.03	.06	.15	.05
δ_{11}	2.76 (1.35)	1.14 (.98)	-.73 (-1.68*)	.30 (1.37)	.34	3.62	.07	2.41	.47	4.07
δ_{22}	2.11 (.91)	1.12 (.92)	-.45 (-.83)	-.02 (-.07)	1.56	.01	.75	1.45	.02	.48
δ_{12}	-2.46 (-1.17)	-1.06 (-.91)	.68 (1.44)	-.11 (-.52)	—b	—b	—b	2.02	—b	2.10
β_1	26.88 (1.50)	16.32 (1.64)	7.16 (1.77*)	1.79 (1.08)	.20	1.11	1.71	.76	2.04	1.37
β_2	-25.88 (-1.45)	-15.32 (-1.54)	-6.16 (-1.52)	-.79 (-.47)	.20	1.11	1.71	.76	2.04	1.37

γ_{11}	-1.84 (-1.33)	-1.58 (-1.97*)	-.58 (-2.04**)	-.37 (-2.55**)	.00	.65	.85	1.47	2.24	.38
γ_{22}	-1.84 (-1.33)	-1.58 (-1.97*)	-.58 (-2.04**)	-.37 (-2.55**)	.00	.65	.85	1.47	2.24	.38
γ_{12}	1.84 (1.33)	1.58 (1.97*)	.58 (2.04**)	.37 (2.55**)	.00	.65	.85	1.47	2.24	.38
ρ_{11}	.83 (.90)	-.66 (-1.06)	-.47 (-.97)	-.29 (-1.06)	1.21	1.11	.82	.06	.56	.10
ρ_{21}	-.83 (-.90)	.66 (1.06)	.47 (.97)	.29 (1.06)	1.21	1.11	.82	.06	.56	.10
ρ_{12}	.52 (.50)	-.48 (-.76)	-.44 (-.83)	-.10 (-.36)	.33	.36	.10	.00	.52	.30
ρ_{22}	-.52 (-.50)	.48 (.76)	.44 (.83)	.10 (.36)	.33	.36	.10	.00	.52	.30
R^2	.87	.89	.93	.89						
F	27.12***	98.95***	102.01***	297.26***						
N	45	117	83	338						

[a] Asterisks indicate significance at the following levels: $*p < .10$; $**p < .05$; $***p < .01$.
[b] Least-squares solutions for the parameters are not unique.

Table 5A–14
1982, Model III (Loans and Deposits)[a]

Coefficients	Group 1 (Farm Banks)	Group 2 (City Banks)	Group 3 (Wholesale Banks)	Group 4 (Retail Banks)	F-Test between Groups 1 & 2	F-Test between Groups 1 & 3	F-Test between Groups 1 & 4	F-Test between Groups 2 & 3	F-Test between Groups 2 & 4	F-Test between Groups 3 & 4
α_0	-237.65 (-2.01*)	-11.12 (-.27)	-17.41 (-.24)	42.68 (.82)	3.35*	2.29	3.89**	.01	.64	.44
α_1	4.76 (.21)	-4.70 (-.81)	-3.25 (-.38)	.48 (.17)	.55	.34	.17	.02	.56	.16
α_2	6.81 (.28)	4.11 (.69)	.67 (.07)	-2.97 (-.98)	.00	.01	.07	.10	.98	.13
δ_{11}	-.35 (-.13)	-.02 (-.03)	-.96 (-1.62)	.33 (1.94*)	.15	2.57	.00	1.19	.23	4.09**
δ_{22}	-1.29 (-.40)	.02 (.03)	-.82 (-1.26)	.28 (1.50)	.41	.12	1.67	.81	.12	2.48
δ_{12}	.69 (.24)	.02 (.04)	.96 (1.59)	-.26 (-1.55)	—[b]	—[b]	—[b]	1.13	.15	3.55*
β_1	24.58 (2.19**)	3.05 (.50)	7.34 (.57)	-2.63 (-.33)	2.91*	.93	3.38*	.10	.31	.42
β_2	-23.58 (-2.10**)	-2.05 (-.33)	-6.34 (-.50)	3.63 (.45)	2.91*	.93	3.38*	.10	.31	.42

	(1)	(2)	(3)	(4)	(5)	(6)	(7)	(8)	(9)	(10)
γ_{11}	.25	.11	.11	1.57	.19	1.37	.02 (.03)	−.69 (−.57)	−.27 (−.52)	−1.40 (−1.74*)
γ_{22}	.25	.11	.11	1.57	.19	1.37	.02 (.03)	−.69 (−.57)	−.27 (−.52)	−1.40 (−1.74*)
γ_{12}	.25	.11	.11	1.57	.19	1.37	−.02 (−.03)	.69 (.57)	.27 (.52)	1.40 (1.74*)
ρ_{11}	.21	.79	.03	.53	.86	1.37	.07 (.33)	−.26 (−.39)	−.40 (−.90)	.86 (.60)
ρ_{21}	.21	.79	.03	.53	.86	1.37	−.07 (−.33)	.26 (.39)	.40 (.90)	−.86 (−.60)
ρ_{12}	.25	1.07	.05	.05	.22	.46	.23 (.96)	−.16 (−.22)	−.34 (−.74)	.36 (.25)
ρ_{22}	.25	1.07	.05	.05	.22	.46	−.23 (−.96)	.16 (.22)	.34 (.74)	−.36 (−.25)
R^2							.89	.91	.91	.89
F							207.69***	107.27***	195.33***	22.95***
N							251	99	175	35

[a]Asterisks indicate significance at the following levels: *p < .10; **p < .05; ***p < .01.

[b]Least-squares solutions for the parameters are not unique.

Table 5A–15
1983, Model III (Loans and Deposits)[a]

Coefficients	Group 1 (Farm Banks)	Group 2 (City Banks)	Group 3 (Wholesale Banks)	Group 4 (Retail Banks)	F-Test between Groups 1 & 2	F-Test between Groups 1 & 3	F-Test between Groups 1 & 4	F-Test between Groups 2 & 3	F-Test between Groups 2 & 4	F-Test between Groups 3 & 4
α_0	-322.33 (-2.38**)	-66.19 (-1.18)	-26.02 (-.39)	50.07 (.72)	3.07*	4.35**	6.46**	.19	1.64	.61
α_1	-37.69 (-2.16**)	-3.40 (-.89)	6.79 (1.03)	7.21 (2.24**)	3.70*	6.55**	7.04***	1.55	4.45**	.00
α_2	48.53 (2.55***)	2.36 (.58)	-10.73 (-1.46)	-7.74 (-2.26**)	5.64**	9.71***	9.30***	2.10	3.53*	.13
δ_{11}	1.31 (1.08)	-.28 (-1.03)	-.05 (-.12)	-.04 (-.23)	1.65	1.30	1.34	.17	.62	.00
δ_{22}	.31 (.21)	-.29 (-.87)	.84 (1.67*)	-.03 (-.23)	.16	.14	.06	3.08*	.50	2.59
δ_{12}	-.87 (-.69)	.32 (1.07)	-.32 (-.69)	.04 (.31)	.83	.19	.56	1.18	.69	.52
β_1	36.60 (2.03**)	13.11 (1.45)	11.02 (1.04)	-5.77 (-.52)	1.37	1.67	4.30**	.02	1.70	1.18
β_2	-35.60 (-1.98*)	-12.11 (-1.34)	-10.02 (-.95)	6.77 (.61)	1.37	1.67	4.30**	.02	1.70	1.18

γ_{11}	−1.99 (−1.29)	−1.15 (−1.57)	−1.08 (−1.21)	.31 (.34)	.24	.29	1.75	.00	1.48	1.15
γ_{22}	−1.99 (−1.29)	−1.15 (−1.57)	−1.08 (−1.21)	.31 (.34)	.24	.29	1.75	.00	1.48	1.15
γ_{12}	1.99 (1.29)	1.15 (1.57)	1.08 (1.21)	−.31 (−.34)	.24	.29	1.75	.00	1.48	1.15
ρ_{11}	−2.60 (−1.87*)	−.22 (−.76)	−.03 (−.05)	.59 (2.22**)	2.82*	3.50	5.61**	.10	4.12	1.10
ρ_{21}	2.60 (1.87*)	.22 (.76)	.03 (.05)	−.59 (−2.22**)	2.82*	3.50	5.61**	.10	4.12	1.10
ρ_{12}	−3.21 (−2.19**)	−.14 (−.45)	.13 (.23)	.68 (2.51**)	4.20**	5.17	7.50***	.15	3.83	.70
ρ_{22}	3.21 (2.19**)	.14 (.45)	−.13 (−.23)	−.68 (−2.51**)	4.20**	5.17	7.50***	.15	3.83	.70
R^2	.90	.91	.95	.93						
F	30.53***	351.76***	193.39***	197.13***						
N	39	310	97	152						

[a]Asterisks indicate significance at the following levels: $^*p < .10$; $^{**}p < .05$; $^{***}p < .01$.
[b]Least-squares solutions for the parameters are not unique.

6
The Cost Structure of Electronic and Computer Technology

A recent study prepared for the Farm Credit System on the business technology and telecommunications environment in 1995 concluded that financial service institutions must successfully operationalize new technology to survive in the future.[1] Those institutions that are able to assimilate new technology to deliver services, attract customers, and minimize expenses are most likely to remain viable in the years to come. The study cited the following financial services as likely to be most affected: credit and lending, transaction processing and cash management, risk management and insurance, investment services, financial planning and advisory services, information services, and marketing services. The growing automation of financial services raises some important questions about the business of banking. For example, does automation lower the costs of producing bank services? Is technology divisible so that it is accessible at any level of output? Can smaller institutions compete effectively with larger organizations in a more automated environment?

There appear to be two different answers to the last question.[2] One viewpoint, the so-called shake-out theory, is that smaller institutions will not be able to acquire adequate capital and management ability to successfully implement complex technological services. Consequently, larger institutions will offer higher quality services at lower costs than those of smaller financial service companies. If this is true, a consolidation of resources can be expected in the banking industry as many small banks either disappear or become affiliated with larger banking organizations. Another viewpoint is the divisibility theory. If small-scale operations can produce technological services at costs per unit output comparable to those of large-scale operations, divisibility would exist and consolidation of resources (if it occurred) could not be attributed to technology. Some of the arguments in favor of divisibility are (1) that small banks can cooperatively purchase expensive equipment to overcome start-up cost barriers to entry, (2) that equipment is becoming more user-friendly, (3) that rapid obsolescence of technology prohibits large investment without substantial risk, and (4) that technology is reducing the size and cost of automated equipment while simultaneously improving its capabilities.

Historically, small banks have contracted larger bank correspondents to supply automated (and other) services, including sale of federal funds, check collections, buying and selling U.S. government and municipal securities, automated clearinghouse services, and electronic data processing services. More recently, small banks have been turning to the bankers' bank for services previously obtained from correspondent banks. A bankers' bank is an institution set up (and owned) by a group of independent community banks. Although it is normally designed to service banks within the state, out-of-state banks may be allowed to subscribe to its services, which would tend to expand the scale and scope of operations. The bankers' bank is a logical alternative in cases in which the correspondent banking organization is a potential competitor of the bank. Also, it allows banks to selectively choose services that fit the unique needs of their respective customers.[3] Other alternatives for cooperatively securing relatively expensive automated services fall under the general description of joint ventures, including franchising relationships, network sharing, and other third-party business agreements. Therefore, small banks have more choices than ever before in acquiring automated services for resale at the retail level. Also, it is likely that increasing third-party arrangements will eventually lead to more competitive pricing of many automated services. Indeed, it is not unreasonable to expect that wholesalers will enter the market to distribute key automated services on a large scale across the nation.

The extent to which banks use outside contracting for automated services in the future depends on how technology affects scale economies. This chapter seeks to provide an overview of past studies on this issue and new evidence based on the Functional Cost Analysis (FCA) program data. We present information on the relative cost of automation for different size banks and then report the findings of statistical analyses of how technology affects demand deposit services. The results of further statistical analyses based on the translog model are also reported for demand deposit and credit card services.

Past Studies of Technology and Bank Costs

In this section, two branches of the literature on bank technology are discussed. The first group of studies examines the effect of technology on bank costs, with particular emphasis on transactions service costs associated with the payments system. The second part of this section discusses the findings of studies dealing with the use of correspondent services. Presumably, smaller banks purchase correspondent services because in-house production based on relatively expensive technology is too costly.

Before proceeding, it would be instructive to review the potential effects of technology on the average cost curve, as illustrated in figure 2–3 (chapter 2). One effect of technology is to lower average unit costs of output, which can be interpreted as an efficiency gain. In figure 2–3, the cost curve labeled AC_1 corresponds to some lower level of technology, and the efficiency gain is depicted by the shift down to AC_2. The second possible effect of technology is a decrease in scale economies. The primary reason for this type of change in the cost curve is greater divisibility in the implementation of technology. Small banks may be able to adapt to new technology at a lower cost than in the past. For example, the advent of desk-top microcomputers, EFT, and ATMs has probably made it easier for small banks to take advantage of the technology that over a decade ago was cost-effectively available only to larger banks. The greater divisibility of modern equipment should cause average cost curves to flatten. As shown in figure 2–3, this effect can be represented by a greater decline in long-run average costs at lower output levels than at higher output levels.

Automated Services and Bank Costs

The first comprehensive study of how technology affects scale economies was reported by Bell and Murphy in 1968.[4] Two purposes motivated this study: (1) to determine the degree of capital intensity in different bank production processes and (2) to assess the extent of indivisibilities that may exist. The second objective was accomplished by investigating the relationship between the adoption of sophisticated processing systems (that is, new technologies) and the bank output scale. A survey of First Federal Reserve District banks collected relevant information from 374 respondents, most with less than $150 million in assets.

As expected, the use of various types of automated equipment—for example, proof machines, check encoders, computerized check-handling equipment, collators, sorters, verifiers, tabulators, and so on—was related directly to the number of demand deposits outstanding. However, a less gradual pattern of adoption was observed for electronic bookkeeping (or tronics) machines. Once banks reached about 15,000 accounts, the use of tronics declined substantially as banks appeared to shift to a computer system. This shift is suggestive of technological indivisibility, to be discussed in more detail shortly. The same patterns emerged for the numbers of different machines used by various bank (output) size groups. Table 6–1 presents the results on machine time per functional output category. The demand deposit function leads the field by far in terms of machine time.

To test for the significance of possible shifts in technology, Bell and Murphy proposed three hierarchical levels of electronic sophistication: (1) conventional bookkeeping machines, combining an adding machine with a typewriter; (2) tronics machines, which have electronic capabilities to auto-

Table 6–1
Percentage Distribution of Annual Machine Time, by Bank Function[a]

Function	Type of Machine						
	Conventional	Tronics	Computer	Punch Card[b]	Computer Equipment	Window Posting	Proof Machines[c]
Demand deposits	34.89	97.19	65.03	27.91	96.32	60.55	98.29
Time deposits	4.66	0.83	3.74	5.66	0.45	26.00	0.68
Installment loans	14.39	0.09	10.73	16.75	—	9.48	0.51
Business loans	17.51	0.41	—	0.37	—	1.30	0.28
Real estate loans	4.76	0.52	0.14	0.18	—	2.67	0.24
Securities	0.16	—	—	—	—	—	—
Trust department	11.31	0.51	5.61	30.48	—	—	—
Safe deposit	0.06	0.01	0.11	—	—	—	—
Business development	—	—	4.18	5.75	2.44	—	—
Administration	12.01	0.38	10.44	9.08	0.80	—	—

Source: Frederick W. Bell and Neil B. Murphy, Costs in Commercial Banking: A Quantitative Analysis of Bank Behavior and Its Relation to Bank Regulation (Boston: Federal Reserve Bank of Boston, April 1968), 124.
[a]Distributions may not add to 100 percent because of rounding.
[b]Includes tabulator, key punch, collator, verifier, and sorter.
[c]Includes proof machine, check encoder, and proof inscriber.

matically update previous account balances; and (3) computer systems, which can automatically update accounts and generate detailed reports. It was hypothesized that the average product of labor (equal to the number of accounts divided by labor costs) would shift as the level of sophistication progressed in tandem with increased output levels. Therefore, the average product of labor should shift with the number of accounts. Test results using a subsample of fifty-three survey respondents with available FCA data indicated the following:

Demand deposits: Changes in labor productivity and scale were positively related to one another; therefore, technological change appears to be a source of increased scale economies.

Time deposits: A negative relationship was found between shifts in labor productivity and scale.

Installment loans: No significant relationship occurred.

Business loans: The technology shift hypothesis was supported.

Real estate loans: No significant relationship occurred.

This evidence therefore indicates that there is a certain amount of indivisibility in banking technology that enables larger banks to increase their returns to scale relative to smaller banks.

The growing presence of electronic funds transfer (EFT) systems in the latter part of the 1960s motivated a rather comprehensive treatment of the subject by Flannery and Jaffee.[5] Their primary interest centered on the economic implications of EFT, as characterized by cash dispensers (CDs), automated teller machines (ATMs), point-of-sale (POS) machines, and automated clearinghouses (ACHs) linked up by regional processing centers and nationwide communication networks that are mostly computer operated. The authors noted that an EFT bank is probably so different in its production process from the conventional bank that past studies of economies of scale may well be irrelevant.[6] Because the widespread adoption of EFT in the banking industry would erode geographic barriers to entry on the liability side of the balance sheet, they (correctly) forecasted an increasingly competitive market for deposit funds. Because of this trend toward pure competition, it was believed that the issue of scale economies would become a critical factor in the survival of smaller institutions. In other words, small banks that were unable to lower operating costs sufficiently because of indivisibilities of technology would disappear or be merged out.

Flannery and Jaffee pointed out that many of the hardware requirements of EFT can be overcome by use of shared systems, cooperatives, distributors, and correspondents. Although most hardware can be obtained from outside sources, the possibility of inefficiencies in purchasing and equipment usage externally by small banks is still a relevant question. Since it is clear that the rising volume of paper-oriented transfers is increasing output costs and since EFT equipment is becoming relatively cheaper to install and operate, small banks must learn both to purchase and to produce services in an EFT environment at competitive costs or be forced to exit the industry.[7]

The continuing development of the EFT payments system has stimulated more recent empirical research. For example, Walker sought to estimate scale economies for retail banking machines, including CDs and ATMs.[8] Survey data were gathered on machine costs and transaction volumes in 1975 for 27 banks with 79 CDs and 91 banks with 505 ATMs. A log-linear model was estimated using ordinary least squares (OLS) to get cost-output (or transactions) elasticities. Variables to control for exogenous factors (for example, urban area, geographic region, number of offices, affiliation with a holding company, bank regulatory status, asset size, sharing of EFT machines with another institution, and on-line status of EFT machines) were included in the model. Also, non-EFT costs of operations were added into the regression equation.

Output for cash dispensers corresponded with the number of cash withdrawals from checking accounts, savings accounts, and advances on credit cards. The elasticity of CD costs with respect to CD output was 0.122, and marginal costs were found to be 0.007. These results implied that the cost of each additional CD transaction is so low as to recommend an initial charge for the sale of a CD card, with free usage thereafter.

ATMs have a variety of different outputs, such as withdrawals, deposits, account transfers, and payments. An OLS regression model similar to the CD model was run, and the cost-output elasticity for ATMs was estimated to be 0.499 (different statistically from both one and zero at the 0.001 level). Therefore, if volume output (or number of machines) doubled, ATM costs would rise by about 50 percent. The marginal cost of an ATM transaction was $0.046, which is high enough to require that added service charges be levied in excess of the initial charge for a card. This cost was observed to be somewhat less than the typical fee per check charged by banks.

Walker inferred from these (and other) results that average costs of retail EFT outputs would continue to decline over the years to come but that non-EFT outputs would experience diseconomies at some point. Furthermore, it was concluded that scale economies are significant, in all likelihood, for retail payments system machines.

Another area of the payments system in which technology has played an important role is check processing. Humphrey has conducted a number of studies exploring the cost characteristics of this behind-the-scenes phase of paper funds transfer. In one study, he examined the costs of Federal Reserve (FR) check-processing operations.[9] Output was measured by total processed checks at FR offices, and inputs included capital structures, labor expenses, capital equipment (mostly computers and check readers/sorters), transportation expenses, and other overhead. These independent variables were regressed on total costs of processing check and return items using a translog cost function. Annual data from thirty-six FR offices over the period 1974–76 were used to run the model. The following cross-sectional results were obtained:

Negative scale economies existed in most FR offices.

The average cost curve was U-shaped, and declining marginal costs were not observed in FR offices.

Average cost curves shifted downward over the 1974–76 period (because of new processing technology and input productivity).

Humphrey concluded that the lack of competition in processing checks, due to zero pricing by the FR, was responsible for the observed diseconomies. Although explicit pricing would resolve part of this problem (which the Monetary Control Act of 1980 mandated), electronic funds transfer at FR automated clearinghouses was recommended as the best long-run solution.

Another study by Humphrey attempted to measure the effect of ACHs on average processing costs compared to paper processing methods.[10] ACH cost and volume data in 1978 and 1979 were gathered for forty ACH processing centers in the United States. The cost function model was a derivative of the aforementioned Humphrey paper, with new variables added to consider the volume of government-issued checks, the number of processing errors, and the amount of magnetic tape usage. Most estimates of scale economies were less than one, which suggests that average costs decline as output increases. Even so, the average cost of electronic (ACH) processing in 1979 was 4.7 cents, compared to only 0.9 cents for paper check processing. Humphrey extrapolated the declining average cost curve findings for ACHs to determine the point at which average costs would be equal for the two processing methods. About 200 million items would be sufficient volume to reach this point of indifference: however, the average ACH office in 1979 processed only about 4 million items. Since smaller FR offices did have paper processing volumes in excess of 200 million, Humphrey concluded that ACH processing may help lower operational costs in the payments system as processing demands continue to rise.[11]

Metzker itemized a variety of expected trends during the remainder of the 1980s with respect to technology, unit costs, and the payments system.[12] The following observations were made:

Computers are becoming smaller, less expensive, and more powerful. This trend should enable even small institutions to have access to considerable computing power.

Software is becoming easier to use and less costly to purchase. Canned or shared software arrangements between institutions may actually lower program expenses in the future.

Electronic communications are likewise experiencing lower costs. As unit costs decline, they will become a more likely substitute for other information transport methods.

Networking will expand in the years to come to link up computer terminals to shared computer, software, and electronic communications systems. Home banking will grow out of this trend.

Branch banking, as characterized by substantial brick-and-mortar investment, will be replaced (or modified) to the extent that ATMs, POSs, and networking in general succeed in gaining public acceptance.

Technological literacy on the part of the general public will spread, requiring that a changing set of services be developed and distributed by financial service companies.

These trends suggest that the unit costs of technology will decline and that smaller institutions will be able to access technology in cases where the fixed costs of proprietary (or in-house) implementation are too high.

On a less encouraging note, not much is known about the effects of converting from a paper-based financial system to an electronic/computer-oriented world. In a special study presented to the Board of Governors of the Federal Reserve System recently, one researcher observed that, in 1982, only about 3 percent of paper transactions had been replaced by EFT methods and projected that 7.5 percent of such transactions would be displaced by 1985.[13] Therefore, it is somewhat early to clearly discern the effects of the EFT era on the structural characteristics of the banking industry. Although many observers forecast a declining role in banking for small institutions, current technology trends cast some doubt on concluding their demise too hastily.

Correspondent Banking and Bank Costs

The most common way of acquiring automated (and technical) services for small banks has been through correspondent relationships with larger banks. Regarding bank costs, Dunham has observed that studies of economies of scale in banking (surveyed in chapter 3) do not consider the potential effects of correspondent activities between banks on estimates of returns to scale.[14] For example, many small and medium-sized (respondent) banks purchase bank services from larger correspondents by "upstreaming" noninterest-earning deposit balances. Because the FCA data are not adjusted for these implicit (opportunity) costs of idle funds, costs for smaller banks may have been underestimated in previous studies. Also, because interbank accounts are more costly to maintain than individual and business accounts and are held generally by larger banks, costs for demand deposits could be overestimated for larger banks as compared to smaller banks. For both of these reasons, Dunham hypothesized that economies of scale for demand deposits have been underestimated in previous studies.

To test for this bias, the first stage of the study used 1978 FCA data to calculate variables for output (number of demand deposit accounts), costs (unadjusted direct allocated costs), input prices (average county wage rates), and homogeneity factors (average account size, number of bank offices, and a service mix variable equal to the number of certificate of deposit accounts divided by the total number of time and savings deposit accounts). Based on information from 277 Federal Reserve members, a log-linear function was fitted to the data, resulting in an elasticity of cost equal to 1.025. The second stage of the study adjusted deposit costs to reflect (1) the opportunity costs of idle balances on deposit at correspondent banks (that is, 75 percent of the product of these balances times the Treasury bill rate) and (2) the costs of only noncorrespondent demand deposit services (that is, about 75 percent of the product of correspondent balances times the Treasury bill rate, subtracted from total demand deposit costs). With all else held the same, the elasticity estimate dropped to 0.899 after these adjustments were made. This finding tends to confirm the hypothesis that demand deposit returns to scale had been underestimated in previous studies and that costs involved in correspondent banking had not been accounted for.

Dunham also attempted to measure the efficiency gain effect of technology on bank costs over the period 1967–79. The following trends were uncovered:

Regular demand deposit has experienced gradually declining average costs since about 1971.

Regular savings accounts have had fairly stable average costs, but a noticeable decline began in about 1977.

Commercial and agricultural loans have had generally increasing average costs over this thirteen-year period.

Real estate mortgage and installment loans have not changed their average cost level.

Therefore, technology appears to have its greatest influence on products and services related to the payments system. Unfortunately, no specific tests for the presence or absence of increased scale efficiencies were performed by Dunham.[15]

Flannery extended Dunham's work by retesting the correspondent cost hypothesis with a translog cost function.[16] Once again, the 1978 FCA data were employed, but 737 member banks from all twelve Federal Reserve districts (as opposed to 277 banks from selected districts) with available data were included in the analyses. Output was measured in two ways: (1) an aggregate index of output weighted by allocated costs for each type of output and (2) an aggregate index weighted by average loan rates. For unit banks, Flannery found that average costs were understated by as much as 15 percent because of the exclusion of correspondent balance opportunity costs. However, unlike Dunham's findings, the elasticity coefficient was unaffected by cost adjustments where output is in aggregate terms (rather than specific to only demand deposits). Apparently, implicit correspondent costs do not vary relative to explicit costs across size groups for unit banks. For branch banks, elasticities were statistically larger after these omitted costs were added than before cost adjustment. In other words, scale economies were overestimated in previous studies. Although this result is opposite of Dunham's finding, the difference can be reconciled by the different samples in addition to the special cost dynamics in the growth of branch banking organizations. And although statistically different elasticities were obtained, Flannery believed that the economic implications of this difference for branch banks was small enough to be of little concern.

In summary, correspondent services appear to affect the measurement of returns to scale for demand deposit services but not for overall returns to scale. Therefore, those performing studies focusing on the payments system may want to consider these implicit costs in their calculations; and researchers concerned about overall bank output costs can forgo the added task of making these adjustments. Regarding the payments system, the evidence has indicated that efficiency gains that are best explained by advancing technology occurred in the 1960s and 1970s. It is not known, however, whether or not correspondent services are purchased by smaller banks to offset indivisibilities that affect returns to scale. (No tests have been conducted to date on the relationship between the degree of correspondent activity and returns to scale among small banks.)

Cost Efficiency and Bank Technology

It is to be expected that automation tends to lower average bank costs. Using 1968 FCA data, Longbrake found that automation did reduce the costs of producing demand deposits for banks with more than $15 million in demand deposits.[17] For other services, including time deposits, installment loans, commercial loans, and mortgage loans, automation increased costs for all but the largest banks. Therefore, reasons other than cost reduction may motivate banks to automate. For example, new technology may be applied to management problems to improve control. Also, it may be necessary at times to install new equipment either to maintain the competitive status quo or to introduce new services in an effort to surpass other financial service sellers. Therefore, the effect of technology on cost efficiency is not unambiguous.

In this section, we approach the issue of technology and bank costs from an empirical standpoint. Since demand deposit services consume a large proportion of a bank's operating expenses, and since they are most readily automated (in terms of both external delivery and internal data processing), we begin by examining the effect of technology on the cost of producing demand deposits. We then consider the scale and scope economies of jointly producing demand deposit and credit card services, since these services are linked to one another (or cross-sold) by many banks. Before moving on to these empirical analyses, however, we provide some descriptive information on bank expenses and technology.

Bank Expenses for Automation

Tables 6–2 and 6–3 compare the extent of banking technology utilization (in expense terms) by banks of different deposit size in 1980 and 1982, respectively, as averaged from FCA data. In 1980, banks with less than $25 million in deposits in both unit and branch states had noticeably higher ratios of computer-related costs (including data processing and software expenses) to total operating expenses than other banks. In 1982, the same trend was obvious in unit banking states but not in branch banking states. The lower ratios of computer costs to both total labor costs and labor costs for demand deposits among small branch state banks suggest that labor is substituted for automation, probably because of an inability to cost-justify the use of technology. Hence, it appears that banks with less than $25 million in deposits generally do not obtain the full benefit of new technologies (because of indivisibilities that lead to idle capacity).

Tables 6–2 and 6–3 also indicate that there are no substantial differences between large banks with more than $400 million in deposits and other banks in automation expenditures. Apparently, as banks expand output, they do not change the technology-to-labor mix in dollar terms. Since computer expenses are approximately 6 percent to 10 percent of total operating expenses and are only about 12 percent to 20 percent of total labor costs, it is clear that labor costs are much greater for banks today than automation costs. The dominance of labor in the input mix probably accounts for the relative stability of the technology utilization ratios in tables 6–2 and 6–3. Although *technology* is an often-cited buzzword in the bank literature, the data demonstrate that banks produce "hand-made," as opposed to "machine-made," services to a large degree.

Table 6–2
Mean Values for Measures of Bank Technology Utilization, 1980

Measures	Deposit Size ($ millions)						
	<25	25–50	50–100	100–200	200–400	>400	All Banks
A. Unit State Banks							
1. Total computer costs/total operating expenses	.092	.064	.067	.076	.069	.079	.071
2. Total computer costs/total labor costs	.178	.127	.126	.145	.125	.153	.135
3. Computer costs/labor costs for demand deposits	.393	.235	.222	.314	.184	.270	.252
B. Branch State Banks							
1. Total computer costs/total operating expenses	.092	.060	.066	.070	.072	.064	.068
2. Total computer costs/total labor costs	.177	.110	.123	.130	.142	.121	.128
3. Computer costs/labor costs for demand deposits	.196	.186	.232	.258	.236	.213	.230

Table 6-3
Mean Values for Measures of Bank Technology Utilization, 1982

Measures	Deposit Size ($ millions)						
	<25	25–50	50–100	100–200	200–400	>400	All Banks
A. Unit State Banks							
1. Total computer costs/total operating expenses	.118	.069	.057	.074	.071	.098	.072
2. Total computer costs/total labor costs	.257	.129	.114	.149	.153	.217	.146
3. Computer costs/labor costs for demand deposits	.363	.201	.209	.245	.256	.355	.238
B. Branch State Banks							
1. Total computer costs/total operating expenses	.059	.063	.066	.059	.094	.082	.069
2. Total computer costs/total labor costs	.112	.117	.128	.116	.187	.161	.135
3. Computer costs/labor costs for demand deposits	.162	.181	.217	.214	.297	.302	.233

Demand Deposits and Technology

Does larger scale allow more cost-efficient use of technology? To answer this question, we conducted a cost-output analysis of demand deposits for 1979, 1980, and 1982 using FCA data. The following translog cost model was estimated for different bank size groups:

$$\ln C_{dd} = \alpha_0 + \alpha_1 \ln DD + \alpha_2 (\ln DD)^2 + \alpha_3 \ln TECH + \mu \quad (6.1)$$

where C_{dd} is allocated demand deposit costs, TECH is the ratio of computer-related cost to labor costs (allocated to demand deposits), and other notations are as before. This model attempts to measure the relationship between the extent of automation and bank costs, holding bank output constant. The α_3 coefficient measures the percentage change in output cost per 1 percent change in the TECH variable, with output held constant.

Tables 6–4, 6–5, and 6–6 give results for equation (6.1).[18] The estimated coefficient for the TECH variable ranged between .87 and .99 and was extremely significant in all cases. This means that increasing the ratio of computer cost to labor cost by 1 percent increased output cost by only .87 percent (for example). A cost savings was therefore gained by substituting technology for labor. In 1979 and 1982, banks with less than $25 million in deposits had relatively lower TECH coefficients than other bank groups, implying that these small banks could gain more by using greater automation in relation to labor than other banks could. This result may explain the relatively higher expenditure on computer-related costs by small banks (especially in unit banking states) reported earlier, in tables 6–2 and 6–3.

There is no evidence of a trend toward greater cost gains by large banks. Instead, excluding banks with less than $25 million in deposits, there is a general trend for all banks to realize about the same modest level of cost gains by increasing their ratios of computer costs to labor expenses (that is, cost gains would be marginal because the coefficients are close to one in most cases). It therefore appears that larger banks have increased their utilization of automation until most (if not all) of the associated cost gains have been exhausted. Smaller banks appear not to have exhausted the gains from utilization of automation, probably because of the relative indivisibility of modern technology at lower output levels.

Joint Production Costs of Demand Deposits
and Credit Cards

In recent years, banks have greatly expanded their credit card operations. Historically, credit cards were offered only to preferred customers by both businesses and banks. The advent of the microcomputer and the subsequent acceleration of business software development has made it feasible for bank

Table 6–4
Parameter Estimates for the Relationship between Allocated Costs for Demand Deposits and Technology, 1979[a]

Variable	Deposit Size ($ millions)						
	<25	25–50	50–100	100–200	200–400	>400	All Banks
Intercept	−4.44	−120.46	−32.87	−28.26	−128.30	8.24	−12.48
	(−.08)	(−1.09)	(−.55)	(−.73)	(−.88)	(.09)	(−3.39***)
ln DD	.87	15.10	4.56	4.06	14.67	.06	2.00
	(.13)	(1.11)	(.65)	(.93)	(.93)	(.01)	(4.74***)
ln DD²	.02	−.85	−.22	−.19	−.75	.03	−.06
	(.04)	(−1.03)	(−.53)	(−.78)	(−.88)	(.06)	(−2.50**)
ln TECH	.88	.99	.97	.91	.91	.96	.95
	(16.15***)	(27.52***)	(43.60***)	(19.75***)	(12.57***)	(13.54***)	(59.57***)
R^2	.95	.96	.97	.89	.87	.92	.97
F	121***	258***	693***	142***	61***	81***	2,441***
N	23	34	66	60	32	26	241

[a]Asterisks indicate significance at the following levels: *$p < .10$; **$p < .05$; ***$p < .01$.
[b]The variable ln DD is the natural log of demand deposits in dollars; the variable ln TECH is the natural log of the ratio of allocated computer costs and labor costs for demand deposits.

Table 6–5
Parameter Estimates for the Relationship between Allocated Costs for Demand Deposits and Technology, 1980[a]

Variable	Deposit Size ($ millions)						
	<25	25–50	50–100	100–200	200–400	>400	All Banks
Intercept	20.56	27.75	10.89	33.42	11.65	18.93	-3.89
	(.13)	(.63)	(.28)	(.90)	(.50)	(-.15)	(-.91)
ln DD	-2.14	-2.77	-.62	-2.90	-.45	2.93	1.02
	(-.11)	(-.51)	(-.14)	(-.69)	(-.17)	(.23)	(2.08**)
ln DD^2	.19	.22	.08	.19	.06	-.12	-.00
	(.16)	(.67)	(.33)	(.84)	(.44)	(-.18)	(-.16)
ln TECH	.93	.90	.95	.87	.92	.99	.92
	(6.59***)	(25.58***)	(33.27***)	(21.22***)	(22.93***)	(10.55***)	(58.31***)
R^2	.95	.97	.94	.91	.96	.91	.97
F	37***	301***	415***	172***	238***	50***	2,154***
N	10	33	77	56	34	19	229

[a]Asterisks indicate significance at the following levels: *$p < .10$; **$p < .05$; ***$p < .01$.
[b]The variable ln DD is the natural log of demand deposits in dollars; the variable ln TECH is the natural log of the ratio of allocated computer costs and labor costs for demand deposits.

Table 6-6
Parameter Estimates for the Relationship between Allocated Costs for Demand Deposits and Technology, 1982[a]

Variable	Deposit Size ($ millions)						
	<25	25–50	50–100	100–200	200–400	>400	All Banks
Intercept	-19.78	43.03	.07	14.47	-27.69	138.66	1.36
	(-.60)	(.58)	(.00)	(.22)	(-.30)	(2.22**)	(.46)
ln DD	3.09	-4.73	.67	-.94	3.93	-13.75	.40
	(.72)	(-.52)	(.12)	(-.40)	(2.13**)	(1.19)	(1.19)
ln DD²	-.14	.34	.01	.10	-.17	.76	.03
	(-.49)	(.61)	(.02)	(.23)	(-.33)	(2.29**)	(1.68*)
ln TECH	.87	.94	.95	.93	.91	.97	.94
	(15.74***)	(24.32***)	(37.91***)	(28.48***)	(17.70***)	(27.39***)	(65.46***)
R^2	.97	.93	.96	.93	.92	.97	.97
F	144***	201***	564***	335***	120***	305***	3,130***
N	18	47	80	80	36	32	293

[a] Asterisks indicate significance at the following levels: $*p < .10$; $**p < .05$; $***p < .01$.
[b] The variable ln DD is the natural log of demand deposits in dollars; the variable ln TECH is the natural log of the ratio of allocated computer costs and labor costs for demand deposits.

cards to be sold to virtually anyone who has good credit standing and a demand deposit account (or related transactions account). Less obvious is the likelihood that the rapid increase in computerized credit card operations has stimulated further technological change in the processing of demand deposits (from the potential for cost sharing). Data processing and reporting requirements for demand deposits and credit cards are almost the same. Indeed, some institutions cross-sell credit cards as a means of providing depositors with automatic overdraft privileges.

Since demand deposits and credit cards should involve a great deal of cost sharing, especially regarding technological inputs, their cost characteristics provide one of the best examples of how technology affects the joint production of bank services. As in chapters 4 and 5, a translog cost model was estimated with the following variables (as calculated from FCA data): (1) allocated costs, (2) demand deposits in dollars, (3) credit card borrowings in dollars, (4) input prices for labor and capital, and (5) each bank's state branching status. Because many banks volunteering data in the FCA program either did not report allocated credit card expenses or did not have credit card operations, the sample size was reduced by about one-third of the FCA bank population. As in the previous translog models, table 6–7 shows that the estimated regression models fitted the data well, with R^2 values around .90.

Part A of table 6–8 gives the estimates of scale and scope economies derived from the cost models. The scale estimates in the unit states reflect a cost curve that is flat at lower output levels and then slopes downward as output is increased beyond $100 million in deposits. In branch states, a relatively flat cost curve was found, which may be attributable to diseconomies at the firm level as the number of branch offices is expanded. Hence, especially in unit states, there are significant and increasing returns to scale in the joint production of demand deposits and credit cards. The positive scope estimates in part B of table 6–8, calculated using equation (4.6) in chapter 4, are quite positive in general. No particular trends are evident between unit and branch states and over time. In combination, the findings on economies of scale and scope imply the possibility that natural monopoly conditions exist in the production of highly automated bank services such as demand deposits and credit cards.

Summary and Conclusions

Technology is usually believed to be a means of reducing operating costs. This reduction can be reflected in various ways in the cost function. For example, the cost curve could be lowered because of improved cost efficiency; it could become flatter because of greater divisibility of factors of production; or it could do both. Past research evidence has supported both

Table 6–7
Estimates of Multiproduct Cost Functions for Demand Deposits and Credit Cards over Time: Unit versus Branch States[a]

Coefficients	1979 Unit States	1979 Branch States	1980 Unit States	1980 Branch States	1982 Unit States	1982 Branch States
α_0	29.53 (0.26)	-108.61 (-1.32)	-245.07 (-2.34**)	-109.70 (-1.46)	124.84 (.58)	-51.51 (-.67)
α_1	-.41 (-.09)	.64 (.38)	4.46 (.91)	2.61 (1.08)	5.62 (.88)	3.00 (1.04)
α_2	0.17 (.11)	-.21 (-.25)	-.42 (-.21)	-.90 (-.63)	-1.63 (-.67)	-1.70 (-.87)
σ_{11}	-.18 (-1.67*)	.04 (1.01)	-.04 (-.29)	.06 (1.07)	-.10 (-.66)	-.21 (-2.67***)
σ_{22}	-.01 (-.70)	.02 (1.88*)	.00 (-.17)	.03 (1.72*)	.04 (1.49)	-.01 (-.54)
σ_{12}	.04 (1.17)	-.03 (-1.68*)	-.01 (-.23)	-.03 (-1.19)	-.04 (-.83)	.10 (2.34**)
β_1	-3.56 (-.19)	18.23 (1.36)	35.73 (2.05**)	16.65 (1.43)	-26.35 (-.78)	7.17 (.51)
β_2	4.56 (1.17)	-17.23 (-1.28)	-34.73 (-2.00**)	-15.65 (-1.34)	27.35 (.81)	-6.17 (-.44)
γ_{11}	-.03 (-.02)	-1.51 (-1.39)	-2.63 (-1.57)	-1.19 (-1.31)	2.40 (.86)	-.62 (-.48)
γ_{22}	-.03 (-.02)	-1.51 (-1.39)	-2.63 (-1.57)	-1.19 (-1.31)	2.40 (.86)	-.62 (-.48)
γ_{12}	.03 (.02)	1.51 (1.39)	2.63 (1.57)	1.19 (1.31)	-2.40 (-.86)	.62 (.48)

Table 6–7 (Continued)

Coefficients	1979 Unit States	1979 Branch States	1980 Unit States	1980 Branch States	1982 Unit States	1982 Branch States
ρ_{11}	-.31 (-.79)	-.00 (-.02)	.24 (.37)	.19 (1.08)	.21 (.43)	-.03 (-.12)
ρ_{12}	.31 (.79)	.00 (.02)	-.24 (-.37)	-.19 (-1.08)	-.21 (-.43)	.03 (.12)
ρ_{21}	-.05 (-.43)	.04 (.58)	.06 (.37)	.09 (.81)	.15 (.69)	.01 (.09)
ρ_{22}	.05 (.43)	-.04 (-.58)	-.06 (-.37)	-.09 (-.81)	-.15 (-.69)	-.01 (-.09)
R^2	.84	.95	.87	.94	.88	.95
F	35.54***	364.19***	27.05***	261.71***	24.80***	257.39***
SSE	7.58	12.35	4.32	11.29	3.70	10.31
N	69	183	47	152	40	141

[a] Asterisks indicate significance at the following levels: $*p < .10$; $**p < .05$; $***p < .01$.

Table 6–8
Estimates of Scale and Scope Economies for the Joint Production of Demand Deposits and Credit Cards over Time: Unit versus Branch States[a]

Bank Deposit Size ($ millions)	1979		1980		1082	
	Unit States	Branch States	Unit States	Branch States	Unit States	Branch States
A. Scale Economies Estimates[b]						
0–25	.94	.96	.85	.91*	1.17	1.07
25–50	.83**	.96	.86	.93**	1.05	.99
50–100	.75***	.95**	.82**	.95**	.97	.98
100–200	.71***	.95**	.75***	.96*	.87*	1.01
200–400	.63***	.95*	.68***	.98	.77*	1.01
>400	.59***	.96	.59**	.99	.65*	.99
B. Scope Economies Estimates						
0–25	.16	1.16	.29	.41	.12	.58
25–50	.28	.42	.36	.64	.72	.69
50–100	.35	.65	.31	.41	.39	.41
100–200	.33	.49	.49	.55	.90	.41
200–400	.26	.49	.51	.39	.56	.33
>400	.75	.82	.91	.41	.81	-.01

[a]All estimates are based on models using input prices.
[b]Asterisks indicate significance at the following levels: *p < .10; **p < .05; ***p < .01.

of these technological effects for payments system activities but not necessarily for other types of bank services. Also, the relatively low use of automation in some phases of payments services (for example, automated clearing services for check handling) suggests that high technology is still not a major factor in the provision of banking services).

We presented new evidence on the potential effects of technology on payments system services based on recent FCA data. Focusing on demand deposits, we found that banks of all sizes could not lower operating costs (on a proportionate basis as output is increased) by increasing their ratio of computer-related costs to labor costs. Banks with less than $25 million in deposits had greater cost benefits available to them than larger banks. The implication here is that very small banks do not obtain the full cost benefit available to them through automation. Consistent with the greater desirability of automating for very small banks, their computer-related expenses relative to total operating expenses were higher than those of larger banks. However, small branch banks did not have relatively higher computer-related expenses in 1982 because of increased use of labor (and associated costs). It is possible that small branch banks may be able to use more low-skilled labor (as a proportion of total labor expenses) than unit banks to serve as a substitute for mechanization. Alternatively, small branch banks may curtail automation in an effort to avoid higher fixed operating expenses. Whatever the case may be, most banks appear to spend about the same proportion of their operating budget on automation and tend to exhaust most (if not all) of the cost benefits that technology may allow them. Thus, we may tentatively conclude from this evidence that banks do employ technology to reduce operating costs; however, small banks with less than $25 million in deposits are exposed to indivisibilities that prevent them from implementing automated services as cost-effectively as larger banks can.

The last part of this chapter examined the cost characteristics of producing two related bank services with a high potential for both automation and jointness—that is, demand deposits and credit cards. According to translog cost model results for 1979, 1980, and 1982, especially in unit states, significant scale economies were found at relatively high levels of output (for example, for banks with over $400 million in deposits, the scale estimates were lower than they were for smaller banks). Since measures of economies of scope were quite positive in most years, it was believed that natural monopoly may exist in the production of these highly automated transactions services. This does not mean that small banks cannot provide such services cost-efficiently, because there is the alternative of purchasing these services to a certain extent from larger producers of automated services. Indeed, our findings are strong evidence in favor of the bankers' bank as a centralized purveyor of automated services that can provide automated services at low cost to small institutions. In this sense, small banks are simply conduits through which automated services are sold upon production in large institutions.

Notes

1. *Business Technology in Finance and Agriculture in 1995* (Denver: Farm Credit System, June 1984).

2. See Paul Metzker, "Future Payments System Technology: Can Small Financial Institutions Compete?" *Economic Review,* Federal Reserve Bank of Atlanta (November 1982), 58–66.

3. For a more complete discussion of bankers' banks, see Pamela Frisbee, "Bankers' Banks: An Institution Whose Time Has Come," *Economic Review,* Federal Reserve Bank of Atlanta (April 1984), 31–35.

4. Frederick W. Bell and Neil B. Murphy, *Costs in Commercial Banking: A Quantitative Analysis of Bank Behavior and Its Relation to Bank Regulation,* (Boston: Federal Reserve Bank of Boston, April 1968), 113–43.

5. Mark J. Flannery and Dwight M. Jaffee, *The Economic Implications of an Electronic Monetary Transfer System* (Lexington, Mass.: Lexington Books, 1973).

6. Ibid., 116.

7. It was estimated at that time that a payroll check could be deposited electronically for about 10 cents less than by manual methods and that electronic bill payment would save about 4 cents per transaction. See *Automated Clearing Houses: An in Depth Analysis* (Atlanta: Atlanta Payments Project, 1974).

8. David A. Walker, "Economies of Scale in Electronic Funds Transfer Systems," *Journal of Banking and Finance* 2(1978): 65–78.

9. David Burras Humphrey, "Economies of Scale in Federal Reserve Check Processing Operations," *Journal of Econometrics* 15(January 1981): 155–73.

10. David Burras Humphrey, "Scale Economies at Automated Clearinghouses," *Journal of Bank Research* 12(Summer 1981): 71–81.

11. Further work by Humphrey has appeared in David Burras Humphrey, *The U.S. Payments System: Costs, Pricing, Competition and Risk* (New York: New York University, Salomon Brothers Center for the Study of Financial Institutions, 1984).

12. Metzker, "Future Payments System Technology."

13. Donald G. Long, "Technological Change and the Small Depository Institution," in *The Future of Small Depository Institutions in an Era of Deregulation, Financial Innovation, and Technological Change,* Proceedings of a Conference of the Board of Governors of the Federal Reserve System, Washington, D.C.: January 1984, 25–46.

14. Constance Dunham, "Commercial Bank Costs and Correspondent Banking," *New England Economic Review,* Federal Reserve Bank of Boston (September-October 1981), 22–36.

15. Dunham also tested other outputs to check the consistency of her results with those of previous studies. In general, the model produced reasonable results, which are not discussed here.

16. Mark J. Flannery, "Correspondent Services and Cost Economies in Commercial Banking," *Journal of Banking and Finance* 7(1983): 83–99.

17. William A. Longbrake, "Computers and the Cost of Producing Various Types of Banking Services," Federal Deposit Insurance Corporation, Working Paper no. 72-17, 1972.

18. Separate regression runs for banks in unit and branch states could not be undertaken because of small sample sizes in some bank size groups.

7
Cost Efficiency and Bank Failure

A fundamental rationale for studying cost efficiency is that it is a critical dimension of survival and success; yet to our knowledge, no research in banking has directly tested this proposition. There has been considerable research, however, on the relationship of bank failure (and problems) to financial ratios and related accounting information. Indeed, the success of statistical models based on ratios for profitability, asset quality, liquidity, capitalization, and efficiency prompted federal bank regulators to adopt them as "early warning systems" (EWSs) to monitor bank condition and to improve the allocation of examination resources.[1]

Although EWS models normally include a rough measure of cost efficiency, such as the ratio of operating expenses to operating income, more precise measures of cost characteristics derived from bank cost curves have not been incorporated. In this chapter, we bring together two branches of bank literature by examining the ability of cost-curve measures to predict bank failure. Our approach is to compare the significance and predictive ability of models that use only financial ratios to those based on either cost measures alone or on financial ratios and cost measures combined. Our research hypothesis is that cost measures are significant indicators of impending bank collapse.

Methodology

The FDIC tapes of income and condition were used to collect data. Since 1985 data were not yet available at the time this study was initiated, and since 1984 had a record seventy-eight bank failures (surpassed only in the Great Depression and in 1985), we chose 1984 as the analysis period. Of these seventy-eight failures, seventy-one banks had had the necessary data available on the 1982 tapes and seventy banks had had them in 1983, which permits tests for one year prior to failure and two years prior to failure. There was no data collection beyond two years prior to failure, because it was believed that further tests were not needed to arrive at a conclusion to our research hypothesis. A second sample of about 8,500 nonfailed banks was chosen from the FDIC list of almost 15,000 federally insured banks that had data available on the tapes for twenty years (from 1964 to 1983). Of these survivor banks, a random sample of about a thousand banks was selected for the analyses.

A total of thirty financial ratios were constructed as an initial step in the development of a ratio EWS model.[2] Past literature and regulatory practice were used as a guide.[3] Statistical analyses with all of these ratios in the model indicated that many variables were highly correlated. To simplify matters and to eliminate redundant variables, twelve ratios were chosen because of both their degree of correlation and their common use in the financial press (including regulatory publications) as measures of financial condition.[4] Table 7–1 lists labels and definitions of these variables.

Table 7–1
Predictor Variables in LOGIT Models

Label	Definition
NOI	Ratio of net operating income to total assets
ROA	Ratio of net income after taxes, securities gains (losses), and extraordinary items to total assets
RNW	Ratio of net income minus preferred stock dividends to common stock, surplus, undivided profits, and contingency and other reserves
LNPD	Ratio of gross loans to total deposits
TSDD	Ratio of time and savings deposits to demand deposits
TREAS	Ratio of U.S. Treasury securities to total assets
LIQ	Ratio of cash and securities to total assets
LOSS	Ratio of gross charge-offs on loans minus recoveries to total loans
LOSSP	Ratio of gross charge-offs on loans minus recoveries to provision for possible loan losses
CAPA	Ratio of total equity plus allowance for possible loan losses to total assets plus allowance for possible loan losses
CAP	Ratio of total equity to total assets
PROV	Ratio of provision for possible loan losses to total operating expenses
SEDT	Scale economies estimate based on translog cost function with demand and time deposits
SESL	Scale economies estimate based on translog cost function with securities and loans
SEDL	Scale economies estimate based on translog cost function with deposits and loans
RDT	Residual cost based on translog cost function with demand and time deposits
RSL	Residual cost based on translog cost function with securities and loans
RDL	Residual cost based on translog cost function with deposits and loans

Six cost measures are also listed in table 7–1. A priori, it was expected that failing banks would have scale economies either above or below unity because of the presence of size inefficiencies. We also expected that at a given level of output, failing banks would have more higher-than-normal average costs than nonfailing banks. In an effort to capture this anticipated difference, the predicted cost of producing bank services was subtracted from the actual cost; the predicted cost was calculated by taking a weighted average of the bank's outputs. The weights (as well as scale economies) for different outputs were estimated from the following translog cost models:

$$\ln \text{TOE} = \alpha_0 + \alpha_1 \ln \text{DD} + \alpha_2 \ln \text{TD} + \frac{1}{2}\delta_{11}(\ln \text{DD})^2$$
$$+ \frac{1}{2}\delta_{22}(\ln \text{TD})^2 + \delta_{12}(\ln \text{DD})(\ln \text{TD}) + \mu \qquad (7.1)$$

$$\ln \text{TOE} = \alpha_0 + \alpha_1 \ln \text{SEC} + \alpha_2 \ln \text{LOAN} + \frac{1}{2}\delta_{11}(\ln \text{SEC})^2$$
$$+ \frac{1}{2}\delta_{22}(\ln \text{LOAN})^2 + \delta_{12}(\ln \text{SEC})(\ln \text{LOAN}) + \mu \quad (7.2)$$

$$\ln \text{TOE} = \alpha_0 + \alpha_1 \ln \text{LOAN} + \alpha_2 \ln \text{DEP} + \frac{1}{2}\delta_{11}(\ln \text{LOAN})^2$$
$$+ \frac{1}{2}\delta_{22}(\ln \text{DEP})^2 + \delta_{12}(\ln \text{LOAN})(\ln \text{DEP}) + \mu \qquad (7.3)$$

where TOE is total operating expenses and all other notations are the same as in chapters 4 and 5. Residual costs for each bank (for demand and time deposits) equal the natural log of actual TOE minus the natural log of predicted TOE. As already mentioned, there should be a positive relationship between residual costs and the probability of failure.

The logistic discrimination method of regression analysis (hereafter the LOGIT model) was used to test the significance and classificatory ability of the variables with respect to the bank failure event. The LOGIT model estimates the probability of failure for each bank as

$$p = \frac{1}{1 + e^{-Z}} \qquad (7.4)$$

where Z is a weighted linear composite of the variables (generally written as βX). To classify banks the researcher must select a critical value for p beyond (below) which banks are identified as failing (nonfailing). To obtain statistical estimates of variable significance, the stepwise routine for the SAS

LOGIT procedure was run.[5] This procedure seeks to find a best set of predictor variables, in the sense that they are significantly related to the probability of failure, uncorrelated with one another, and explain most of the variance of the probability of failure. First, chi-square statistics are computed for each predictor, and the most significant predictor is selected (where a .10 level of significance was set as a minimum). Next, adjusted chi-square statistics are calculated for all predictors that are not in the model on the basis of their relationship to residual variance that is unexplained by the first predictor selected. This process is reiterated until the residual variance is insignificant (at the .10 level).

There are other methods of developing an EWS model. For example, past researchers have employed linear probability models, discriminant analysis models, and PROBIT models. These models, like the LOGIT model, have in common the calculation of a Z-score as

$$Z = \beta_0 + \beta_1 X_1 + \beta_2 X_2 + \cdots + \beta_m X_k \tag{7.5}$$

The Z-score reduces the multidimensional nature of bank condition into a single measure. Discriminant models can be derived from quadratic equations as well as from linear forms such as equation (7.5). However, linear probability and discriminant models, unlike PROBIT and LOGIT models, require multivariate normality among predictors. Therefore, PROBIT and LOGIT models are more general; however, they do require that the probability of failure be normal and logistic, respectively, given the predictors in the model. Since the normal and logistic distributions differ mainly in the extreme values, there is not much difference between them from a practical standpoint. We chose to use LOGIT because of its relatively simple implementation on SAS.

According to Collins and Green, LOGIT (as well as PROBIT) is also theoretically more appealing than other methods because it tends to use a "threshold" probability to forecast failure.[6] Figure 7–1 illustrates this advantage. If the bank had a Z-score below 0.6, the probability of failure would be relatively low (for example, $p = .10$). Beyond $Z = 0.6$, the probability of failure increases at an increasing rate (because of the shape of the cumulative distribution function), suggesting that the critical value for p should be set by the researcher at about .60.

Table 7–2 gives the parameter estimates for the predictors that were selected by the stepwise routine. The high overall chi-square values for the models indicate that both financial ratios and cost measures are highly related to bank failure. For the ratio models, the parameter estimates were almost the same for 1982 and 1983. In both years before failure, the net operating income to total assets ratio (NOI) and cash plus securities to total assets ratio

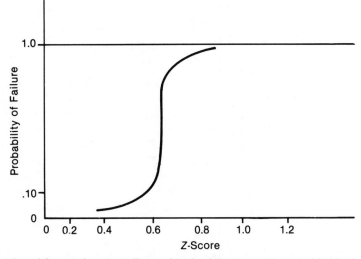

Source: Adapted from Robert A. Collins and Richard D. Green, "Statistical Methods for Bankruptcy Forecasting," *Journal of Economics and Business* 34(1982): 352.

Figure 7–1. The LOGIT Cumulative Distribution Function

(LIQ) were highly significant. The 1983 model did have a higher chi-square statistic than the 1982 model, which suggests that as the failure event becomes more remote, the significance of the ratio measures declines. On the surface at least, the ratio models imply that failing banks have relatively low profitability and asset liquidity.

The cost models contribute further insight into the failure process. The negative signs for the scale economies estimates for demand and time deposits (SEDT) and deposits and loans (SEDL), for example, suggest that most small banks were smaller than the average nonfailed bank. By contrast, the scale economies estimates for securities and loans (SESL) are positive; that is, banks with higher SESL values had greater probabilities of failure. This outcome implies that failing banks were experiencing diseconomies on the asset side of the balance sheet. Given the aforementioned size bias in the scale economies variables, this finding is particularly noteworthy.

The residual cost measures also exhibited mixed coefficient signs in the regression models. The residual cost measure for demand and time deposits (RDT) was higher for failing banks than for nonfailing banks. This means that, in relation to their level of deposit funding, according to equation (7.1), operating expenses for failing banks were relatively high. One potential reason for high operating expenses is loan losses. Alternatively, nondeposit

Table 7-2
Coefficient Estimates for Stepwise LOGIT Models[a]

Predictor Variables	Ratio Models		Cost Models		Ratio and Cost Models	
	I (1982)	II (1983)	III (1982)	IV (1983)	V (1982)	VI (1983)
Intercept	2.46 (23.32***)	1.82 (9.14***)	42.75 (12.02***)	33.95 (14.00***)	28.85 (19.94***)	1.74 (8.57***)
NOI	−38.34 (21.04***)	−52.27 (61.56***)				
ROA					−51.10 (7.93***)	−54.13 (54.54***)
RNW						
LNDP					5.02 (5.99**)	
TSDD						
TREAS						
LIQ	−14.63 (70.96***)	−13.66 (45.72***)				−13.48 (45.23***)
LOSS					−114.50 (11.47***)	

LOSSP						
CAPA						
CAP					−18.47 (4.46**)	
PROV					18.53 (7.04***)	
SEDT			−73.48 (22.07***)	−39.52 (17.09***)	−33.46 (24.22***)	
SESL			103.62 (17.89***)			
SEDL			−76.14 (6.94***)			
RDT			23.14 (33.65***)	19.25 (91.40***)	14.78 (14.95***)	
RSL						
RDL			−18.89 (22.05***)	−12.58 (41.46***)	−12.38 (10.54***)	
χ^2	149***	40***	170***	253***	205***	232***

a Asterisks indicate the significance levels for the chi-square statistics in parentheses: *$p <$ .10; **$p <$ .05; ***$p <$ .01.

expenses may be increasing because of a liquidity squeeze (as supported by the lower liquidity ratios for failing banks in the ratio models).

The residual cost measure for deposits and loans (RDL) was lower among failing banks than among nonfailing banks. It therefore appears that failing banks attempt to conserve on operating expenses, since their expenditures were below the expected level that would have been incurred normally at their level of loan and deposit output. Austerity programs might be implemented to cut costs and forestall impending collapse.

The results of the combination ratio and cost predictors models in table 7–2 point to loan losses as the chief cause of failure. In the 1982 model, the ratio of net charge-offs on loans to total loans and the ratio of the provision for possible loan losses to total operating expenses increased with the probability of failure. The loan losses undoubtedly depressed the profitability and capital of the failing banks, as indicated by the negative signs for the ROA and CAP variables.

It is interesting that the residual cost measures RDT and RDL were significant, given the ratio of loans to deposits (LNDP) that was in the 1982 model. This implies not only that failing banks have high loan-to-deposit ratios but that cost-control problems appear on both sides of the balance sheet. A likely scenario that emerges from our analyses is that failing banks suffer loan losses that cause their asset liquidity, profitability, and capitalization to deteriorate. Increased nondeposit funding occurs, probably in response to lower asset liquidity. These balance sheet changes cause further problems, such as inefficiencies in the production of deposits, loans, and securities.

The 1983 combination model results in table 7–2 reveal that in the year immediately preceeding the failure event, only profitability and liquidity were significant. We interpret this to imply that just before collapse, failing banks have such severe difficulties that the causes (loan losses) overwhelm the symptoms (cost abnormalities).

Table 7–3 shows the classification results for the three alternative models in 1982 and 1983. Results are given for critical values for the probability of failure set at both .10 and .15. When $p = .10$, between 80 percent and 89 percent of the failed banks were correctly identified, while from 86 percent and 93 percent of nonfailed banks were classified correctly. When we set $p = .15$, a higher (lower) percentage of nonfailed (failed) banks were correctly classified. In general, this classification accuracy is quite high compared to previous bank failure studies. We can infer, therefore, that the LOGIT models did a fairly good job of finding ratio and cost measures that identify failing banks. Because the classification accuracy of the cost models was comparable to that of the ratio models, we believe that cost characteristics of banks are closely related to their probability of success.

Table 7-3
Classification Results for LOGIT Models: Number of Banks in Group X Classified into Group Y

LOGIT Models	1982				1983			
	NF(NF)	F(F)	NF(F)	F(NF)	NF(NF)	F(F)	NF(F)	F(NF)
A. Classification of Nonfailed (NF) and Failed (F) Banks: Critical Value $p = .10$								
Ratio	846	57	139	14	886	60	76	10
Cost	860	56	125	15	897	59	64	11
Ratio and cost	860	55	119	16	881	62	80	8
B. Classification of Nonfailed (NF) and Failed (F) Banks: Critical Value $p = .15$								
Ratio	907	49	78	22	921	56	41	14
Cost	907	48	78	23	920	53	41	17
Ratio and cost	910	53	75	18	923	56	38	14

Summary and Conclusions

In this chapter we tested the long-standing belief that cost efficiency is related to bank viability. More specifically, we hypothesized that banks failing in 1984 would have abnormal cost characteristics relative to banks with a long record of success (as proxied by having been in business since 1964). LOGIT model analyses of cost measures for scale and the level of costs were compared to results based on financial ratios. The results on cost control indicated the following:

1. Failing banks were smaller, on average, compared to the general banking population, which accounted for their smaller-scale economy estimates for demand and time deposits and for deposits and loans (that is, they had not exhausted scale benefits that cause costs to be higher than otherwise).
2. Despite the size bias, failing banks had higher-scale economy estimates for securities and loans than did nonfailing banks, which would imply that diseconomies were present.
3. Failing banks had excessive operating costs relative to their base.
4. Failing banks had lower than expected operating costs given the level of their loans outstanding and deposit base. The larger proportions of loans and nondeposit funds probably led to some of the cost inefficiencies that were found.

The classification results for the models gave strong evidence in support of our cost control hypothesis. Models using cost measures demonstrated high classification accuracy for both failed and nonfailed banks. Additionally, the cost models performed as well as the financial ratio models, which proxy the EWS approach taken by federal bank regulators. The LOGIT model results and associated classification results led us to the conclusion that cost control plays a vital role in the survival of banks.

Notes

1. For an excellent overview of the literature and current practice regarding EWS models in banking, see "Warning Lights for Bank Soundness: Special Issue on Commercial Bank Surveillance," *Economic Review* 68, Federal Reserve Bank of Atlanta (November 1983). Recently, the FDIC has proposed a risk-based deposit insurance system that would rely in part upon an EWS model to rate the riskiness of each insured bank. This objective score would be combined with the examiners' subjective assessments of each bank's risk to get an overall risk measure. Different ranges of risk would be associated with various deposit insurance premium and rebate schedules. This pro-

posal had not been implemented at the time of this writing, but it is likely that risk-based deposit insurance will be required in the near future.

2. For a list of financial ratios used in previous studies cited widely in the literature, see Donald R. Fraser and James W. Kolari, *The Future of Small Banks in a Deregulated Environment* (Cambridge, Mass.: Ballinger, 1985), 181–6.

3. For a list of financial ratios employed by federal regulators, see Barron H. Putnam, "Early Warning Systems and Financial Analysis in Bank Monitoring," *Economic Review* 68, Federal Reserve Bank of Atlanta (November 1983), 6–12.

4. The ratio of net operating income to total assets was highly correlated with the efficiency ratio of operating expenses to operating income and thus proxies management's efficient usage of bank assets.

5. *SAS Supplementary Library User's Guide* (Cary, N.C.: SAS Institute, 1982), 181–202.

6. Robert A. Collins and Richard D. Green, "Statistical Methods for Bankruptcy Forecasting," *Journal of Economics and Business* 34 (1982): 349–54.

8
Bank Costs and Implications

Today's banking environment is less stable than it was in the past. Nonbank competitors are positioning themselves to expand their market shares in services that are traditionally bank-supplied. At the time of this writing, the Supreme Court had unanimously voted to prevent the Federal Reserve Board from regulating nonbank banks (that is, major brokerage firms, insurance companies, department stores, and other businesses), thereby allowing dozens of commercial companies to begin offering limited financial services. However, two other federal court cases that have ruled against nonbank banks are expected to reach the Supreme Court eventually.

Another uncertainty for banks in the marketplace is the extent of interstate banking and the speed with which it will proceed in the future. Of course, large bank holding companies may employ the nonbank bank loophole in order to engage in interstate activities. Another important avenue, however, is through regional interstate banking compacts. These compacts were recently challenged for their constitutionality, but in June 1985, the Supreme Court approved their legality. As was shown in table 1–10 (chapter 1), regional interstate banking is fairly pervasive already. Therefore, in the short run at least, interstate banking will continue to spread. Whether or not Congress will act in the near future to deregulate interstate banking on either a regional or national level is still unknown.

Another source of change is the volatile interest rate environment of the late 1970s and early 1980s. Will this volatility be repeated in the future? Deposit rate deregulation has forced banks to manage the maturity structures of assets and liability more carefully than they did in the past. A less obvious but potentially more important effect of interest rate deregulation on the banking industry is the possibility of surges in competitive vigor when interest rates increase above normal levels. In the past few years, interest rate levels have subsided and with them the extent of competition and market innovation. The uncertainty associated with changes in the regulatory environment and consequent shifts in competitive pressures may increase the risk inherent in the enterprise of banking in the long run.

Product line deregulation is perhaps the least predictable environmental change. Bankers are lobbying Congress for repeal or modification of the Glass-Steagall Act, which separates investment and commercial banking. Besides their securities brokerage and underwriting activities, bankers are also seeking to expand their line of services in the areas of insurance and real estate. However, considerable opposition is being encountered from various industry groups. Since congressional action will be needed to move ahead on new bank products and services, their fate is left to the political nuances of prolonged debate and hard-won compromise.

Finally, the internal processes of creating bank services and then delivering them to the public are being altered substantially by the increase in the pace at which technology is advancing in the banking industry. There is a much greater public acceptance of electronic funds transfer (EFT) methods today than there was a decade ago. Indeed, many consumers and businesses are forming expectations of continued evolution and increased adoption of automated bank services in the future. We can expect that whenever competition increases (because of rising interest rates, further deregulation, entry of financial-service sellers, and so forth), there will be motivation for added technological innovation in banking in an attempt to cut costs. Therefore, the "plant vintage" of a typical bank will change in the years to come, particularly when competition strains resource costs and profitable management.

It has been the theme of this book that the aforementioned external and internal changes in banking and the resultant new competition in the industry will require banks to operate as efficiently as possible. Attention has been drawn to the fact that banks must move away from simply providing accounts to customers when asked and toward developing a more complete relationship that is based on marketing (or sales) principles. Comparatively little attention, though, has been directed toward the more fundamental concept of cost control. Without knowledge of costs, it is not possible to appropriately price products and services for profitable sale to bank customers. Therefore, as a starting point, it is crucial for bankers to understand the cost characteristics of their business.

As was discussed in chapter 1, the cost economics of banking are also fundamental to the public policy issue of optimal industry structure. Exactly what constitutes optimality in the number and size distribution of banks is not a simple matter to determine. It would be generally agreed, however, that we want the banking system to efficiently allocate savings to investment (that is, the most successful businesses) and to do this at minimum cost. Operational efficiency can serve to lower interest rates charged to borrowers and to raise interest rates offered to lenders in the financial system, so that the saving-and-investment process is fostered.

A related public policy argument for cost efficiency in banking is that in order for society's savings to flow efficiently to investments, they first need to be channeled to those institutions (including banks) that are most likely to efficiently allocate loanable funds to business firms. In this regard, it is reasonable to believe that those banks that are most efficient tend to best fulfill this desired investment function. Therefore, public policy, by implication, should promote a bank industry structure that encourages efficient bank operations.

But what if very large banks operate most efficiently because of significant scale economies? A question then arises regarding the potential cost benefits of concentrating bank resources in only a few giant sellers and the potential disadvantages of anticompetitive behavior (due to oligopoly or monopoly pricing) that could offset these cost benefits. This fear has been voiced many times in the past but it is probably more relevant today, in view of the vast changes occurring in the financial services industry. Of course, if scale economies are exhausted fairly rapidly as bank output increases, the possible deleterious consequences of a consolidation movement in banking become moot issues. Giant banks would be less able to exercise their market power to the extent that small banks can produce and sell products and services at competitive prices.

For these reasons, the subject of bank costs should be of broad interest not only to bank managers, owners, and regulators but also to the public at large. In this last chapter, we seek to provide an overview of what we have learned from the literature and empirical evidence presented in previous chapters. The final section discusses the implications of bank costs and the research on this topic.

Overview of Past and Present Bank Cost Evidence

Early studies on bank costs based on Call Report data found that small banks had cost inefficiencies in the 1930s and 1940s. Studies in the 1960s and 1970s that used econometric methods found comparable results. These studies also reported evidence of diseconomies for branch banks at higher output levels, which were normally attributed to problems in coordinating a decentralized organizational form. The consensus of this literature was that small banks were at a cost disadvantage compared to large banks but that the difference was not so large as to prevent them from competing effectively in their particular market niches.

Recent studies of bank costs involving the translog cost model have improved on past research in two ways. First, more than one output is considered at a time. This approach is one step closer to the actual production process of banks, because, as a rule, multiple services are produced. The second advantage is the test for and estimation of potential cost benefits that may accompany the joint production of bank services. In general, the studies reported U-shaped cost curves for banks, with scale benefits exhausted at only $10 million to $25 million in deposits. There was some evidence of flat cost curves in branch states also. To a certain degree, these results are contrary to earlier studies; that is, very small banks were found to be cost-efficient for the most part, and in the case of branch bank states, instead of diseconomies at higher output levels, a flat cost curve was encountered.

The evidence on scope economies was ambiguous. In one study, jointness was not generally uncovered, whereas some other studies found positive evidence in favor of jointness, although they concluded that scope benefits were not substantial enough to alter the scale results. Unfortunately, none of the studies obtained estimates of the extent of scope, and this left open the question of how important scope is in the production of banking services. For example, how much are costs reduced by expanding output through joint production as opposed to through production of one output at a time? Also, does the degree of jointness vary with the size of the bank?

Another gap in the literature concerned the possibility that output mix may influence the cost characteristics of banks. Farm banks produce a mix of outputs that is obviously different from the output mix of large, downtown banks. Consequently, since studies do not differentiate between banks with diverse output mixes, their results may well not be meaningful to practitioners (and possibly others interested in certain segments of the banking population).

In chapters 4 and 5, we presented updated analyses of FCA cost data for the period 1979–83. One purpose of these analyses was to reconsider the cost characteristics of banks in light of the many changes that have transformed the internal cost structure of banks over the past decade. A second purpose of this research was to propose a new measure for calculating the extent of scope economies, one that overcomes some of the problems with the standard method used in the past. Third, and last, we sought to group banks by their output mix and conduct separate cost analyses of each major group of banks.

One important point of departure of this research was the use of dollars rather than number of accounts to measure output. In brief, we argued that in a competitive marketplace, the cost of acquiring a dollar of deposit funding was the same at the margin for both small and large accounts. Although past studies adjusted for different account sizes when the number of accounts was used to measure output, this methodology assumes that there is a perfect relationship between the number and size of accounts. For this reason, studies in the past have reported scale estimates for different ranges of deposits in dollar terms, rather than in terms of the number of accounts. To the extent that this assumed relationship between the number and size of accounts does not hold, the interpretation of the results for scale economies over different deposit size ranges is clouded (given that the numbers of accounts is the appropriate measure of output). Other reasons also favor the use of dollars in measuring output. For instance, the introduction of the average size of deposits in a multiple regression equation with the numbers of accounts in the model might lead to multicollinearity that can bias the estimation of the parameters for outputs. On a more fundamental level, bankers themselves are likely to seek *dollars of accounts* because they are employed in gauging their relative market shares. Whether the output is deposits, loans, or securities, the one common denominator is the dollar amounts of such accounts. Consequently, analyses of costs were conducted with output denominated in dollars.

The findings of our research on bank costs differed in a variety of ways from recently published work that was based on the translog cost model. First, cost curves in unit banking states were consistently flat, with no economies or diseconomies evident. In branch banking states, the cost curves were normally either U-shaped or upward-sloping. If it is true that diseconomies at the firm level were responsible for these shapes, the cost curves of branch banks on the plant level could be inferred as being approximately the same shape as those for unit banks. An alternative possibility, which was supported in part by the results, is that interest rate regulation motivated branch banks to expand their office facilities as a means of providing implicit, or service, returns to customers above the regulated ceiling rate that applied to explicit, or interest, returns. As deregulation of deposit rates proceeded in the late 1970s and early 1980s, branch banks trimmed their office facilities so that greater explicit returns could be paid out to customers. In 1982, there did appear to be a trend toward a flattening of the cost curve for securities and loans, which lends some support to our argument that deregulation is changing the cost structure of branch banks to more closely parallel that of unit banks.

Our jointness tests for banks in unit and branch states indicated that there are significant cost complementarities in the joint production of loans and deposits but not in securities and loans or demand and time deposits, at least from a statistical standpoint. We interpreted these results to imply that as financial intermediaries, banks reap cost benefits by vertically integrating the production of outputs in stage one (deposits) and stage two (assets) of their overall business. Measures of the extent of scope economies based on our proposed methodology suggested that the economic significance of joint production of outputs was substantial in all stages of the production process. Also, no clear trend was observed linking bank size and the degree of scope economies. There was a tendency for unit states to have somewhat higher scope estimates than branch states, but it is not known why such a difference should exist (other than perhaps because inputs can be managed more efficiently in unit banks because of greater centralization).

In chapter 5, the results were reported for four different types of banks (as determined by their grouping according to output mix, using the statistical technique of cluster analysis). Farm banks were found to be unique, in that their cost curves were normally flat, in contrast to the U-shaped, upward-sloping, and L-shaped cost curves uncovered in other groups. Additionally, farm banks tended to have scope economies that were related to deposit size, but the other groups did not exhibit such a trend. Retail banks were also different in that their scope measures were, on average, smaller than those for other bank groups. Since retail banks were distinguished by their relatively large proportionate investments in securities, it was tentatively inferred that securities operations are more specialized than other key bank services, which might explain the inability to share the cost of their production with other outputs. City banks and wholesale banks had comparable cost characteristics, which is not surprising, since both groups were distinguished by their relatively high amount of commercial and industrial loans as a percentage of assets. It is important to note that all four bank groups appeared to have higher scope economies in the joint production of deposits and loans than in other combinations of either liabilities or assets.

In chapter 6, we discussed studies dealing with the effects of technology on the production of banking services. These studies showed, in general, that automation tends to reduce costs of operations. We then presented new tests for the relationship between automation and bank costs that indicated the following: (1) small banks cannot cost-effectively utilize modern technology to produce demand deposits and tend to have relatively high computer-related expenses compared to other banks; (2) large banks did not appear to have a cost advantage over smaller banks in the production of demand deposits; and (3) large banks do appear to have a cost advantage over smaller banks in the joint production of demand deposits and credit card services. The third result implies that there are scale economies at even relatively large output levels, which, in conjunction with the finding of fairly positive scope measures between demand deposits and credit cards, suggests that natural monopoly conditions may be present in the production of automated services in banking.

Implications

This book has attempted to provide the reader with a broad understanding of the cost economics of banking. As often noted, the study of bank costs has important implications for the structure and performance of the banking industry. In this section, we seek to put in perspective the research results that have been reported throughout the text, with an emphasis on these implications.

Public Policy

As a society that desires a higher standard of living, we should recognize the importance of the fact that an improved banking system will pay dividends through greater economic development. The integral nature of economic and financial systems has been painfully recorded in U.S. history many times. Of course, just as the competitive pressure generated by numerous sellers has fueled economic prosperity, the increase in competition among banks and other financial-service sellers in the past decade has led to improved and expanded financial services for the public as a whole. For the purpose of public policy, the question that arises, however, is whether increased competition in the financial sector will lead to a consolidation of resources that could have important implications for various private and public sectors of the United States. If the cost economics of the banking industry are such that natural monopoly can be expected to occur in the years to come, are the potential cost benefits of this kind of industry structure sufficient to outweigh the potential uncertainties that may crop up in the form of monopolistic pricing of financial services, declining financial services, and the market power that may be exercised in the private as well as public sector?

The cost evidence reviewed in this book implies that this public policy concern is a moot issue for the most part. For natural monopoly to occur, both scale and scope economies would have to be present in large banks. We found that scope economies are important in reducing production costs for all sizes of banks; however, cost curves were flat or U-shaped in most cases, rather than downward-sloping over a large range of output. We should note here that the production of demand deposits and credit cards did have cost characteristics that conformed, for the most part, to those of natural monopoly. This does not mean that freer competition will drive out small competitors; instead, it implies that small banks are better suited to the delivery of highly automated transactions services (purchased from larger financial institutions) than to their production. As it is in so many other industries, the production process in banking is composed of stages. The evidence on demand deposit and credit card services suggests that there are phases to stage one of the production process (the acquisition of deposits) that small banks would best leave for the large institutions. It does not imply anything about stage two of the production process (the administration of assets) or about the relationship of these two stages.

Bank Management

Bank management is ultimately responsible for controlling costs. For this reason, bankers themselves are directly affected by the cost economics of their business. Those banks that do not manage their costs appropriately will probably replace personnel as a first attempt to bring costs into line with revenues. Of course, continued problems with cost control would reduce the bank's competitiveness and possibly encourage acquisition or merger with a rival bank.

The implication of our research findings detailed in previous chapters is that many different sizes of banks should be able to coexist in today's financial marketplace. The lesson to be learned from the cost findings is that banks need to seek market niches that do not overlap with those of other sellers and then produce services demanded by their clientele as cost-efficiently as possible. Even if larger banks could produce the same services more cheaply, this advantage may be irrelevant because they serve a different market segment. Indeed, we found that the output mix of banks differs noticeably and that these differences are associated with different cost characteristics. A farm bank, for example, need not be concerned about the cost efficiency of a bank that is devoted to corporate clientele. These two types of banks serve different market segments and have distinct cost characteristics. A business-oriented bank may improve its cost efficiency by expanding output, but this does not appear to be the case in farm banking.

The scope findings imply that all banks can lower their costs per unit output by expanding a number of products jointly. Except for farm banks, size is not related to the achievement of scope economies. It is the mix of outputs that is important. Bank management should be aware of cost complementarities in the production of financial services and should seek to maximize scope economies by viewing different product lines as separate profit centers but also as interrelated products that must be jointly maximized for profitability.

Bank Shareholders

Bank owners are often also managers, so that their motivations for cost control overlap. To the extent that management and ownership are separate, however, their goals may diverge. Bank shareholders seek to maximize their wealth, as reflected in the share price of the institution. If cost-efficient operations are not being maintained by management, it may be a signal to shareholders that management is not seeking the same wealth-maximization goal. In a regulated banking environment, bank shareholders may be less concerned about cost efficiency, because regulators may monitor the cost control of the bank's managers. However, in a more competitive banking market, as is the trend today, there is a greater need for shareholders to evaluate the cost management of the bank.

Research

There are a number of implications for future research in the field of bank costs, structure, and performance that follow from the findings and conclusions of this text. One potential area of research would be to expand on the study of different segments of the banking population. More specifically, future research should consider the effect of state branching status, which was ignored in our analyses because of small sample sizes. Another avenue for future research would be to develop a statistical test for whether or not the measure of scope is significantly different from zero. Our scope measure indicates the percentage cost reduction from expansion through joint production as opposed to production of outputs one at a time, but it is not known whether these estimates are statistically significant. Other areas of research would include more detailed analyses of different outputs (such as commercial loans, installment loans, and so forth) with respect to their scope characteristics, examination of bank costs in institutions with distinct organizational features (such as multibank holding companies and branch banks), and the study of technology and new bank services (such as money market funds management, interest-bearing checking accounts, telephone bill payment services, and so on).

Bibliography

Adar, Zvi; Tamir Agmon; and Yair E. Orgler. "Output Mix and Jointness in Production in the Banking Firm." *Journal of Money, Credit and Banking* 7 (May 1975): 235–43.

Alhadeff, David. *Monopoly and Competition in Banking.* Berkeley: University of California Press, 1954.

Arrow, K.B.; H.B. Chenery; B. Minhas; and R.M. Solow. "Capital Labor Substitution and Economic Efficiency." *Review of Economics and Statistics* 43 (August 1961):225–50.

Atlanta Payments Project. *Automated Clearing Houses: An In Depth Analysis,* Atlandta, 1974.

Baer, Herbert; Gillian Garcia; and Simon Pak. "The Effect of Promotional Pricing on Dynamic Adjustment in the Market for MMMFs and MMDAs." *Proceedings of a Conference on Bank Structure and Competition,* Federal Reserve Bank of Chicago (April 1984), 153–83.

Baltensperger, Ernst. "Costs of Banking Activities—Interactions Between Risk and Operating Costs. *Journal of Money, Credit and Banking* 4 (August 1972): 592–611.

Baumol, William J. "The Transaction Demand for Cash: An Inventory Theoretic Approach." *Quarterly Journal of Economics* 66 (November 1952):545–56.

Baumol, William J. "On the Proper Tests for Natural Monopoly in a Multiproduct Industry." *American Economic Review* 67 (December 1977):809–22.

Baumol, William J.; John Panzar; and Robert Willig. *Contestable Markets and the Theory of Industry Structure.* New York: Harcourt Brace Jovanovich, 1982.

Bell, Frederick W., and Neil B. Murphy. "Bank Service Charges and Costs." *National Banking Review* 4 (June 1967):449–57.

Bell, Frederick W., and Neil B. Murphy. *Costs in Commercial Banking: A Quantitative Analysis of Bank Behavior and Its Relation to Bank Regulation.* Boston: Federal Reserve Bank of Boston, April 1968.

Bell, Frederick W., and Neil B. Murphy. "Economies of Scale and Division of Labor in Commercial Lending." 6 *National Banking Review* (October 1969):131–39.

Benston, George J. "Branch Banking and Economies of Scale." *Journal of Finance* 20 (May 1965):312–31.

Benston, George J. "Economies of Scale and Marginal Costs in Banking Operations." *National Banking Review* 2 (June 1965):507–49.

Benston, George J. "Economies of Scale in Financial Institutions." *Journal of Money, Credit and Banking* 4 (May 1972):312–41.

Benston, George J. "Graduated Interest Rate Ceilings and Operating Costs by Size of Small Consumer Cash Loans." *Journal of Finance* 32 (June 1977):695–707.

Benston, George J.; Allen N. Berger; Gerald A. Hanweck; and David B. Humphrey. "Economies of Scale and Scope in Banking." *Proceedings of a Conference on Bank Structure and Competition,* Federal Reserve Bank of Chicago (May 1983), 432–61.

Benston, George J.; Gerald Hanweck; and David Humphrey. "Scale Economies in Banking: A Restructuring and Reassessment. *Journal of Money, Credit and Banking* 14 (November 1982):435–56.

Borts, G.H. "The Benston Paper, Some Comments." *Journal of Money, Credit and Banking* 4 (May 1972):419–21.

Borts, G.H. "Costs of Bank Activities: Interactions Between Risk and Operating Costs, A Comment." *Journal of Money, Credit and Banking* 4 (August 1972): 612–13.

Bothwell, James L., and Thomas F. Cooley. "Efficiency in the Provision of Health Care: An Analysis of Health Care Organizations." *Southern Economic Journal* 45 (April 1982):970–84.

Braunstein, Y.M., and L.B. Pulley. "Flexible Multiproduct Cost Functions: An Empirical Investigation." Brandeis University, Department of Economics, October 1981. Mimeographed.

Brown, Randall S.; Douglas W. Caves; and Laurits R. Christensen. "Modelling the Structure of Cost and Production in Multiproduct Firms." *Southern Economic Journal* 46 (July 1979):256–76.

Caves, Douglas W.; Laurits R. Christensen; and Michael W. Tretheway. "Flexible Cost Functions for Multiproduct Firms." *The Review of Economics and Statistics* 62 (August 1980):477–81.

Christensen, Laurits R., and William H. Greene. "Economies of Scale in U.S. Electric Power Generation." *Journal of Political Economy* 84 (August 1976):655–76.

Christensen, Laurits R.; Dale W. Jorgenson; and Lawrence J. Lau. "Transcendental Logarithmic Production Frontiers." *Review of Economics and Statistics* 55 (February 1973):28–45.

Christophe, Cleveland A. *Competition in Financial Services.* New York, First National Corporation, March 1974.

Clark, Jeffrey A. "Estimation of Economies of Scale in Banking Using a Generalized Functional Form." *Journal of Money, Credit and Banking* 16 (February 1984):53–68.

Collins, Robert A., and Richard D. Green. "Statistical Methods for Bankruptcy Forecasting." *Journal of Economics and Business* 34 (1982):349–54.

Daniel, Donnie L.; William A. Longbrake; and Neil B. Murphy. "The Effect of Technology on Bank Economies of Scale for Demand Deposits." *Journal of Finance* 28 (March 1973):131–46.

Diewert, W. Erwin. "Exact and Superlative Index Numbers." *Journal of Econometrics* 14 (May 1976):115–45.

Dunham, Constance. "Commercial Bank Costs and Correspondent Banking." *New England Economic Review,* Federal Reserve Bank of Boston, (September-October 1981), 22–36.

Durkin, Thomas A. "Consumer Loan Costs and the Regulatory Basis of Loan Sharking." *Journal of Bank Research* 8 (Denver: Summer 1977):108–17.

Farm Credit System. *Business Technology in Finance and Agriculture in 1995,* June 1984.

Federal Reserve Bank of Atlanta. "Warning Lights for Bank Soundness: Special Issue on Commercial Bank Surveillance." *Economic Review* 68 (November 1983).

Federal Reserve Bank of Kansas City. *Monthly Review* (February, March, April, December 1961 and February 1962).

Federal Reserve Bank of Kansas City. *Financial Letter.* Adapted from testimony of Paul Volcker, Chairman of the Board of Governors of the Federal Reserve System, before the Senate Committee on Banking, Housing, and Urban Affairs, May 8, 1985.

Flannery, Mark J. "The Impact of Interest Rates on Small Commercial Banks." Rodney L. White Center of Financial Research, Working Paper No. 10-81 (August 1981).

Flannery, Mark J. "Market Interest Rates and Commercial Bank Profitability: An Empirical Investigation." *Journal of Finance* 36 (December 1981):1085–1101.

Flannery, Mark J. "Correspondent Services and Cost Economies in Commercial Banking." *Journal of Banking and Finance* 7 (1983):83–99.

Flannery, Mark J. "Removing Deposit Rate Ceilings: How Will Bank Profits Fare?" *Business Review,* Federal Reserve Bank of Philadelphia (March-April 1983), 13–31.

Flannery, Mark J. "The Social Cost of Unit Banking Restrictions." *Journal of Monetary Economics* 13 (1984):237–49.

Flannery, Mark J., and Dwight M. Jaffee. *The Economic Implications of an Electronic Monetary Transfer System.* Lexington, Mass.: Lexington Books, 1973.

Fraser, Donald R., and James W. Kolari. *The Future of Small Banks in a Deregulated Environment.* Cambridge, Mass.: Ballinger, 1985:181–6.

Fraser, Donald R., and Gene S. Uselton. "The Omnibus Banking Act." *MSU Business Topics* 28 (Autumn 1980):5–14.

Frisbee, Pamela. "Bankers' Banks: An Institution Whose Time Has Come." *Economic Review,* Federal Reserve Bank of Atlanta (April 1984), 31–35.

Fuss, Melvyn, and Leonard Waverman. "Regulation and the Multiproduct Firm: The Case of Telecommunications in Canada." In Melvyn Fuss and Daniel McFadden, eds., *Production Economics: A Dual Approach to Theory and Application.* New York: North-Holland, 1978. 384.

Gady, Richard L. "Anatomy of Profitable Medium-Size Banks in the Fourth District, 1966–1970." *Economic Review,* Federal Reserve Bank of Cleveland (October-November 1972), 20–32.

Garcia, Gillian, et al. "Financial Deregulation: Historical Perspective and Impact of the Garn-St. Germain Depository Institutions Act of 1982." Staff Study 83-2, Federal Reserve Bank of Chicago (1983).

Garcia, Gillian, et al. "The Garn-St. Germain Depository Institutions Act of 1982." *Economic Perspectives,* Federal Reserve Bank of Chicago (March-April 1983).

Gilligan, Thomas W., and Michael L. Smirlock." An Empirical Study of Joint Production and Scale Economies in Commercial Banking." *Journal of Banking and Finance* 8 (1984):67–77.

Gilligan, Thomas W.; Michael L. Smirlock; and William Marshall. "Scale and Scope

Economies in the Multiproduct Banking Firm." *Journal of Monetary Economics* 13 (1984):393–405.

Gramley, Lyle E. *A Study of Scale Economies in Banking*. Kansas City: Federal Reserve Bank of Kansas City, 1962.

Greenbaum, Stuart I. "Competition and Efficiency in the Banking System: Empirical Research and Its Policy Implications." *Journal of Political Economy* 75 (1967): 461–81.

Greenbaum, Stuart I. "A Study of Bank Cost." *National Banking Review* 4 (June 1967):415–34.

Haslem, John A., and William A. Longbrake. "A Discriminant Analysis of Commercial Bank Profitability." *Quarterly Review of Economics and Business* 11 (Autumn 1971):39–46.

Heggestad, Arnold A., and John J. Mingo. "On the Usefulness of Functional Cost Analysis Data." *Journal of Bank Research* 9 (Winter 1978):251–56.

Horvitz, Paul M. "Economies of Scale in Banking." In *Private Financial Institutions*. Englewood Cliffs, N.J.: Prentice-Hall, 1962.

Humphrey, David Burras. "Economies of Scale in Federal Reserve Check Processing Operations." *Journal of Econometrics* 15 (January 1981):155–73.

Humphrey, David Burras. "Scale Economies at Automated Clearinghouses." *Journal of Bank Research* 12 (Summer 1981):71–81.

Humphrey, David Burras. *The U.S. Payments System: Costs, Pricing, Competition, and Risk*. New York: New York University, Salomon Brothers Center for the Study of Financial Institutions, 1984.

Jackson, Raymond. "The Consideration of Economies in Merger Cases." *Journal of Business* 43 (October 1970):439–47.

Kalish, Lionel, III, and R. Alton Gilbert. "An Analysis of Efficiency of Scale and Organizational Form in Commercial Banking." *Journal of Industrial Economics* 21 (July 1973):293–307.

Kane, Edward J. "Accelerating Inflation, Technological Innovation, and the Decreasing Effectiveness of Bank Regulation." *Journal of Finance* 36 (May 1981): 355–67.

Kaufman, George; Larry Mote; and Harvey Rosenblum." Implications of Deregulation for Product Lines and Geographic Markets of Financial Institutions." *Journal of Bank Research* 14 (Summer 1983):8–21.

Kim, Moshe. "Scale Economies in Banking: A Methodological Note." *Journal of Money, Credit and Banking* 17 (February 1985):96–102.

Koch, Donald L. "The Emerging Financial Services Industry: Challenge Innovation." *Economic Review*, Federal Reserve Bank of Atlanta (April 1984), 26.

Kolari, James, and Asghar Zardkoohi. "Small Banks in a Changing Financial Market." Small Business Administration Study, Grant Contract No. SBA-8564-04-84, May 1986.

Kwast, Myron L., and John T. Rose. "Pricing, Operating Efficiency, and Profitability Among Large Commercial Banks." *Journal of Banking and Finance* 6 (1982): 233–54.

Long, Donald G. "Technological Change and the Small Depository Institution." *The Future of Small Depository Institutions in an Era of Deregulation, Financial Innovation, and Technological Change,* Proceedings of a Conference of the Board of

Governors of the Federal Reserve System, Washington, D.C., January 1984, 25–46.

Longbrake, William A. "Computers and the Cost of Producing Various Types of Banking Services." Federal Deposit Insurance Corporation, Working Paper No. 72-17 (1972).

Longbrake, William A., and John A. Haslem. "Productive Efficiency in Commercial Banking." *Journal of Money, Credit and Banking* 7 (August 1975):317–30.

Mayo, John W. "Multiproduct Monopoly, Regulation, and Firm Costs." *Southern Economic Journal* 51 (July 1984):208–18.

McCord, Thomas. "The Depository Institutions Deregulation and Monetary Control Act of 1980." *Issues in Bank Regulation* 3 (Spring 1980):3–7.

McFadden, D.L. "Further Results on C.E.S. Functions." *Review of Economic Studies* 30 (June 1963):73–83.

McNeill, Charles R. "The Depository Institutions Deregulation and Monetary Control Act of 1980." *Federal Reserve Bulletin* 66 (June 1980):444–53.

Metzker, Paul. "Future Payments System Technology: Can Small Financial Institutions Compete?" *Economic Review,* Federal Reserve Bank of Atlanta (November 1982), 58–66.

Mullineaux, Donald J. "Economies of Scale of Financial Institutions." *Journal of Monetary Economics* 1 (April 1975):233–40.

Mullineaux, Donald J. "Economies of Scale and Organizational Efficiency in Banking: A Profit-Function Approach." *Journal of Finance* 33 (March 1978):259–80.

Murphy, Neil B. "Costs of Banking Activities: Interactions Between Risk and Operating Costs, A Comment." *Journal of Money, Credit and Banking* 4 (August 1972): 614–15.

Murphy, Neil B. "A Reestimation of the Benston-Bell Murphy Cost Functions for a Larger Sample with Greater Size and Geographic Dispersion." *Journal of Financial and Quantitative Analysis* 7 (December 1972):2097–105.

Nagata, Ernest A. "The Cost Structure of Consumer Finance Small-Loan Operations." *Journal of Finance* 28 (December 1973):1327–37.

Nelson, Richard W. "Branching, Scale Economies, and Banking Costs." *Journal of Banking and Finance* 9 (1985):177–91.

Nerlove, Marc. "Returns to Scale in Electricity Supply." In F. Carl Christ, *Measurement in Economics,* 167–98. Stanford, Calif.: Stanford University Press, 1963.

Panzar, John C., and Robert Willig. "Economies of Scope, Product Specific Returns to Scale, and Multiproduct Competitive Industries." Unpublished paper, Bell Laboratories. Murray Hill, N.J., 1978.

Polakoff, Murray E.; Thomas A. Durkin; and Others. *Financial Institutions and Markets,* 2nd ed. Boston: Houghton Mifflin, 1981.

Powers, John Anthony. "Branch Versus Unit Banking: Output and Cost Economies." *Southern Economic Journal* 36 (October 1969):153–64.

Putnam, Barron H. "Early Warning Systems and Financial Analysis in Bank Monitoring." *Economic Review* 68, Federal Reserve Bank of Atlanta (November 1983), 6–12.

Rhoades, Stephen A. "Limitations of Antitrust Laws for the Analysis of Market Extension Mergers." Unpublished paper, Federal Reserve System, 1981.

Rosenblum, Harvey, and Christine Pavel. "Financial Services in Transition: The

Effects of Nonbank Competitors." Staff Study 84-1, Federal Reserve Bank of Chicago (1984).

Rosenblum, Harvey, and Diane Siegel. "Competition in Financial Services: The Impact of Nonbank Entry." Staff Study 83-1, Federal Reserve Bank of Chicago (1983).

SAS Supplementary Library User's Guide. Cary, N.C.: SAS Institute, 1982.

SAS User's Guide: Statistics. Cary, N.C.: SAS Institute, 1982.

Scherer, Charles R. *Estimating Electric Power Marginal Costs.* Amsterdam: North-Holland, 1977.

Scherer, F.M. *Industrial Market Structure and Economic Performance,* 2nd ed. Chicago: Rand McNally, 1980, 5.

Schweiger, Irving, and John McGee. "Chicago Banking: The Structure of Banks and Related Financial Institutions in Chicago and Other Area." *Journal of Business* 34 (July 1961):203–366.

Schweitzer, Stuart A. "Economies of Scale and Holding Company Affiliation in Banking." *Southern Economic Journal* 39 (1972):258–66.

Shull, Bernard, and Paul M. Horvitz. "Branch Banking and the Structure of Competition." *National Banking Review* 1 (December 1964):143–88.

Silber, William L. "The Process of Financial Innovation." *American Economic Review* 73 (May 1983):89–95.

Smirlock, Michael. "An Analysis of Bank Risk and Deposit Rate Ceilings: Evidence from the Capital Markets." *Journal of Monetary Economics* 13 (1984):195–210.

Stigler, George J. *The Theory of Price.* New York: Macmillan, 1966.

Uzawa, H. "Production Functions with Constant Elasticity of Substitution." *Review of Economic Studies* 29 (October 1962):291–99.

Walker, David A. "Economies of Scale in Electronics Funds Transfer Systems." *Journal of Banking and Finance* 2 (1978):65–78.

Walker, John A. *Bank Costs for Decision Making.* Boston: BP, 1970.

Waite, Donald C., III. "Deregulation in the Banking Industry." *The Bankers Magazine* 165 (January/February 1982):26–35.

Whitehead, David. "Interstate Banking: Taking Inventory." *Economic Review,* Federal Reserve Bank of Atlanta (May 1983), 4–20.

Whitehead, David. "A Guide to Interstate Banking, 1983." Staff study, Federal Reserve Bank of Atlanta (1983).

Whitehead, David. "Can Interstate Banking Increase Competitive Market Performance." *Economic Review,* Federal Reserve Bank of Atlanta (January 1984).

Willig, Robert D. "Multiproduct Technology and Market Structure." *American Economic Review* 69 (May 1979):346.

Zwick, Jack. "A Cross-Section Study of Industry Costs and Savings." In John M. Chapman and Robert P. Shay, eds., *The Consumer Finance Industry: Its Costs and Regulations.* New York: Columbia University Press, 1965.

Index

Adar, Zvi, 79
Agmon, Tamir, 79
Agricultural banks. *See* Farm banks
Alhadeff, David, 64–65, 68, 70, 90
Allocable versus nonallocable costs, 31–32
Allstate Insurance Company, 2
Analysis: cluster, 127–129, 145;
     discriminant, 208; Functional Cost,
     37, 70–71, 75, 80, 82, 83, 87, 90, 97,
     98, 102, 111, 182, 185, 188–190,
     191, 194, 198, 202, 220; regression,
     207–208, 212
Automated clearinghouses (ACHs), 1, 182,
     185, 187, 202
Automated teller machines, (ATMs), 1,
     183, 185–186, 188
Average costs: bank failure and, 207;
     bank-cost studies and, 64–65, 67, 76,
     85, 90, 183, 186, 187, 207; economies
     of scale and, 33, 47, 183, 207;
     long-run, 33, 54, 183; multiproduct
     firms and, 46; ray, 47; short-run, 33

Baltensperger, Ernst, 89–90
BancOne, 17
Bank of America, 14
Bank Holding Company Act of 1956,
     Douglas Amendment to the, 19
Bank-cost studies: Adar's 79; Agmon's, 79;
     Alhadeff's, 64–65, 68, 70, 90; average
     costs and, 64–65, 67, 76, 85, 90, 183,
     186, 187, 207; Baltensperger's, 89–90;
     bank competition and, 85, 86, 111,
     118–119, 123–124, 191, 224; bank
     consolidation and, 73, 74, 123; bank
     failure and, 205–209, 212, 214;
     Baumol's, 47, 58; Bell's 74–75, 183,
     185; Benston's, 37, 50–51, 59, 70–74,
     75, 80–81, 82, 83–85, 87, 88,
     90–91; Berger's, 80–81, 82, 83, 85,
     91; Borts's, 89; branch banks and,
     64–65, 67–68, 72–74, 83–86, 87–88,
90, 91, 110, 111, 118–122, 122–123,
190, 191, 198, 202, 219, 220, 221,
225; Braunstein's, 58; Call Reports of
Income and Condition and, 37, 76, 82,
85, 90, 219; Caves's, 57–58;
Christensen's, 45, 57–58; Clark's, 85;
Cobb-Douglas, 75, 85, 90; Collins's,
208; constant returns to scale and, 65;
consumer loan costs and, 87; credit
cards and, 198, 202, 222; decreasing
returns to scale and, 76; demand
deposits and, 91, 123, 145, 183, 185,
189, 190–191, 194, 198, 202, 209,
214, 221, 222; deregulation and, 76,
79, 86, 118–119, 123; Divisia index and,
83; Dunham's, 188–190; early, 64–65,
67–68, 70, 90, 91, 219; economies of
scale and, 65, 71–72, 73, 75, 76, 79,
80, 82, 83, 84, 85–86, 88, 90–91, 97,
98–105, 108–110, 111, 118–122,
122–123, 145–146, 183, 188–189,
190, 194, 198, 202, 207, 209, 214;
economies of scope and, 80–81, 82, 83,
91–92, 97, 98–105, 108–110, 111,
118–122, 123, 145–146, 198, 202,
220, 225; electronic funds transfer and,
185–188; Federal Deposit Insurance
Corporation and, 63, 205, 206; Federal
Home Loan Bank Board and, 63;
Federal Reserve System and, 63, 64, 65,
67, 68, 70–71, 82, 183, 186–188,
189; Flannery's, 87–88, 185–186,
189–190; Functional Cost Analysis and,
70–71, 75, 80, 82, 83, 87, 90, 97, 102,
111, 182, 185, 188–190, 191, 194,
198, 202, 220; Fuss's, 48–49, 57–58,
59; Gilligan's, 37, 81–83, 91;
Gramley's, 68, 70, 71; Green's, 208;
Greenbaum's, 36, 37, 39, 74, 76, 91;
Hanweck's, 50–51, 59, 80–81, 82,
83–85, 88, 91; Horvitz's, 65, 67–68,
70, 90; Humphrey's, 50–51, 59, 80–81,

Bank-cost studies: *(continued)*
82, 83–85, 88, 91, 186–187; increasing
    returns to scale and, 65, 76; Jaffee's,
    185–186; jointness and, 82, 83, 85, 90,
    91–92, 108, 110, 120–122, 123,
    145–146, 198, 202, 220, 221, 222;
    Jorgenson's, 45; Kane's, 16; Kim's, 51,
    54, 59–61; Kwast's, 88–89; large
    banks and, 54, 65, 67, 68, 70, 71–72,
    75, 82, 83, 85–86, 88, 89, 90,
    104–105, 108, 120, 121, 123–124,
    145–146, 188–189, 202–203, 219,
    224; Lau's, 45; Longbrake's, 190;
    McGee's, 68, 70; McKinsey &
    Company's, 22, 86; marginal costs and,
    59–60, 71, 72, 75, 80, 82, 83, 85, 86,
    89, 186, 194; marginal revenues and,
    59–60; Marshall's, 82–83; Mayo's, 58;
    Melzker's, 187–188; money market
    mutual funds and, 225; Mullineaux's,
    76, 83, 88; multiproduct firms and,
    59–60, 80, 90, 145; Murphy's,
    74–75, 89–90, 183, 185; Nelson's,
    85–86; Nerlove's, 43; in the 1960s,
    70–76, 90, 219; in the 1970s, 76, 79,
    219; nonbank competition and, 123,
    124, 224; Office of the Comptroller of
    the Currency and, 63; Orgler's, 79;
    Panzar's, 49, 58; Powers's, 74, 76;
    product costs and profitability and,
    88–89; product costs and risk and,
    89–90; Pulley's, 58; recent, 79–86, 90,
    91, 122–123; Rose's, 88–89;
    Rosenblum's, 14; Schweiger's, 68, 70;
    Schweitzer's, 91; SEDL and, 209;
    SEDT and, 209; SESL and, 209;
    Siegel's, 14; small banks and, 65, 67,
    68, 70, 74, 75, 76, 82, 83, 85–86,
    89–90, 104, 119–120, 121, 123–124,
    187, 188–189, 190, 202–203, 209,
    220; Smirlock's, 37, 81–83, 91; social
    costs of structure restraints and, 87–88;
    technology and, 54, 74, 75, 108,
    119–120, 123, 182–183, 185–191,
    194, 198, 201–202, 222; translog
    functions and, 53, 54, 57–58, 59–60,
    80, 82, 83, 87–88, 90, 97, 100–110,
    111, 122, 190, 194, 198, 202, 207,
    219–220, 221; Tretheway's, 57–58;
    unit banks and, 64–65, 68, 72–74,
    83–85, 87–88, 90, 91, 110, 111,
    118–122, 122–123, 190, 191, 198,
    202, 221; Waite's, 22; Walker's, 186;
    Waverman's, 48–49, 57–58, 59;
    Willig's, 49–50, 58
Banking Act of 1933, 8
Banking Act of 1935, 8
Baumol, William, 47, 58

Bell, Frederick, W., 74–75, 183, 185
Benston, George J., 37, 50–51, 59, 70–74,
    75, 80–81, 82, 83–85, 87, 88, 90–91
Berger, Allen N., 80–81, 82, 83, 85, 91
Borts, George, 89
Branch banks: bank competition and, 118;
    bank-cost studies and, 64–65, 67–68,
    72–74, 83–86, 87–88, 90, 91, 110,
    111, 118–122, 122–123, 190, 191,
    198, 202, 219, 220, 221, 225; cost
    economics of, 64–65, 67–68, 72–74,
    83–86, 87–88, 90, 91, 110, 111,
    118–122, 122–123, 127, 132, 190,
    191, 198, 202, 220, 221, 225;
    deregulation and, 118–119, 123, 221;
    economies of scale and, 91, 111,
    118–122, 122–123, 127, 198, 219,
    220; economies of scope and, 91, 111,
    118–122, 123, 198, 221; farm banks
    as, 132; interest rates and, 123, 221;
    jointness and, 91, 221; Regulation Q
    and, 118; technology and, 123, 191,
    198, 202; unit banks compared to,
    64–65, 72–74, 83–85, 87–88, 90, 91,
    98, 110, 111, 118–122, 122–123, 190,
    191, 198, 202, 221
Braunstein, Y.M., 58

Caldwell Banker, 2
Call Reports of Income and Condition, 37,
    76, 82, 85, 90, 219
CAP (ratio of total equity to total assets),
    212
Cash dispensers (CDs), 185–186
Cash Management Account, 14
Cash management systems, corporate, 1
Caves, Douglas W., 57–58
Certificates of Deposit (CDs), 16
Christensen, Laurits R., 45, 57–58
Chrysler Corporation, 14
City banks: characteristics of, 129, 145,
    220, 222, 224; cost economics of, 129,
    133, 137–138, 145, 222, 224;
    economies of scale and, 133, 137–138,
    145; economies of scope and, 138, 145,
    222, 224; jointness and, 222, 224
Clark, Jeffrey A., 85
Cluster analysis, 127–129, 145; FASTCLUS
    and, 128
Cobb-Douglas functions, 41–43, 44, 45,
    53; bank-cost studies and, 75, 85, 90
Collins, Robert A., 208
Competition, bank: bank-cost studies and,
    85, 86, 111, 118–119, 123–124, 191,
    224; branch banks and, 118;
    deregulation and, 25–26, 63, 86, 97,
    118–119, 221, 224; interstate banking
    and, 26, 123; public policy issues and,

23–25, 219, 223, 224; technology and, 191, 218

Competition, nonbank: bank-cost studies and, 123, 124, 224; deregulation and, 2, 4, 19, 25–26, 79, 97, 224; dimensions of, 10, 14, 16–17, 19, 21–22; insurance companies and, 1–2, 10, 17, 124, 217; manufacturers and, 10, 14; money market mutual funds and, 1, 2, 14, 16, 79, 98, 123; origins of, 5–6, 8–10; public policy issues and, 23–25, 223, 224; retailers and, 1–2, 10, 14, 124, 217; securities dealers and, 1–2, 10, 14, 16, 217; technology and, 218; U.S. Supreme Court and regulation of, 217

Comptroller of the Currency, Office of the, 63

Computers: cost economics and, 52, 75, 108, 183, 185, 187–188, 191, 194, 198, 202, 222; credit cards and, 194, 198; large banks and, 53, 75, 108, 185, 194, 202; micro-, 52, 183, 194, 198; small banks and, 52, 75, 183, 185, 187–188, 191, 194, 202, 222

Consolidation, bank: bank-cost studies and, 73, 74, 123; economies of scale and, 23–25, 73, 74; economies of scope and, 25; interstate banking and, 23, 124, 217; public policy issues and, 146, 219; technology and, 181

Constant elasticity of substitution (CES) functions, 44–45, 53

Constant returns to scale, 41, 65

Consumer loan costs, 87

Cost economics: allocable versus non-allocable cost, 31–32; average costs, 33, 46, 47, 54, 64–65, 67, 76, 85, 90, 183, 186, 187, 207; bank failure and, 205–209, 212, 214; branch banks and, 64–65, 67–68, 72–74, 83–86, 87–88, 90, 91, 110, 111, 118–122, 122–123, 127, 132, 190, 191, 198, 202, 219, 220, 221, 225; city banks and, 129, 133, 137–138, 145, 222, 224; computers and, 52, 75, 108, 183, 185, 187–188, 191, 194, 198, 202, 222; consumer loans and, 87; credit cards and, 194, 198, 202, 222, 223; demand deposits and, 91, 123, 145, 183, 185, 189, 190–191, 194, 198, 202, 209, 212, 214, 221, 222, 223; Divisia index and, 51, 83; electronic funds transfer and, 185–188; endogeneity and, 50–52, 53–54; farm banks and, 127, 129, 132, 133, 137, 138, 140, 144, 145, 222, 224; fixed versus variable costs, 30; importance of, 29; interest rates and,

19, 21–22, 98, 108, 123, 217; jointness and, 30–31, 80, 82, 83, 85, 91–92, 108, 110, 120–122, 123, 138–140, 144, 145, 194, 198, 202, 220, 221, 222, 224; large banks and, 24–25, 26, 33, 50, 52, 54, 65, 67, 68, 70, 71–72, 73, 74, 75, 82, 83, 85–86, 88, 89, 90–91, 104–105, 108, 120, 121, 123–124, 146, 188–189, 202–203, 219, 222, 223, 224; long-run average costs, 33, 54; long-run marginal costs, 33, 34; marginal costs, 33, 34, 46–50, 53, 59–60, 71, 72, 75, 80, 82, 83, 85, 86, 89, 186, 194; marginal revenues, 59–60; measurement of, 35–46; product costs and profitability, 88–89; product costs and risk, 89–90; public policy issues and, 23–25, 218–219; ray average costs, 47; retail banks and, 129, 132, 137, 138, 144, 145, 222, 224; scale and, 23–25, 26, 32–54, 65, 70, 71–72, 73, 74, 75, 79, 80, 82, 83, 84, 85–86, 88, 90–91, 97, 98–105, 108–110, 111, 118–122, 122–123, 127, 133, 137–138, 145–146, 182, 183, 185, 186, 187, 188–189, 190, 194, 198, 202, 207, 209, 214, 219, 220–221, 222, 223; scope and, 25, 51–52, 53, 54, 80–81, 82, 83, 91–92, 97, 98–105, 108–110, 111, 118–122, 123, 138–140, 144–145, 146, 198, 202, 220, 221, 222, 223, 224, 225; short-run average costs, 33; short-run marginal costs, 33; small banks and, 24, 26, 33, 52, 54, 65, 67, 68, 70, 74, 75, 76, 82, 83, 85–86, 89–90, 90–91, 104, 119–120, 121, 123–124, 183, 187, 188–189, 190, 191, 202–203, 209, 219, 220, 222, 223; social costs of structure restraints, 87–88; technology and, 1, 51–52, 75, 108, 181–183, 185–191, 194, 198, 202, 222; types of banks and, 38; unit banks and, 64–65, 68, 72–74, 83–85, 87–88, 90, 91, 110, 111, 118–122, 122–123, 132, 190, 191, 198, 202, 221; wholesale banks and, 129, 133, 137, 138, 145, 222, 224. *See also* Bank-cost studies

Credit cards: bank-cost studies and, 198, 202, 222; computers and, 194, 198; cost economics of, 194, 198, 202, 222, 223; demand deposits produced jointly with, 194, 198, 222; economies of scale and, 222; economies of scope and, 222; jointness and, 194, 198, 202, 222; technology and, 1, 194, 198, 202, 222

Dean Witter Reynolds, 2

Decreasing returns to scale, 76
Demand deposits: bank-cost studies and,
    91, 123, 145, 183, 185, 189, 190–191,
    194, 198, 202, 209, 212, 214, 221,
    222; cost economics and, 91, 123, 145,
    183, 185, 189, 190–191, 194, 198,
    202, 209, 212, 214, 221, 222, 223;
    credit cards produced jointly with, 194,
    198, 222; economies of scale and, 209,
    222; economies of scope and, 222;
    jointness and, 91, 123, 145, 194, 198,
    202, 221, 222; RDT and, 209, 212;
    SEDT and, 209; technology and, 183,
    185, 189, 190–191, 194, 198, 202, 222
Depository Institutions Deregulation
    Committee, 2
Depository Institutions Deregulation and
    Monetary Control Act (DIDMCA) of
    1980, 2, 97
Deregulation: bank competition and,
    25–26, 63, 86, 97, 118–119, 221, 224;
    bank-cost studies and, 76, 79, 86,
    118–119, 123; branch banks and, 123,
    221; interest rates and, 19, 21–22, 76,
    79, 123, 217, 221; interstate banking
    and, 26, 217; nonbank competition
    and, 2, 4, 19, 25–26, 79, 97, 224
Discriminant analysis models, 208
Divisia index: bank-cost studies and, 83;
    economies of scale and, 51, 83
Douglas Amendment to the Bank Holding
    Company Act of 1956, 19
Drive-in teller facilities, 1, 79
Dunham, Constance, 188–190

Early warning systems (EWSs): bank failure
    and, 205–209, 212, 214; CAP and,
    212; discriminant analysis models and,
    208; linear probability models and, 208;
    LIQ ratio and, 208–209; LNDP and,
    212; LOGIT models and, 207–208,
    212, 214; NOI ratio and, 208–209;
    PROBIT models and, 208; RDL and,
    212; RDT and, 209, 212; ROA and,
    212; SEDT and, 209; SEDL and, 209;
    SESL and, 209; Z-score and, 208
Economics, cost. *See* Cost economics
Electronic funds transfer (EFT), 52, 79;
    automated clearinghouses, 1, 182, 185,
    187, 202; automated teller machines, 1,
    183, 185–186; bank-cost studies and,
    185–188; cash dispensers, 185–186;
    cost economics and, 185–188;
    increasing public acceptance of, 218;
    point-of-sale machines, 185
Endogeneity, 50–52, 53–54

Failure, bank: bank-cost studies and,
    205–209, 212, 214; cost economics
    and, 205–209, 212, 214; early warning
    systems and, 205–209, 212, 214;
    economies of scale and, 207, 209, 214;
    Federal Deposit Insurance Corporation
    and, 205, 206; small banks and, 209;
    translog functions and, 207
Farm banks: branch banks as, 132;
    characteristics of, 38, 127, 129, 140,
    144, 145, 220, 224; cost economics of,
    127, 129, 132, 133, 137, 138, 144,
    145, 146, 222, 224; economies of scale
    and, 127, 133, 137, 145; economies of
    scope and, 138, 144, 145, 222, 224;
    jointness and, 222, 224; unit banks as,
    132
Farm Credit System, 181
FASTCLUS, 128
Federal Deposit Insurance Corporation
    (FDIC), 8; bank-cost studies and the,
    63, 205, 206; bank failure and the,
    205, 206
Federal Home Loan Bank Board, 63
Federal Reserve Bank of: Kansas City, 65,
    82; San Francisco, 64
Federal Reserve System, 6, 8; bank-cost
    studies and the, 63, 64, 65, 67, 68,
    70–71, 82, 183, 186–188, 189;
    regulation of nonbank banks and the,
    217
Fixed versus variable costs, 30
Flannery, Mark J., 87–88, 185–186,
    189–190
Ford Motor Company, 10, 14
Functional Cost Analysis (FCA), 37, 98;
    bank-cost studies and, 70–71, 75, 80,
    82, 83, 87, 90, 97, 102, 111, 182, 185,
    188–190, 191, 194, 198, 202, 220;
    technology and, 182, 191, 194, 198,
    202
Functions: Cobb-Douglas, 41–43, 44, 45,
    53, 75, 85; constant elasticity of
    substitution, 44–45, 53; hybrid, 57–58;
    quadratic, 58; Shephard's Lemma, 60;
    translog, 45–46, 50, 53, 57–58, 59–60,
    80, 82, 83, 87–88, 90, 100–102,
    108–110, 111, 122, 190, 194, 198,
    202, 207, 219–220, 221
Fuss, Melvyn, 48–49, 57–58, 59

Garn–St. Germain Depository Institutions
    Act of 1982, 2, 97, 124
General Electric, 10
General Motors, 10, 14
Gilligan, Thomas W., 37, 81–83, 91

Glass-Steagall Act, 25, 218
Gramley, Lyle E., 68, 70, 71
Green, Richard D., 208
Greenbaum, Stuart I., 36, 37, 39, 74, 76, 91

Hanweck, Gerald, 50–51, 59, 80–81, 82, 83–85, 88, 91
Horvitz, Paul M., 65, 67–68, 70, 90
Humphrey, David, 50–51, 59, 80–81, 82, 83–85, 88, 91, 186–187
Hybrid translog functions, 57–58

Increasing returns to scale, 32–33, 53, 65, 76
Inflation, money market mutual funds and, 1
Insurance companies, competition from, 1–2, 10, 17, 124, 217
Interest Rate Adjustment Act of 1966, 9
Interest rates: branch banks and, 123, 221; deregulation and, 19, 21–22, 76, 79, 123, 217, 221; operating costs and, 19, 21–22, 98, 108; public policy issues and, 218; Regulation Q and, 1, 2, 8–9, 16, 79; volatility of, 217
Interstate banking: bank competition and, 26, 123; bank consolidation and, 23, 124, 217; deregulation and, 26, 217; federal legislation and, 19, 23; future of, 217; public policy issues and, 146; regional compacts for, 217; U.S. Supreme Court and, 19, 217

Jaffee, Dwight M., 185–186
Jointness, 30–31, 80; bank-cost studies and, 82, 83, 85, 90, 91, 108, 110, 120–122, 123, 145, 198, 202, 220, 221, 222; branch banks and, 91, 221; city banks and, 222, 224; credit cards and, 194, 198, 202, 222; demand deposits and, 91, 123, 145, 194, 198, 202, 221, 222; economies of scale and, 120–122, 198, 202, 220, 222; economies of scope and, 25, 91–92, 108, 110, 120–122, 123, 138–140, 144, 198, 202, 220, 221, 224; farm banks and, 222, 224; large banks and, 120, 121, 122, 123, 146, 202, 222; retail banks and, 222, 224; small banks and, 121, 122, 123, 202; translog functions and, 90, 202, 220; unit banks and, 91, 221; wholesale banks and, 222, 224
Jorgenson, Dale W., 45

Kane, Edward J., 16
Kim, Moshe, 51, 54, 59–61
Kwast, Myron L., 88–89

Large banks: bank-cost studies and, 54, 65, 67, 68, 70, 71–72, 73, 74, 75, 82, 83, 85–86, 88, 89, 90, 104–105, 108, 120, 121, 123–124, 146, 188–189, 202–203, 219, 224; computers and, 52, 75, 108, 185, 194, 202; cost economics of, 24–25, 26, 33, 50, 52, 54, 65, 67, 68, 70, 71–72, 73, 74, 75, 82, 83, 85–86, 88, 89, 104–105, 108, 120, 121, 123–124, 146, 188–189, 202–203, 219, 222, 223, 224; economies of scale and, 24–25, 26, 33, 50, 52, 70, 71–72, 74, 75, 82, 83, 85–86, 88, 90–91, 104–105, 108, 123, 146, 188–189, 194, 202, 219, 222, 223; economies of scope and, 25, 52, 83, 123, 202, 223; jointness and, 120, 121, 122, 123, 146, 202, 222; marginal costs and, 89, 194; public policy issues and, 146, 219, 223, 224; technology and, 52, 71, 75, 108, 181–182, 185, 194, 202–203
Lau, Lawrence J., 45
Legislation, banking: Bank Holding Company Act of 1956, 19; Banking Act of 1933, 8; Banking Act of 1935, 8; Depository Institutions Deregulation and Monetary Control Act (DIDMCA) of 1980, 2, 97; Douglas Amendment to the Bank Holding Company Act of 1956, 19; Garn–St. Germain Depository Institutions Act of 1982, 2, 97, 124; Glass-Steagall Act, 25, 218; Interest Rate Adjustment Act of 1966; 9; McFadden Branch Banking Act of 1927, 8, 19; Monetary Control Act of 1980, 187
Linear probability models, 208
LIQ (cash plus securities to total assets) ratio, 208–209
LNDP (ratio of loans to deposits), 212
Logistic discrimination method of regression analysis (LOGIT model), 207–208, 212, 214
Longbrake, William A., 190
Long-run average costs (LAC), 33, 54, 183
Long-run marginal costs (LMC), 33, 34

McFadden Branch Banking Act of 1927, 8, 19
McGee, John, 68, 70
McKinsey & Company, 22, 86

Manufacturers, competition from, 10, 14
Marginal costs: bank-cost studies and, 59–60, 71, 72, 75, 80, 82, 83, 85, 86, 89, 186, 194; economies of scope and, 53; large banks and, 89, 194; long-run, 33, 34; multiproduct firms and, 46–50, 53, 59–60, 80; short-run, 33; small banks and, 89; translog functions and, 53, 59–60
Marginal revenues, 59–90
Marshall, William, 82–83
Mayo, John W., 58
Merrill Lynch, 2, 14, 16
Metzker, Paul, 187–188
Microcomputers, 52, 183, 194, 198
Monetary Control Act of 1980, 187
Money market certificates (MMCs), 79
Money market deposit accounts (MMDAs), 2, 16, 98
Money market mutual funds (MMMFs): bank-cost studies and, 225; competition from, 1, 2, 14, 16, 79, 98, 123; inflation and, 1
Mullineaux, Donald J., 76, 83, 88
Multibank holding companies (MBHCs), 88, 91, 124, 217, 225
Multiproduct firms: average costs and, 46; bank-cost studies and, 59–60, 80, 90, 146; economies of scale and, 46–50, 98–105, 108–110, 145; economies of scope and, 53, 98–105, 108–110, 145; marginal costs and, 46–50, 53, 59–60, 80; marginal revenues and, 59–60; translog functions and, 59–60
Murphy, Neil B., 74–75, 89–90, 183, 185

Nationwide Insurance, 17
Nelson, Richard W., 85–86
Nerlove, Marc, 43
NOI (net operating income to total assets) ratio, 208–209
Nonallocable versus allocable costs, 31–32
Nonbank competition. *See* Competition, nonbank
NOW (negotiable order of withdrawal) accounts, 2; Super-NOW accounts, 2, 16, 98

Operating costs. *See* Cost economics
Orgler, Yair E., 79

Paine Webber, 2
Panzar, John C., 49, 58
Penney, J.C., 10
Phone, banking by. *See* Telephone banking
Point-of-sale (POS) machines, 185, 188
Powers, John Anthony, 39, 74, 76
PROBIT models, 208

Product costs: profitability and, 88–89; risk and, 89–90
Profitability, product costs and, 88–89
Public policy issues: bank competition and, 23–25, 219, 223, 224; bank consolidation and, 146, 219; economies of scale and, 23–25, 219, 223; economies of scope and, 25, 223; interest rates and, 218; interstate banking and, 146; large banks and, 146, 219, 223, 224; nonbank competition and, 23–25, 223, 224; small banks and, 219
Pulley, L.B., 58

Q, Regulation. *See* Regulation Q
Quadratic function, 57

Ray average costs (RAC), 47
RDL (residual cost measure for demand and time deposits), 209, 212
RDT (residual cost measure for deposits and loans), 212
Reader-sorters, 52
Regression analysis, 207–208, 212
Regulation Q, 1, 2, 8, 16, 79; branch banks and, 118
Retail banks: characteristics of, 129, 145, 222, 224; cost economics of, 129, 137, 138, 144, 145, 222, 224; economies of scale and, 137, 138, 145; economies of scope and, 144, 222, 224; jointness and, 222, 224
Retailers, competition from, 1–2, 10, 14, 124, 217
Returns to scale, 188, 189, 190; constant, 41, 65; decreasing, 76; increasing, 32–33, 53, 65, 76
Risk, product costs and, 89–90
ROA (ratio of net income after taxes, securities gains [losses], and extraordinary items to total assets, 212
Rose, John T., 88–89
Rosenblum, Harvey, 14

SAS, 101, 207–208; FASTCLUS procedure of, 128
Scale, economies of: average costs and, 33, 47, 183, 207; bank consolidation and, 23–25, 73, 74; bank failure and, 207, 209, 214; bank-cost studies and, 65, 71–72, 73, 76, 79, 80, 82, 83, 84, 85–86, 88, 90–91, 97, 98–105, 108–110, 111, 118–122, 122–123, 145–146, 183, 188–189, 190, 194, 198, 202, 207, 209, 214, 220–221; branch banks and, 91, 111, 118–122, 122–123, 127, 198, 219, 220; city

banks and, 133, 137–138, 145; Cobb-Douglas functions and, 41–43, 44, 45; constant elasticity of substitution functions and, 44–45; constant returns to scale, 41, 65; credit cards and, 222; decreasing returns to scale, 76; definition of, 24; demand deposits and, 209, 222; Divisia index and, 51, 83; farm banks and, 127, 133, 137, 145; increasing returns to scale, 32–33, 53, 65, 76; jointness and, 120–122, 198, 202, 220, 222; large banks and, 24–25, 26, 33, 50, 52, 70, 71–72, 74, 75, 82, 83, 85–86, 88, 90–91, 104–105, 108, 123, 146, 188–189, 194, 202, 219, 222, 223; limitations on, 33–34; long-run average costs and, 33, 183; long-run marginal costs and, 33, 34; marginal costs and, 33, 34; measurement of, 35–46; multiproduct firms and, 46–50, 98–105, 108–110, 145; public policy issues and, 23–25, 219, 223; ray average costs and, 47; retail banks and, 137, 138; returns to scale, 32–33, 41, 65, 76, 188, 189, 190; SEDL and, 209; SEDT and, 209; SESL and, 209; short-run average costs and, 33; short-run marginal costs and, 33; small banks and, 24, 33, 52, 70, 74, 76, 82, 83, 85–86, 90–91, 104, 123, 194, 202, 219, 220; stocks versus flows and, 38–40; Taylor series expansions and, 45–46; technology and, 51–52, 71, 75, 182, 183, 185, 186, 194, 198, 202, 222; translog functions and, 45–46, 50, 53, 82, 83, 194, 198, 202, 207, 220; types of banks and, 36; unit banks and, 91, 111, 118–122, 122–123, 198; wholesale banks and, 137, 138, 145

Schweiger, Irving, 68, 70

Schweitzer, Stuart A., 91

Scope, economies of: bank consolidation and, 25; bank-cost studies and, 80–81, 82, 83, 91–92, 97, 98–105, 108–110, 111, 118–122, 123, 145–146, 198, 202, 220, 225; branch banks and, 91, 111, 118–122, 123, 198, 221; city banks and, 138, 145, 222, 224; credit cards and, 222; definition of, 25; demand deposits and, 91, 222; farm banks and, 138, 144, 145, 222, 224; jointness and, 25, 91–92, 108, 110, 120–122, 123, 138–140, 144, 198, 202, 220, 221, 224; large banks and, 25, 52, 83, 123, 202, 223; marginal costs and, 53; multiproduct firms and, 53, 98–105, 108–110, 145; public

policy issues and, 25, 223; retail banks and, 144, 222, 224; small banks and, 52, 54, 123, 202; Taylor series expansions and, 108; technology and, 51–52, 54, 198, 202, 222; translog functions and, 53, 97, 108–110, 198, 202; unit banks and, 91, 111, 118–122, 198, 221; wholesale banks and, 145, 222, 224

Sears, Roebuck and Company, 2, 10

Securities dealers, competition from, 1–2, 10, 14, 16, 217

SEDL (scale economies estimates for deposits and loans), 209

SEDT (scale economies estimates for demand and time deposits), 209

SESL (scale economies estimates for securities and loans), 209

Shephard's Lemma, 60

Short-run average costs (SAC), 33

Short-run marginal costs (SMC), 33

Siegel, Diane, 14

Small banks: bank failure and, 209; bank-cost studies and, 65, 67, 68, 70, 74, 75, 76, 82, 83, 85–86, 89–90, 90–91, 104, 119–120, 121, 123–124, 187, 188–189, 190, 191, 202–203, 209, 219, 220; computers and, 52, 75, 183, 185, 187–188, 191, 194, 202, 222; cost economics of, 24, 26, 33, 52, 54, 65, 67, 68, 70, 74, 75, 76, 82, 83, 85–86, 89–90, 90–91, 104, 119–120, 121, 123–124, 183, 187, 188–189, 190, 191, 202–203, 209, 219, 220, 222, 223; economies of scale and, 24, 33, 52, 70, 74, 76, 82, 83, 85–86, 90–91, 104, 123, 188–189, 194, 202, 219, 220; economies of scope and, 52, 54, 123, 202; jointness and, 121, 122, 123, 202; marginal costs and, 89; public policy issues and, 219; technology and, 52, 54, 74, 75, 85, 119–120, 181–182, 183, 187–188, 191, 194, 202–203, 222

Smirlock, Michael L., 37, 81–83, 91

Structure restraints, social costs of, 87–88

Super-NOW accounts, 2, 16, 98

Taylor series expansions, 45–46, 108

Technology: automated clearinghouses, 1, 182, 185, 187; automated teller machines, 1, 183, 185–186, 188; bank competition and, 191, 218; bank consolidation and, 181; bank-cost studies and, 54, 74, 75, 108, 123, 182–183, 185–191, 194, 198, 201–202, 222; branch banks and, 123, 191, 198, 202; computers, 52, 75, 108, 183, 185, 187–188, 191, 194, 198,

Technology *(continued)*
202, 222, corporate cash management systems, 1; cost economics and, 1, 51–52, 75, 108, 181–183, 185–191, 194, 198, 202, 222; credit cards and, 1, 194, 198, 202, 222; demand deposits and, 183, 185, 189, 190–191, 194, 198, 202, 222; drive-in teller facilities, 1, 79; economies of scale and, 51–52, 71, 75, 182, 183, 185, 186, 194, 198, 202, 222; economies of scope and, 51–52, 198, 202, 222; electronic funds transfer, 52, 79, 183, 185–188; Functional Cost Analysis and, 182, 191, 194, 198, 202; large banks and, 52, 71, 75, 108, 181–182, 185, 194, 202–203; microcomputers, 52, 183, 194, 198; nonbank competition and, 218; point-of-sale machines, 185, 188; reader-sorters, 52; small banks and, 52, 54, 74, 75, 85, 119–120, 181–182, 183, 187–188, 191, 194, 202–203, 222; telecommunications, 108; telephone banking, 1, 79, 225; unit banks and, 191, 198, 202
Telecommunications, 108
Telephone banking, 1, 79, 225
Total operating expenses (TOE), 207
Translog functions: advantages of, 53, 219–220; bank failure and, 207; bank-cost studies and, 53, 54, 57–58, 59–60, 80, 82, 83, 87–88, 90, 97, 100–102, 108–110, 111, 122, 190, 194, 198, 202, 207, 219–220, 221; disadvantages of, 53, 57; economies of scale and, 45–46, 50, 53, 82, 83, 194, 198, 202, 207, 220; economies of scope and, 53, 97, 108–110, 198, 202; hybrid, 57–58; jointness and, 90, 202, 220; multiproduct firms and, 59–60; quadratic, 58

Travelers Insurance, 2
Tretheway, Michael W., 57–58

Unit banks: bank-cost studies and, 64–65, 68, 72–74, 83–85, 87–88, 90, 91, 110, 111, 118–122, 122–123, 190, 191, 198, 202, 221; branch banks compared to, 64–65, 72–74, 83–85, 87–88, 90, 91, 98, 110, 111, 118–122, 122–123, 190, 191, 198, 202, 221; cost economics of, 64–65, 68, 72–74, 83–85, 87–88, 90, 91, 110, 111, 118–122, 122–123, 132, 190, 191, 198, 202, 221; economies of scale and, 91, 111, 118–122, 122–123, 198; economies of scope and, 91, 111, 118–122, 123, 198, 221; farm banks as, 132; jointness and, 91, 221; technology and, 191, 198, 202
Urban banks. *See* City banks
U.S. Supreme Court: interstate banking and the, 19, 217; regulation of nonbank banks and the, 217
U.S. Treasury, 6

Variable versus fixed costs, 30

Waite, Donald C., III, 22
Walker, David A., 186
Waverman, Leonard, 48–49, 57–58, 59
Westinghouse, 10
Wholesale banks: characteristics of, 129, 145, 222, 224; cost economics of, 129, 133, 137, 138, 144, 222, 224; economies of scale and, 137, 138, 145; economies of scope and, 145, 222, 224; jointness and, 222, 224
Willig, Robert, 49–50, 58

Z-score, 208

About the Authors

James Kolari received his Ph.D. in finance from Arizona State University and is Assistant Professor of Finance at Texas A&M University. His teaching responsibilities include undergraduate and graduate courses in financial institutions and financial markets. He has published over 25 articles in these areas in refereed journals, in addition to a recent book entitled *The Future of Small Banks in a Deregulated Environment*, co-authored with Donald R. Fraser. Dr. Kolari has taken leaves of absence from Texas A&M University to serve as Visiting Scholar at the Federal Reserve Bank of Chicago and Fulbright Scholar at the University of Helsinki, Finland. He has worked as a bank consultant to the U.S. Small Business Administration under grant contracts on small banks and bank service costs, as well as the American Bankers Association and Independent Bankers Association of America.

Asghar Zardkoohi joined the faculty of the Business and Public Policy Group in the Department of Management at Texas A&M University in 1981 after spending four years on the faculty of Department of Economics at Auburn University. Dr. Zardkoohi teaches graduate and undergraduate courses in public policy and markets. He holds a Ph.D. in economics from Virginia Polytechnic Institute and State University. Under a grant contract, Dr. Zardkoohi has worked as a bank consultant to the U.S. Small Business Administration, examining the effect of the changing financial environment on bank efficiency. His research interests are in economic analysis of law, banking, industrial organization, and government regulation. Dr. Zardkoohi's research in a variety of economic and public policy issues has been published in a number of leading economic journals.